The Devil You Knew

The myths around depression, and why your best days are ahead of you

Prof. Ian Hickie

Co-director, Brain & Mind Centre, University of Sydney

PENGUIN BOOKS

PENGUIN BOOKS

UK | USA | Canada | Ireland | Australia
India | New Zealand | South Africa | China

Penguin Books is part of the Penguin Random House group of companies whose addresses can be found at global.penguinrandomhouse.com

Penguin Random House Australia

First published by Penguin Books in 2023

Cover design by Lisa White © Penguin Random House Australia Pty Ltd
Figure 1 (p. 217) courtesy of Science Photo Library/Alamy
Typeset in 11/17 pt ITC New Baskerville by Midland Typesetters, Australia
Printed and bound in Australia by Griffin Press, an accredited ISO AS/NZS 14001 Environmental Management Systems printer

NATIONAL LIBRARY OF AUSTRALIA
A catalogue record for this book is available from the National Library of Australia

ISBN 978 1 76104 274 4

penguin.com.au

FSC www.fsc.org MIX Paper | Supporting responsible forestry FSC® C018684

We at Penguin Random House Australia acknowledge that Aboriginal and Torres Strait Islander peoples are the Traditional Custodians and the first storytellers of the lands on which we live and work. We honour Aboriginal and Torres Strait Islander peoples' continuous connection to Country, waters, skies and communities. We celebrate Aboriginal and Torres Strait Islander stories, traditions and living cultures; and we pay our respects to Elders past and present.

For Johnno and Noelene, who supported me to learn and encouraged me to act. For Liz, who has been my constant companion. For my kids, who tolerate me. Most importantly, for the many people who have shared their personal journeys with me.

Contents

Introduction

This book has a clear mission. It's designed to assist individuals of any age affected by clinical depression, and their families. It provides up-to-date and useful information that can help you out of a deep hole and then do everything you can to stay out of that hole.

Hopefully, it does that job in a straightforward way. It's been my experience that a variety of information sources are needed – notably, things that come from the brain and behavioural sciences, alongside very personal accounts of what works. The science isn't over. It continues to grow and change. While there is much consensus, there is still much to be revealed.

The personal stories that have been selected here are illustrative of the ways different people have gained insights into their own individual journeys. I've highlighted aspects and strategies that have really made a difference. They are not the same for everybody. It's important to know what others have tried, what's worked and what have been dead-ends.

The structure of the book moves through the major topic areas (clinical illness characteristics, brain science, theories of causation, most useful treatment approaches) and areas of controversy (what works, what myths can be discounted). At times it's complex because our emotions, thinking and behaviours are complex.

But feel free to start anywhere – to find the explanations or answers that are most relevant to you. Read the personal stories. Do they connect with your own experiences? Go straight to the take-out tips if you want to take immediate action. Try the different strategies that I'm promoting (sleep-wake cycle modification, anxiety reduction, best-matched medications, skilled psychological therapy, knowing your own long-term vulnerability), or ones that have helped others who've been stuck in the same place.

Though we all believe we are very familiar with our own internal worlds, and that we already have all the answers, the experience of mental ill-health often forces us to rethink our assumptions. That personal journey has the potential to be life-changing. My goal is to assist those making that journey to discover new truths and use those insights to lead a longer and more productive life.

PART 1

CLINICAL DEPRESSION: A JOURNEY TO RECOVERY

1

Is There Really a Need for Another Book about Depression?

Is it worth you spending your valuable time reading this book? Will you learn things and find strategies you can apply in your own life? I certainly hope so – it's the main game. There are some things we *all* need to know, if we're to travel together on this journey – and it could also be worth your family's while to look over your shoulder as you read on.

Things we all need to know include:

- If you don't have physical symptoms like really severe fatigue, muscle aches and pains, a disturbed gut or a racing heartbeat, you're not really depressed;
- No, depression is not always due to childhood trauma;
- Yes, it's likely that part of your own vulnerability is genetic, inherited from your parents, your grandparents and wherever else your DNA has come from over the generations;
- Yes, there is a clear connection between your childhood anxiety, your teenage depression and your adult alcohol abuse;
- Yes, lack of pleasure in life, not a depressed mood, is what clinical depression is all about;

- No, you weren't a lazy teenager who just couldn't get out of bed;
- Getting the right medication, at the right time, combined with the psychological or behavioural therapy that works, is the best way out of this hole and the best way not to go back this way again;
- No, it's not work stress, but it's the change in seasons that's killing you;
- No, exercising more and eating healthy is not enough to keep you well;
- No, your weight-gain problem is not just about over-eating;
- Yes, there are a whole lot of new treatments out there, but they're not all equally good;
- It's not that you've gone off your partner, but your new medication is killing your libido.

Many good books have been written about clinical depression. As community awareness has increased over the past two decades, more people have now come forward for help. Many have received effective medical treatments or psychological therapies and are getting on with their lives. Many have shared their personal stories, at least among their close family and friends. From the way most people reacted positively to these advances, I thought that the public communication of the underlying science, and the real progress that was made, was headed in the right direction.

But more than 20 years into the 21st century, I'm no longer convinced that 'the arc of progress' (to paraphrase Martin Luther King Jr) is heading to a more inclusive, or even more accurate place. Information sources are now very chaotic. The place of good clinical care is increasingly crowded out by many competing voices. Disreputable options are presented as miracle cures, sold actively to an unsuspecting or naive general public. At the same time intriguing new options are dismissed as medical mirages, or are only available to those who have access to critical knowledge or the capacity to pay large additional fees.

Over the past decade, the broader mental health of nations has taken some unexpected turns. Most notably, the rates of psychological distress and self-harming behaviours, particularly in younger women, have shot up. But does this really indicate that rates of clinical depression and other major disorders are rising? Are those changes due to the adverse impacts of new social media? Or is there something much more pernicious afoot in our wider society? Why are young people apparently bearing the burden of these major shifts in mental health problems and related self-harm? And all this started long before the unexpected arrival of COVID-19.

The mental health of every country has been impacted by the pandemic, even Australia and New Zealand, which evaded the massive physical health impacts. Suicide rates have remained stubbornly high, despite greater public awareness and preventive health initiatives. Most health systems were unable to meet the increasing demand for mental health care pre-COVID-19. How will they cope now? Will those in need of high-quality clinical care be worse off?

An unexpected upside from the COVID-19 pandemic is a growing public interest in mental health and wellbeing. Most of us were perturbed as our basic assumptions about work, education, financial security, physical health, family and community cohesion, travel and planning for the future went out the window. Community surveys about anxiety and depression, alcohol use, calls to helplines and the use of emergency mental health services, all show we are living in more troubled times.

If, during these tough periods, we do retreat from the arc of progress on common mental disorders, it is those with clinical depression, and their families and carers, who will most likely feel the hurt. This book aims to put their experiences and their need for real information back at the centre of mental health care.

The questions addressed here are most frequently raised with me by people who have clinical depression and their families. I hope to dispel common myths, such as: antidepressants don't work, or that they cause suicide; depression is due to childhood trauma; teaching kids resilience will prevent all depressions. But I will also make clear what we don't yet know and what areas of scientific research, brain science and social enquiry can deliver new insights.

We also need to consider the impacts of bad information on those engaged in providing care – across the health, education and other social services systems, these places where the daily impacts of these illnesses play out. Some health care providers may find this book informative and a tool to assist in open discussion with people with depression and their families. If so, I hope they share it directly with their clientele.

I am well aware that policymakers are also under considerable pressure to provide more appropriate financial and smarter social support, and expanded health systems, to meet the needs of those affected by clinical depression. This book may offer some useful insights and recommendations. Hopefully that includes what *not* to do! It's all too easy to respond to public demand with simple solutions that don't work, or even make the situation worse.

Last of all, this book is intended for our wider community. As with many other major health problems, we are all diminished (personally, financially and socially) when we neglect the legitimate needs of others. I do not underestimate the genuine interest of those who really do care about the future mental health and wellbeing of the communities in which we live.

Clinical depression is not a single disease

Most important are the needs of those seeking health care, and their families. They have the most urgent need for access to deep knowledge, the type that can genuinely assist a person to undertake the perilous journey to recovery. I argue that they often can't access that knowledge due to a list of big factors. Those things are not going to shift unless we develop a common understanding of the real nature of the problems we face.

'Clinical depression' or 'major depression' is not a single entity. So, although the public marketing of depression over the past 30 years has been a great success, it is no longer consistent with the main challenges faced by those who actually have the illness or those who try to provide treatments.

In the 21st century, we are no longer focused on simply providing average one-size-fits-all care (which in truth is more low-level than average). Instead, our focus is on much greater personalisation of care, making the most of modern technologies and the use of measurement-based care – tracking what happens to *you*, individually, over time. So, high-quality care for clinical depression is now entirely about you and your own unique journey – that is, finding as quickly as possible what best characterises your illness and which interventions work for you.

If you're a teenager and you have a circadian (relating to your body clock) depression rather than anxious depression, common forms of antidepressant medication, or psychological therapy, are not your best options. If your postnatal or menopausal depression is related to changes in estrogen levels, hormonal interventions may be critical. If your depression came on for the first time at age 65, you need a brain scan and a search for an underlying medical cause rather than being brushed off with some lame story about the inevitable impacts of retirement or growing old.

Over the past two decades we have seen rapid development in the basic biomedical, psychological and social sciences that underpin early intervention, effective treatments and prevention of recurrence of depressive disorders. These things are constantly changing. I spend many days at international conferences just trying to stay abreast of this new knowledge. Only trouble is, many information sources for the general public don't provide any real update on these new facts.

Much media, and sadly some health professionals, perpetuate old stereotypes and convenient myths. Each day I'll find a new report that says, 'Major depression was invented by the American Psychiatric Association in the 1980s – it's really just a social disease.' Or: antidepressants are just placebos; antidepressants are addictive; antidepressants cause more physical health problems than they cure. Another prevailing myth is that all we need to do is toughen up our kids – they've become too soft. Or, that the widespread public discussion of depression as an illness is just a front for the greedy pharmaceutical industry. Depression could be mitigated if we were nicer to our kids, increased welfare payments, ended poverty, prevented interpersonal trauma or had better diets. Teaching psychological skills in schools will be enough to curb the sudden increase in distress in younger generations.

Even publications by major health bodies tend to promote stories about more severe depressions being due to genetic vulnerabilities, while less severe depressions are not biological. That nature versus nurture divide is too simplistic, as is the idea that antidepressants and psychological therapies are equally effective for everybody.

There is now a rapidly changing landscape of who is most affected by these conditions. In the developed world, the greatest challenges are now with younger people who are coming to care or engaging in self-harming behaviours at ever-younger ages. For young people generally, their specific needs are still poorly recognised.

The next most neglected group are those who are ageing. As the sheer number of older persons in developing countries increases, the differentiation of later-life from mid-life becomes ever more important. Re-reading my favourite pieces from the early 20th century about clinical depression, I've noticed there is almost no mention of the specific issues as they relate to the young or the old. Even very up-to-date clinical guidelines for best practice largely focus on the needs of those aged 25 to 60 years.

New groups are emerging and demand appropriate attention. These include younger people with concurrent medical problems, most notably those affected by immune-related conditions. Other well-recognised groups are still being neglected – including younger and older women, where exposure to sexual violence and domestic assaults, alongside key hormonal perspectives, need urgent attention.

Sadly, we live in the era of disinformation, of 'alternative facts' and 'fake news'. So, when you seek information about clinical depression, it is highly likely you'll be exposed to material that for commercial, ideological or socio-political reasons is just wrong. To quote the great American comedian and political commentator Stephen Colbert, 'Truthiness reigns!' If it feels right but it's wrong, it's still okay to promote it. Hence, much of this book is devoted to dispelling those myths that I thought were dead 20 years ago.

The digital revolution provides an enormous opportunity to become much more engaged in your own health care. As a person, a patient, a client or a consumer, or for your family and carers, you can now become more active in (and hopefully central to) the management of your own condition or your loved one's mental health.

But to do that successfully, you need to know what questions to ask, what aspects of your health to monitor and how to recognise the best care available. You need to be well informed and hold the health system to account. More broadly, this book is designed to provide the rest of us with the opportunity to support those in need.

This book is based on my 35 years as a clinical psychiatrist and an active biomedical and social researcher, listening to the experiences of many people affected, and speaking publicly as an advocate for better care. It is intended to be engaging, provocative and challenging. It includes many take-out tips that will hopefully be of practical use to those most affected.

A taste of what's to come

If you're keen to get a sense of what you may not have heard before and ideas that challenge your assumptions, the following chapters include things like:

- It's a long journey, so find yourself the best clinicians and take the trip to recovery with them, your intimates and your family.
- Clinical depression is much more physiological than psychological. You really are sick. Actually, if you don't have physical symptoms, you're not depressed.
- It's your 24-hour sleep–wake (circadian) cycle that is the real 'on–off' switch for many severe episodes, not a whole lot of other 'psychological' stuff.
- Bad childhood experiences are not the common causes of adult depression. Other genetic and environmental factors are much more relevant.
- While trauma is a major risk factor, not everyone (or even most people) with depression has been traumatised.
- The more we improve the social environment, the less alike we become and the more individual differences explain the onset and course of illness.
- Beware the salesman for individually focused resilience training. It doesn't really work socially or biologically.
- Older people in good health are at much lower risk of depression than younger people – their cheerfulness keeps shining through.
- The emotional circuitry of the brain, and not the thinking cortex, is in the driver's seat. You can't just think (or talk) yourself out of it.

- Most people who take antidepressants benefit from them, even when they are living with significant side-effects.
- Misrepresentation of the placebo response to antidepressants does great harm, not only to those taking treatments but also to those who would benefit from seeking care.
- True prevention has a long way to go – there are no simple biomedical, psychological or social vaccines.
- Effective early intervention, and secondary prevention, are our best bets for reducing the personal impact of clinical depression.
- There are many new experimental treatments on the way – make sure you live long enough to enjoy them!

Feel free to dive in and out of the various chapters. This book is not linear. It doesn't move methodically through one straight narrative. The science of depression doesn't fit one simple story. It has many layers and defies easy conclusions. To assist, there are four main sections. Upfront is the why get involved with my world view (Chapters 1–8). In the middle two sections, there's all the stuff related to causation and the underlying neurobiological mechanisms (Chapters 9–17). Up the back is my summary of where treatment options are at right now (Chapters 18–24). If you prefer to start at the back, and then read forwards, go right ahead!

2

So, What Is Clinical Depression?

To dispense with one central myth, clinical depression is not everywhere and does not afflict everyone.

And, to dispense with one other, clinical depression is not a modern invention of 20th century psychiatry. It was not conceived by the American Psychiatric Association, or its DSM-III 1980 taskforce. It has existed, and been well recognised and managed by physicians for thousands of years.

We now live in an era of almost universal recognition of psychological distress. News items are commonly preceded by warnings of their potential to trigger distress and are followed by links to relevant crisis lines. However, it remains the case that the great majority of us will never be clinically depressed.

Clinical depression is not, and has never been, limited to Western countries or developed economies. The notion that it doesn't occur in traditional, typically poorer or rural communities is nonsense.

Clinical depression has a long history, and the central features have occurred across cultures and recorded time periods. While its prevalence varies with known environmental risks (childhood abuse, physical ill-health), the underlying rate of genetic vulnerability is unlikely to vary.

Perhaps, most importantly, sadness is not the key feature. Sadness is a normal human emotion and an entirely appropriate response to many life difficulties. When it is prolonged, causing considerable distress and resulting in withdrawal from the world or lost opportunities, some of those strategies that are effective for depression can really help: increased exercise, reaching out to friends and families, staying engaged with education or work.

But, the easiest place to start is by saying what clinical depression is *not*.

Clinical depression is not a normal emotional state.

It is not normal grief.

It is not a normal emotional response to acute life difficulties, losses or disappointments.

It is not the normal emotional response to catastrophic life events (loss of financial assets, loss of home through disaster) or physical health challenges (diagnosis of life-threatening cancer, acute spinal cord injury).

Clinical depression is not normal psychological distress in the face of life's challenges

While perhaps one in five of us will develop clinical depression in our lifetime, we will all experience periods of prolonged sadness or psychological distress at some stage.

If this period of psychological distress is prolonged (say, weeks to months) or is having a big impact on your life (you can't get to work or to school) or is messing with your close relationships, then we are likely to shift gear and go ahead and call that a mental disorder.

We might even add more descriptive labels such as 'anxiety' or 'depression' to it, to recognise its most common psychological features (fear, arousal, sadness, hopelessness).

If the episode happens in a very specific life context, we may well make it sound even more technical by adding the label 'adjustment' to the 'disorder' bit – and then you have 'an adjustment disorder with depressed mood'.

The very small number who claim never to have felt this way, often because they assert that they are bulletproof or so resilient, may need to check in with those around them.

The overt expression of distress has the distinct social and biological (and probably evolutionary) advantage of eliciting a caring, protective response from your close social network. As humans function best as part of small, cohesive social groups, this capacity to respond rapidly to a member who is struggling has clear benefits. One day I might need your help, but tomorrow I'll be well enough to help you.

Normal distress, and many brief mental disorders, often occur in the context of a major life disruption such as marriage breakdown, loss of an important relationship, job loss or career disruption, or family conflict.

This very real distress may be accompanied by tears, sadness, loss of motivation, poor sleep and even thoughts that life is not worth living. Without help, or at least recognition and appropriate actions by those you are close to, it may lead to other major difficulties – alcohol or other drug use, antisocial behaviour, irritability, work difficulties, relationship breakdowns.

As is revealed by many long-term community studies, we are all likely to be psychologically destabilised at some stage in our life. That is not remarkable. 'Life is tough and then you die.'

Recovery, not destablisation, is really interesting!

What is interesting is how readily most people recover from periods of very significant upheaval in their lives. With time, support and a break from other responsibilities, we can recover from these psychological challenges in the same way we do from other physical health problems, like a severe headache, back injuries, torn muscles and the other cuts, breaks and strains inflicted throughout life's journey. Most of us will recover from common mental disorders spontaneously or with some appropriate help.

But unlike mental disorders, for common physical injuries we don't turn around and say, 'You weren't hurt; you didn't need help; you just need to fix it yourself!' As a society, we provide the necessary first-aid, symptomatic interventions (ice, analgesia, rest) and practical support.

We also try to prevent painful and disabling physical disorders as best we can. Much of the preventive work championed in our own public mental health campaigns also has the capacity to reduce the onset of common mental disorders.

Many of us who assume that we are very resilient, simply because we have not fallen apart previously, can be surprised when, for the first time, in relation to some specific event (job loss, relationship breakdown), we not only fall apart but also fail to recover quickly.

For common mental disorders, there are also interesting developmental (that's lifespan-speak for differences in childhood, youth, adult and ageing phases of life) factors at work. For many years, the concept of 'psychological immunisation' has existed, meaning that with increasing age and experience of major life events, we become more immune to their devastating psychological impacts. For example, the break-up of a first major intimate relationship is often much more distressing than subsequent disruptions.

Contrary to popular myth, community surveys have shown that older, physically healthy people experience far less psychological distress than younger people. As is often relayed to me by older persons, 'You may be surprised to hear, but I have dealt with those [fill in here the appropriate qualifier – 'relationship', 'identity', 'financial'] problems more than once before in my life!'

To my great relief, older people are often far less judgemental than their middle-aged children and far less ferocious than their youthful grandchildren. They are also far less impressed with the psychobabble and other simplistic or homespun psychological theories of causes of their difficulties that others espouse.

While those people who don't recover within weeks (either for the first time in their life or on repeated occasions) constitute the minority of those who experience common mental disorders, they are some of the people who are then at risk of developing a major illness such as clinical depression.

Your 'vulnerability' to develop clinical depression is intrinsic, enduring and not the same as being exposed to risk

While those life events that land you in the hole of psychological distress may be quite evident, they are not necessarily the reason you stay unwell.

Other enduring vulnerabilities need to be at work to transform severe or prolonged psychological distress into what we recognise as clinical depression.

As with all other illnesses, even when you have been exposed to a highly toxic environmental event (e.g. smoking and lung cancer, asbestos and lung disease) you can't go back and change your exposure to those risks. For mental health, we often focus on repeated sexual abuse as a child or prolonged unemployment as an adult.

The extent to which those exposures, on their own, truly caused the onset of clinical depression is unknown. Often, those things we do know about the past and current circumstances do *not* provide the whole story. Even more importantly, they do *not* necessarily guide us to the best way out!

Unravelling each person's own vulnerability is much more critical than the endless search for any simplistic psychological (say, a single traumatic event) or biological (say, serotonin imbalance) cause.

To put it simply, finding the right road out of town doesn't mean you go back down the road that led you in! For travellers it's fairly obvious that retracing your steps is less productive than forging ahead. Where you started this process is not the desired destination – which is moving on to a more functional and productive life.

The black hole of clinical depression

To be clear, the black hole of clinical depression is a distinct syndrome, not a checklist of loosely linked psychological symptoms, like sadness, anxiety, tiredness, sleep disturbance and a sense of hopelessness or helplessness.

You don't have clinical depression as a consequence of managing to nominate five of nine possible symptoms. If you have to scratch around to tick all the boxes, then you definitely haven't got this problem. You may well have psychological distress, or even a different mental health problem, but you don't have clinical depression.

Some years ago, while conducting focus groups with people with depression, the following key insights flowed:

- For women: 'When I'm distressed, I first go to family and friends for support and help – and sometimes alcohol and sedatives. When it doesn't get better [weeks to months], then I go to the doctor. It didn't start yesterday. By this stage, I expect the doctor to do something really useful – not just tell me to be more active, get out and spend more time with my family and friends!'

- For men: 'When distressed, I don't go anywhere – not to friends, families or doctors. I drink and stay alone. When it gets worse [job loss, partner leaves, children distraught] I drink more. Finally, when dragged to the doctor [by partner, mother or child], I don't need to be told simply to stop drinking first, or that it's just because I've lost my job. It didn't start yesterday. I need serious help, quickly!'
- For both sexes: 'It didn't start yesterday – even though that's what my doctor thinks. Sure, there was a crisis that got me to their office today [lost job, partner left, made plan to kill myself, made disastrous business or life decision] but that is *not* the cause of my depression – it's just one of the consequences. Telling me to wait a few more weeks to see what happens next is no help at all!'

What's the 'clinical syndrome of depression'?

The medical concept of a 'clinical syndrome' is important.

These are the people you see, or anyone else you can recognise, as being very ill. Historically, these people were often treated in medical or clinical settings, hence the notion of the illness being 'clinical' – or requiring expert care, not just kinder families, non-specific support or professional hand-holding.

When you see these people in a family practice, a specialist clinic, a hospital or in an emergency department, you can recognise the non-verbal cues (slumped body posture, gestures of distress, monotonal voice, downcast eyes, lack of facial responses, self-preoccupation) that are consistent with a profound loss of normal cognitive, emotional and physical function.

The story of how the person got there is not the main game – the psychological and physical state that they now occupy is the main concern. Specifically, the 'syndrome' concept is the co-occurrence (all at the same time) of key features. These include loss of pleasure, physical ill-health due to extensive physiological changes, exhaustion, characteristic feelings and thoughts (guilt, shame, hopelessness and helplessness), cognitive dysfunction (reduced attention, impaired problem-solving, recurring intrusive thoughts), dysphoric mood (depressed, irritable, anxious), observable behavioural changes (motor slowing and social withdrawal) and suicidal thoughts and behaviours.

That is, the whole thing comes crashing down on you – the physical, the psychological and the social impact. Life comes to an abrupt fork in the road! Just carrying on as if everything is normal is not possible, despite your best efforts to hold it all together.

William Styron writes in *Darkness Visible* that the 'pain of severe depression is quite unimaginable to those who have not suffered it, and it kills in many instances because it cannot be borne'.

The syndrome persists, typically over weeks or months, rather independently of changes in life circumstances. Left untreated, it often leads to other psychological, medical and substance misuse complications.

The clinical syndrome of depression has ten very different characteristics to that of other common forms of psychological distress. These are:

1. It is associated with disruption of the whole self – mind (brain) and body. It's a state of severe and prolonged changes to fundamental neurobiological, hormonal, immune and metabolic systems.

> It was the worst experience of my life. More terrible even than watching my wife die of cancer. I am ashamed to admit that my depression felt worse than her death but it is true. I was in a state that bears no resemblance to anything I had experienced before. It was not just feeling very low, depressed in the commonly used sense of the word. I was seriously ill.
>
> – Lewis Wolpert, author and developmental biologist

Many individuals I've treated with clinical depression start the conversation by saying, 'I'm not "depressed" (meaning normally sad or distressed), I'm sick!'

My response is, 'Yes, you are really sick – and in ways you probably haven't even thought of.'

To which the person's response is, 'So, you *don't* think it's all in my head?'

My response: 'It's in your head, it's in your brain *and* it's in your body. Your brain runs all the functions in your body, so every other part of your body is out of sync. Your whole system is way off course – physiologically, emotionally and cognitively.

'No, I don't think it is simply your psychological response to difficult life circumstances or that you should tell yourself to get your thinking straight.'

This is the entry point to one of the most important distinctions between clinical depression and normal psychological distress.

Clinical depression is accompanied by a wide array of physical symptoms. The most prominent is prolonged fatigue and loss of energy – that is, exhaustion. This debilitating state is not relieved by sleep, rest or other positive interactions with the world. It persists right across the 24-hour sleep–wake cycle and continues, unabated, from day to day. Other physical symptoms include muscle aches and pains, headaches, disturbed gastro-intestinal function, change in bowel habits and changes in appetite and weight.

Distinguishing physical from psychological symptoms is a very Western concept. In most cultures, and at most points in human history, it has been a meaningless distinction. The ongoing promotion of the mind–body distinction has many downsides, including the belief that the problem is primarily psychological – it is occurring in some very distant place from the rest of your body.

If you see depression as being entirely psychological, you will fall into the trap of believing that it is easily fixed by simple psychological, social or behavioural interventions. To this day, an overly psychological perspective dominates much public discussion.

Clearly, if the problem is entirely cognitive (i.e. of the mind) it requires cognitive therapy. If the problem is entirely social, it requires sociological interventions. In these conceptualisations of the mind–body split, the problem is never biological, so it never requires medication or other medical interventions.

Perhaps an even more pernicious consequence of the separation of psychological and physical symptoms is the failure to see clinical depression as an upheaval of the whole system, manifested most commonly as a profound loss of normal wellbeing.

To maintain your wellbeing, you need all your cognitive, emotional and physiological elements to be harmoniously aligned, not only across the 24-hour sleep–wake cycle, but also over seasons and across the various stages of your life.

Not surprisingly, many people experiencing the physical symptoms of clinical depression for the first time will consult a medical practitioner. They may be very concerned that they have developed a serious medical illness, like cancer.

This way of thinking is likely when you can't immediately link your illness with some other social or personal crisis. People, including most health practitioners, don't consider depression unless they can think of a recent causal life event.

I can't count the number of men I've treated who've cried, 'But I don't have a reason to be depressed. I'm married, financially secure and have good health – what can I possibly be depressed about?'

Or, to have read once again in the news of a famous person who has just revealed their depressive illness or, worse, died from suicide: 'He was the last person in the world you would expect to be depressed. Wealthy, successful, everything to live for . . .'

Inevitably, when faced with these very physical presentations of clinical depression, medical practitioners will arrange relevant blood or other screening tests to exclude other causes. One would also hope that they actively enquire as to the broader psychological and physiological state of the individual.

When the blood tests come back normal, this does not mean you are not sick! It just means that the common blood tests we have for anaemia, diabetes or liver or thyroid disease do not detect or diagnose a complex disorder of the whole system like clinical depression.

As one of my most insightful children would say when I get frustrated with the complexity of brain science compared with the easier diagnoses in other areas of medicine: 'Dad, psychiatrists have just got to get a good (blood, brain or other body) test!'

Hang in there. One day, fairly soon, we will use combinations of blood and brain-specific tests to confirm the diagnosis of clinical depression(s) and exclude other serious medical conditions.

I am often tempted to say to my medical colleagues: 'Why don't you do the more fancy brain or blood tests we already have to show your patient's degree of "unwellness"?'

Three answers dominate:

1. 'I don't need those tests to tell me the person is depressed – I can see it with my own eyes!'
2. 'The government doesn't pay for those tests – because they are not diagnostic!'
3. 'The test isn't going to guide my treatment choice.'

Interestingly, most doctors never ask those with the condition, or their relatives, whether they want more extensive tests. We do hand out diagnoses pretty readily, and pretty much every professor and specialist clinic has their own favourite diagnosis, so changing diagnoses is very common. Assigning a diagnosis does help to validate your illness experience, guide your treatment selection and help you navigate the wider social world.

New tests that increase our capacity to indicate the extent to which a person is physically ill with depression, what type of depression they have, whether they are responding to treatment or are at ongoing risk of the above are potential game-changers.

When I say to patients, 'Well, even though I am an old and fairly experienced professor, I'm not sure about some important aspects of your illness and I want to conduct some important tests', it's unusual for them to say, 'No thanks.'

Mostly it's, 'Really? I didn't know there were tests that could be done'.

Looking at the doctors' responses above, the second part of their answer is true. While depression is associated with abnormal blood tests and brain scans, none of them is specific to depression. So, they are not diagnostic. They do not prove you have depression and not some other major mental or physical illness. But that rather misses the point. It's the person with the illness who really needs to know that they are physically sick, as well as psychologically sick, and get themselves and their health care providers out of the lost world of mind versus body.

The third answer is only partly true – and one of the areas of most active clinical research.

Four small examples from my own clinical research include:

1. For a young person with severe atypical (or 24-hour sleep–wake or 'circadian') depression, an overnight study of their production of the sleep hormone melatonin can demonstrate that its release (normally in the afternoon) is delayed in time and reduced in size. That's a good reason to choose a melatonin-based medication in combination with morning light exposure and regularisation of the 24-hour sleep–wake cycle.
2. For a young woman with severe depression, weight gain and autoimmune diseases, the detection of high blood levels of inflammatory markers or specific antibodies could lead to the prescription of immune regulatory therapies.
3. For a woman with severe depression in her early 40s who also had recurrent cyclical depression as a teenager and postnatal depression after childbirth, blood tests of her hormonal status could lead to additional estrogen-based treatments.
4. For an older person with sudden onset of severe depression, a magnetic resonance imaging (MRI) brain scan that reveals extensive changes in the connecting cables ('white matter') running between the thinking parts ('grey matter') of the brain changes the therapeutic approach. Response to treatment is slower and is often associated with more side-effects (confusion, memory disturbance) and therapy may well need to occur in more supervised environments, like a hospital ward.

2. Clinical depression has key psychological characteristics – but not the ones most people associate with it.

Anhedonia, the absence of pleasure (from the Greek *an*, 'without', and *hedone*, 'pleasure') and not sadness, is the key emotional feature of depression. It is often experienced as the complete absence of emotion or at least a profound loss of emotional responsiveness to normally pleasurable events.

People with clinical depression often say:

'Doctor, I'm just dead inside.'

'I'm not depressed, just empty.'

'I see the people I love, but I just don't respond anymore.'

'I'm not sad, I'm not crying, I'm just existing.'

'I'm moving, I'm talking, I'm doing, but I'm not feeling anything – just dread.'

Humans, just like other animals, rely very strongly on the pleasure we derive from everyday activities to reinforce our most useful behaviours – eating, drinking, sex and caring for others.

Across cultures, and across time, a focus on the loss of pleasure from those most essential human tasks has been at the heart of a very rich clinical and public literature about the depressive experience. By contrast, it's the modern preoccupation with sadness that has underpinned many futile arguments about the validity of the concept of depression as an illness.

Let's be clear: to be sad, in the face of major losses or disappointments, is normal. To express that emotion in the presence of friends and family is normal. The active management of clinical depression has nothing to do with a desire to suppress normal sadness or promote endless happiness in the face of genuine adversity.

In his very personal and scholarly discourse on depression, developmental biologist Lewis Wolpert coined the term (and named his book) *Malignant Sadness,* 'to emphasise the very serious nature of a depressive illness and also to reflect my conviction that normal sadness is to depression what normal growth is to cancer'.

To be blunt, there is no overlap between the everyday turnover of body cells and malignant cancers. Similarly, there is no real overlap between normal sadness, which we all experience, and the despair unique to those with clinical depression.

While the actual cancer process is a bit more complicated, so are the boundaries between prolonged sadness, abnormal grief states, chronic anxiety and clinical depression. But, when the process has clearly gone well beyond the boundaries of normality, the threat to life and limb is clear.

Some cultures place great value on suppressing the active and outward expression of normal sadness, distress or grief – the 'stiff upper lip'. Consequently, they can convey the wrong idea that an absence of sadness is normal.

In other cultures where crying out, tearfulness and the wider public expression of distress and grief is normal, it would hardly ever be considered abnormal to experience these emotions when faced with really challenging life circumstances or major interpersonal losses.

So what distinguishes clinical depression is not that it is a state of being overly sensitive, or persistently sad or tearful, but rather that it is a loss of that normal sensitivity to those things we most value – loved ones, family, social connections, work or career.

The absence of tears is a far more worrying sign of severe depression than the flood of tears that usually accompanies genuine grief, loss and the breaking of fundamental and intimate attachments.

By contrast, it's hard to imagine being able to continue living life without experiencing the ordinary and everyday pleasures that we get from our basic needs, our responses to our physical environment (the rising sun, the beach, the surf, the bushland, the forests), our human rituals (dining, drinking, dancing, praying, performing, singing) or our purposeful activities (work, career, social investments).

While I always have a box of tissues placed strategically in my office, it's much more important to enquire about the degree of pleasure an individual derives from the things they normally value, than any other emotional or psychological characteristic. The return of tears, and normal emotional responsiveness, may well indicate recovery.

As put so eloquently by one grandfather: 'I knew I was better when my grandson landed on my lap, and tears flowed freely from my eyes.'

Or a mother: 'My partner knew I was well again when I burst into tears during some silly rom-com we were watching.'

It's the experience of pleasure, on a daily basis, that keeps us in the game. It also helps us to maintain our most important psychological defence against depression – namely, the optimistic estimation that normal people have about their own abilities, the qualities of their intimate relationships and their positive contribution to their wider world.

Other classical characteristics of depression include feelings of worthlessness, hopelessness, guilt, shame and loss of motivation. Thoughts of life not being worth living, active thoughts of death and contemplation of suicide may become common, intrusive and increasingly difficult to resist. These psychological characteristics, like anhedonia, cannot be easily explained by current life circumstances. The extent to which these feelings are *not* justified or proportionate to life circumstances is often clear to other family members.

Further psychological features include:

- ruminations (typically defined as excessive, repetitive or recurrently intrusive thoughts about previous negative experiences, feelings or actions);

- obsessional thoughts (recurrent, often irrational ideas about infection, injury, harm or threat);
- anxious preoccupation (persistent dread that harm will come to the self or others, being constantly vigilant to the external environment, with the unwarranted expectation of imminent harm); and
- not responding emotionally or cognitively to environmental stimuli that would normally distract, enlighten or provide relief from such distressing phenomena.

3. The behavioural changes that accompany clinical depression are often observed by family, carers and health professionals. The classical behavioural changes that accompany clinical depression are in motor behaviour, often slowed beyond that explained by age or other illness. These motor changes may be observed in physical activities like slowed walking or slowed speech. The actual speed of speech is not the same as the speed of thought, which itself may be slowed. When severe, slowed motor behaviour may resemble that seen in those suffering from Parkinson's disease, and is most likely due to biochemical or structural changes within the same motor circuits of the brain that control these movements, and may respond to the same therapeutic agent (dopamine).

This slowness may be interspersed with periods of purposeless and repetitive overactivity or agitation, resulting in pacing, picking or other stereotypical motor movements ('psychomotor agitation'). The motor agitation is typically accompanied by distressing thoughts, ruminations, obsessions, overwhelming guilt, hopelessness, thoughts of impending doom or thoughts of death. Most importantly, this state is so distressing that it is often accompanied by more impulsive and highly dangerous suicidal behaviour.

With the advent of new personal monitoring devices that include very sensitive measures of motor movement, we now have a capacity to track these motor changes over the various phases of illness onset and recovery. Such devices will be used to detect early signs of recurrence and help individuals to take preventive actions.

4. Distorted thinking processes in attention, memory, planning, mental flexibility and rational thinking are common.

For those with clinical depression, the normal cognitive processes of the brain are often disturbed. Attention is poor, and the person often appears distracted and less responsive to their usual social or emotional stimuli. Mental processing can seem slowed and, subjectively, the affected person can often describe the extra effort needed to do simple things (read, recall daily facts, concentrate at work, study effectively). In older persons, these changes are sometimes mistaken, by the person themselves or family, for the onset of dementia. In younger persons, these difficulties can be misattributed to attention problems or laziness.

Importantly, these cognitive difficulties are temporary – meaning that they occur during the episode of depression, and then largely remit following the end of the illness. However, as these key brain functions were disrupted during the episode, you may be unable to remember key aspects of the illness experience or events that took place during that time.

The identification of changes in those brain regions which facilitate these cognitive functions (for example, in the hippocampus, which supports memory, or within the frontal lobes, which support more complex planning and conceptual thinking) has been the subject of active research over recent decades.

An intriguing line of investigation has been the extent to which the efficacy of antidepressant medications may depend on their capacity to support the regeneration of nerve cell connections ('synaptogenesis') or nerve cells themselves ('neurogenesis') within these brain areas. Other interventions, such as physical exercise, increased social interaction and cognitive training, have also been linked to the promotion of neurogenesis or synaptogenesis.

5. Physiological change, notably to the 24-hour sleep–wake cycle, accompanies clinical depression.

Humans are diurnal mammals, meaning they have a 24-hour daily cycle where most activity occurs during the daylight phase and sleep occurs mainly during the nightime phase. We rely strongly on this cycle being in sync with the daily rotation of the planet to maintain good physical and mental health.

The impact of disrupted circadian systems on general health and wellbeing is a relatively new area of medical research, with fundamental discoveries of its basic machinery resulting in the Nobel Prize in Medicine in 2017. When your circadian system (or 'body clock') is off, you are likely to report waking unrefreshed from sleep, morning weariness when everyone else is energetic, daytime fatigue, irritability or reduced pleasure in life, and a sleep–wake cycle that is easily disrupted by life circumstances.

If you've ever suffered severe jet lag, then you know how miserable a disturbed circadian cycle can be. You can't function (emotionally, physically, cognitively) normally for three to ten days until your brain and body functions come back and sync with the day–night cycle in the place you've landed! You can't just overcome it by telling yourself to feel better, act differently or think straight. But you can take active steps (light exposure, daytime physical activity, timing of meals) to make the adjustment as quickly as possible.

When asked what clinical depression really feels like by people who have never had it, I often respond by saying, just imagine you suddenly had the worst jet lag, and it lasted for weeks on end. That is, you couldn't easily explain why there was such a profound shift in your daily body or brain functions. Just imagine how you would feel. What would you think had happened to you? Where would you go for help or to seek an explanation? How long do you think you could live productively in that state? Would you think that the explanation may be something called 'clinical depression'?

If not jet lag, think about other experiences where your normal daily cycle could be severely disrupted by life circumstances – rotating shift work, childbirth, physical illness, caring responsibilities, study. These circumstances also frequently result in prolonged fatigue, irritability, emotional lability, musculoskeletal pain, headaches, loss of wellbeing and other physiological changes like chaotic eating behaviours and weight gain.

So, during clinical depression, the normal 24-hour synchrony between internal body rhythms and the light-dark cycle – and the tightly linked rhythms of physical activity, sleep, eating behaviour, brain restoration and regeneration, hormonal release, metabolic signals, immune activation, bowel function and, most importantly, our overall sense of wellbeing – are all fundamentally disrupted.

As a result most people with clinical depression experience not only difficulties falling asleep, but restless sleep, non-restorative sleep (feeling just as tired when you wake up as when you went to sleep), marked changes in sleep timing (earlier sleep with early-morning wakening in older persons, as compared with later sleep, oversleeping and delayed waking in younger persons), reduced daytime physical activity (accompanied by severe fatigue or loss of energy) and disturbed or reduced gastro-intestinal function (in particular, constipation).

For those who are suddenly awake at 3am, agitated, preoccupied with death, feeling overwhelming guilt or shame and contemplating suicide, making the rational link that such distress may be underpinned by a perturbed body clock is not easy. However, often in discussion with that same person at 3pm in the afternoon, when they feel much less distressed and more attentive to their external world, this physiological link is entirely plausible.

Many people I see have experienced a disturbed circadian system for several years – just like that described by Australia's former Trade Minister Andrew Robb (see below) – but had never considered that they may have had a depressive illness. In most circumstances, they had also seen a doctor or psychologist – but since they did not report sadness, depressed mood, tearfulness, traumatic life events, distressing life circumstances or adverse childhood experiences, the diagnosis of clinical depression was not considered.

It is two years since I started enjoying the best mornings I have had since childhood, after finally finding a treatment for my underlying depressive condition.

I was 12 years old when I first recognised that something was hampering my ability to function properly early in the day. I would wake up feeling very negative, lacking confidence, indecisive, and just wanting to stay within myself. But I would find that, after having been up and about for a few hours, my state of mind would dramatically improve. I would become positive, a decisionmaker, happy to take responsibility.

For years, I simply put my malaise down to 'not being a good morning person', but as I got older, the fog would take longer to clear. It started to have an impact well into my working day.

I didn't want to admit, even to myself, that I had a depressive condition. Rather than seeking professional help, I did my utmost to self-manage my condition, to try to get myself going. I employed a range of quite bizarre techniques, including staring at the sun to make myself sneeze, because I felt that would help with the release of endorphins and give me a lift.

It took me 43 years to confront my condition. Initially, I went to see a local general practitioner. I was told not to bother taking pills, as they didn't really work — it's all in the head! I left the consultation feeling deflated and thinking, 'Get over it, it's something I'll just have to live with'.

It took six months of experimentation with different types of medication, but I finally found a treatment that worked. I now combine this with daily exercise. I'm one of those questionable people who jump in the bay at dawn to swim 1200 to 1500 metres, even in the middle of winter. There is no better way to get the heart started.

Andrew Robb from *Medical Journal of Australia,* Oct 2013

6. Suicidal thoughts and behaviour are common.

With each person I see with clinical depression, I assume that they are experiencing active suicidal thoughts and may be contemplating suicide. Estimates of the rate of death by suicide, unexplained accidents (single vehicle road accidents, falls from high buildings or cliffs), other lethal injuries (walking in front of a car) or 'unintended' overdoses among persons with clinical depression vary depending on the group of people that have been followed up or diagnosed by a health professional before death.

Conservative estimates are in the range of five to 15 per cent among those who have been actively treated. I was reminded of the conservative nature of these estimates in a recent case where a young woman stabbed herself in the chest after contacting various mental health agencies and helplines, and writing extensively about her depression and her wish to die. The coroner decided that she was too young to have formed a clear view that her actions would most likely result in her death. Her death by her own hand was not classed as a suicide but rather as an accident.

Of course a wider variety of social, cultural and religious taboos have operated to suppress not only suicidal behaviour but also naming suicide as the cause of death. Death by suicide has also typically brought great shame on families, along with intensifying feelings of guilt. Consequently, many family members and friends are still very reluctant to have a death recorded as suicide, seemingly to protect the reputation of the deceased.

So many instances of 'accidental overdose', particularly among celebrities or those in the public eye, in those who have had clear mental health difficulties and access to care and prescription medications, alcohol or illicit drugs, are frequently not counted. From my perspective, they have still died prematurely as a direct result of a potentially treatable depressive illness.

Interestingly, most ways of recording suicidal thoughts tend to undercount the phenomena. Most people are terrified to tell others – family, friends or health professionals – what is really happening inside their head. Often they are not only scared of the possible consequences of disclosure (involuntary detention in a psychiatric facility) but are simply, overwhelmingly distressed by the intrusive, persistent and irrational nature of the thoughts.

Other methods, like self-reporting on questionnaires or computer programs, typically detect higher rates. Whenever someone with clinical depression asserts that they're not experiencing or have never experienced such feelings or thoughts, I put on my most quizzical or confused face and say, 'Really, that's so very unusual . . .'

Often, a great sigh of relief and active disclosure follows – at least from those who are comfortable with me and are certain that I am unlikely to judge them harshly.

When suicidal thoughts or behaviours are experienced for the first time, a person may also be unaware that depression – not life circumstances – are really driving the phenomena. The thoughts are so unacceptable and the potential consequences of acting on the thoughts so dire, that they may intensify other distressing features such as guilt, shame and worthlessness. When accompanied by severe agitation, the thoughts may be extremely difficult to resist and the person may be driven to act in some self-destructive fashion, quite impulsively, simply to relieve their overwhelming distress.

As former Australian Prime Minister Malcolm Turnbull noted in his biography *A Bigger Picture*:

> I'd never given any thought to my mental health before – mental illness was something others had to worry about. And while I'd had periods of real gloom, especially after the defeat of the republic referendum, what I felt enveloping me now was much more serious. For the first time in my life, suicidal thoughts started to enter my mind, unbidden and unwanted.

In a diary note that he made during this dark period, he wrote:

> I feel at present like a complete and utter failure . . . Having lost the leadership I sank deeper and deeper into depression, couldn't make up my mind to stay or go . . . I could backflip and run again and stay in parliament. But for what? More humiliation? A rebirth? Unlikely. The answer is that the pain will end at some point – suicide is a permanent solution to a temporary (we hope) problem. But frankly I am thinking about dying all the time.

Whenever someone reassures me that they will not act on their suicidal ideas because of the adverse impacts on their family, children or friends, or because of their religious or other social beliefs, I remain largely sceptical. Such assurances assume that the person will act rationally or at least act in ways that would be more typical of their non-depressed self. It misunderstands the fundamental state of mind that lies behind the experience of clinical depression, and its active link to life-threatening behaviours.

Not everyone is convinced that persistent suicidal thoughts and behaviours are an intrinsic, and potentially lethal, part of the condition. Other explanations are advanced, including that they are a consequence of:

- the adverse effects of treatment with medication, or the cessation of medications, to treat the condition;
- the adverse life circumstances that have accompanied the onset of the episode (relationship breakdown) or the illness's ongoing impacts on their broader world (social isolation, financial loss);
- other independent risk factors such as childhood trauma;
- other psychological (personality disorder, post-traumatic stress) or medical (chronic pain) difficulties that can co-occur with depression; or,
- concurrent use of other medications (sleeping sedatives), alcohol or other substances (stimulants, cannabis).

While a number of these factors may certainly increase the risk of suicidal behaviour, all downplay the intrinsic relationship with the illness itself and, consequently, the need to ensure active and rapid engagement with effective treatments.

As described by former MP and playwright Neil Cole, reflecting his personal experience, when the cloud of suicidality blows in, uninvited, it is deep and disturbing. It demonstrates no particular rhyme or reason. Rational thinking and active attempts to wish it away are largely ineffective. When it's there, like the weather, you can't be sure when it will pass and the sun (optimism for life) will reappear. The essential task for the person affected is to stay alive until tomorrow.

As captured beautifully in Neil's fictional portrayal of bipolar depression in his novel *Colonel Surry's Insanity*, while everyone else has an explanation, the person at the centre of the experience often remains entirely unconvinced that there is any direct link between their life circumstances and the episode itself, or the depth of despair that accompanies it.

So, why do so many people seek to break the obvious link between clinical depression and suicidal behaviour? Perhaps at the heart of the problem is not only our lack of empathy for those most affected but also our own deep desire to believe that such behaviour can be explained rationally.

From a suicide prevention perspective, it has also become part of a wider movement to see suicide more broadly as a social and political issue. While this does have particular benefits in terms of reducing known population-level risks (unemployment, financial hardship, social isolation), it has a clear downside – justifying the ongoing lack of access of most people with clinical depression to highly effective treatments.

7. Clinical depression is associated with a range of distressing mood states, not simply sadness.

One of the major problems with the diagnosis of clinical depression is the specific linking with the mood state of depression. Depression is a common and non-specific expression in the English language ('depressed economy'). It is also used to describe a feeling that almost all of us have at some stage in life. It fails to communicate the depth, severity or unusual nature of the various moods experienced by people with clinical depression.

While it might be fair to say that everyone gets depressed, so everyone knows what depression is, it might also be fairer to say that most of us really have no idea what it is really like to feel *clinically* depressed.

To complicate matters further, many people (notably men!) don't really identify with the concept of normal depression or sadness. Very frequently, when clinically depressed they are likely to report other mood states, such as irritability, frustration, emptiness or a more pervasive gloom.

8. Clinical depression is prolonged and often unrelenting, not easily impacted by day-to-day events.

While periods of psychological distress are common, and associated with upheavals in our personal lives, they usually end within relatively short periods. Psychological distress, particularly when expressed externally through tears, words, feelings and behaviour, evokes a caring response from our close social network and our wider social world. Fortunately, for many of us, the troops usually do rally to support the injured party. Most distressed people who are not clinically depressed remain reactive to those positive, day-to-day changes in the external environment.

By contrast, those with clinical depression become less responsive and less reactive. So, even when those external events that seemed to precipitate the onset have been resolved, they may well have very little impact on the course of the illness itself.

So, all major definitions of clinical depression have a duration criteria of at least two weeks. Some would suggest at least four weeks is a more appropriate benchmark. But, if you are actually in the state (and also actively suicidal), even two weeks can be a very long time.

Prior to the advent of specific treatments, episodes typically lasted for several months and, when severe, several years. Those periods did often end spontaneously, sometimes correlating with an external factor like a change in seasons (remissions being more likely in spring) but frequently quite independently of any significant change in the person's circumstances. Sadly, those who experience prolonged episodes are also at very high risk of recurrent episodes throughout life.

9. Clinical depression is debilitating, making it very difficult to continue with daily social, interpersonal or economic tasks.

> I was totally self-involved, negative and thought about suicide most of the time. I could not think properly, let alone work, and wanted to remain curled up in bed all day. I could not ride my bicycle or go out on my own.
>
> – Lewis Wolpert

For most of us, as highlighted by psychoanalyst and lapsed neurologist Sigmund Freud, the general purpose of life is 'to love and work'. So, an illness that robs you of either of these capacities undermines the basic reasons that we get out of bed each day and derive pleasure from our otherwise very challenging existence.

When people say that they are depressed but haven't noticed any impact on their normal work life or their intimate relationships, I suggest to them (very kindly) 'Actually, you're not depressed . . . You may be very unhappy or distressed, but not *clinically* depressed.'

10. Clinical depression rapidly leads to other serious complications.

Those who have been clinically depressed for any significant length of time don't just stay that way.

Men who are depressed resort very quickly to substances (for example, alcohol and cannabis) that provide some relief. Women, more typically, use not only alcohol but also easy-to-obtain prescription medications (for anxiety, sleep and pain relief).

The younger people we now see much earlier in the course of these illnesses have ready access to alcohol and a wide range of substances (stimulants, sedatives, cannabis, psychedelics).

One of the funniest interactions I've had with many people (young and old) is the statement: 'I'm not taking your toxic medicines – I've heard about all the harms they cause: suicide, addiction, obesity and diabetes.'

My reply: 'And the substances you prefer, they do *what* exactly? And what of the illness itself – if left untreated?'

At that stage I reach for the endless research publications I've been associated with over the past 30 years, indicating that the direct medical consequences of depression include: suicide, alcoholism, premature heart disease, diabetes and other metabolic conditions and dementia.

Most people are still disbelieving when I then provide the substantial evidence that effective treatment of depression is associated with a reduction in all these bad outcomes.

Sadly, by the time many middle-aged people first come to care they have already developed several of these medical complications, along with a whole lot of other consequences in their personal lives (failed marriages and relationships, disrupted friendships and social networks), their career (lost jobs, poor finances) and their social existence (isolation, detachment from other social connections).

Additionally, if past psychological trauma was not one of the original casuses for their condition, then they have been extremely traumatised by its consequences. One of the most important justifications for earlier intervention, particularly in the teenage years, is not simply to prevent progression of this malignant sadness (that is, to save lives!) but also to reduce the secondary trauma that results if left to run its natural course.

It staggers me that many professional and social critics still promote this really bad option: 'Just let it run its natural course', largely because those who don't really have a clinical condition will probably resolve spontaneously at some time. I doubt any physician in the 21st century seriously says that to a person with cancer, heart disease, asthma or diabetes.

Before we had any effective modern treatments, the natural course of clinical depression was that after some very prolonged period, a significant proportion did spontaneously resolve – if you were still alive!

3

Frustrated and Angry: 'So Much More That We Can Do?'

On some nights during my professional career, I've been really angry and frustrated. Given the support of the media and public for people living with depression, why do I have these nights? Well, I'd just heard a dad who recently lost his teenage son to suicide be asked the same dumb, grossly insensitive question: 'What more could you or your family have done?' The implicit question by the naive interviewer was, 'What more *should you* have done?'

Having sat with too many distressed parents who have gone through something similar and cried out, 'What more could we have done?', I find this profound lack of empathy, and basic understanding, intolerable. My personal response is, 'You did everything you could. The real question is whether we (the community, the health care system) did everything we could.' My overwhelming answer is that collectively our efforts have not come close. In darker times, I might add, 'What's worse is that we speak kind words but have no real agenda for urgent actions.'

Over the past 25 years I've often been out in the public domain, as a clinician, academic and inaugural CEO of Beyond Blue (our national depression awareness campaign), discussing multiple aspects of clinical depression. This has included the concept of depression as an illness, its symptoms, major negative impacts – disability, premature death, and links with suicide, alcohol and drug use, and accidents and injury – potential causes, natural course and best treatments available.

Overall, we have been fortunate in Australia that our media has provided a very balanced and open approach to this community dialogue. This has been greatly assisted by the willingness of many people, from all walks of life, to share their deep and very personal experiences with the wider public. Consequently, public sympathy for those affected has grown, and government and community leaders have become more conversant with the basic facts. ('It's very common, many people are affected, we really should do more.')

Unfortunately, Australia has progressively seen a loss of local media production over that period and has relied heavily on importing overseas-produced material. As part of that process, we now import more of the deliberately provocative, hyper-polarised reporting styles that are so popular among US and some UK-based media organisations.

Erica's story: 'Come back to emergency care when you're well!'

On another occasion, my partner, Dr Elizabeth Scott, spent most of her weekend trying to arrange the safe passage into hospital of one young woman, Erica, who had a severe form of clinical depression. Erica had just made another attempt on her own life, the fifth that year. Despite Elizabeth having attended the hospital in person over the weekend, spoken to four senior psychiatrists at each of the two public institutions funded to provide care, and senior emergency physicians at each of the two emergency departments involved, come Monday morning Erica was discharged home to her parents' care – as if they had the resources, skill and knowledge to cope with an illness that our health care system could not. As if her life was not in immediate danger. And with no clear plan of what would happen next. But, here's the really bizarre part – Erica's parents were told that if she became less suicidal and less impulsive, only *then* could she come back to the hospital for care!

The contrast with cancer care for children and young people in Australia could not be more stark. Quite appropriately, we are now committed to the most advanced care possible for every child facing that life-threatening health crisis. We have the best clinicians, working in partnerships with the best researchers, linked to international best-in-the world clinical trials of new treatments. Every child is their own unique research study. No child is abandoned as just being too hard, or beyond the scope of medical discovery, innovation and best care.

During the COVID-19 pandemic we rallied our national health infrastructure to respond. Huge efforts were made to purchase and distribute vaccines. In the building right next door to my office, an older space was completely refitted by local area health services within two weeks. It immediately delivered vaccines to hundreds of us in need, through the hands of fully trained staff. It was all backed by sophisticated information technologies.

As we walked past this amazing example of collective action, one of my research staff, who had been working ferociously on improving mental health services for young people over the last five years, laughed and remarked (without bitterness), 'Imagine if that much effort was focused on the mental health needs of young people!'

All the things we're told can't be done, or will take another five to ten years, can be fixed in a resource-rich country – that is, when we choose to fix them, and when we have the people, infrastructure, workforces and shared values. We can see it happening in front of our eyes for those who live with childhood cancer or in the national health response to the pandemic.

Are those with clinical depression just 'children of a lesser god'?

In the past, children who had a disability were described as 'children of a lesser god'. Society expressed sympathy then looked the other way. Is the same thing happening to those with depression, as a consequence of ignorance about the nature of these conditions?

Are we still blaming the parents, the young person themself or the adult who lives with one of these conditions? 'Really, it's your fault – you *should* have done more!' The implied belief is that, in some way, those affected are complicit with the illness itself. I can't think of a situation where a child or young person with a life-threatening cancer or overwhelming infection would be sent home with their parents, with no treatment plan, and then told they can come back to care when they improve!

So, back to Erica's abandonment by the health care system: how could this have happened? Well, the local emergency mental health care team simply re-diagnosed the young woman as being not depressed, instead deciding that she had a disorder of self. Consequently, they decided she didn't require further specialised or hospital-based care. As a young psychiatry trainee doctor informed me recently, her job wasn't to treat the illness but simply to clear the bed!

In most areas of medicine, emergency rooms are the fast track to effective and often life-saving care. They are not a short-cut to the exit door! Emergency departments use smart and well-trained clinicians, clear protocols for rapid response and connect you to other parts of the health care system to ensure your safety and continuity of care. The problem here is not the emergency room physicians – it's the public ignorance of what is really possible, the collusion of inadequately resourced and poorly co-ordinated mental health systems, and the promotion of ferociously anti-clinical sentiments by other interests.

My sharp response to journalists, professional sceptics or well-meaning but inactive politicians, public servants and health care providers is, 'What did you do to prevent these most tragic events?' If they are not sufficiently provoked, I'm inclined to go one step further: 'Did your actions, by pushing the responsibility back to the parents or the young person themselves, actually contribute to the neglect of these life-threatening conditions? Did you perpetuate the myth that such tragedies are so complex that little can be done to prevent them?'

Although these problems are not new, we now have a brand-new distraction: the aftermath of the COVID-19 pandemic. Actually, it's not really a distraction, because as the economic and social repercussions continue to play out long after the immediate health crisis, the mental health of our nations will be near the top of the list of major difficulties.

While mental health and suicide prevention are recognised as important, most responses are led by more awareness campaigns, promotion of self-help strategies (stay connected, don't abuse alcohol, get lots of exercise), increased support for helplines and rather generic messages about reaching out for professional help (if you can't self-manage). The evidence suggests that not only do these feel-good strategies not deliver much benefit but also, inadvertently, they may make the situation a lot worse for those who really do need access to high-quality or emergency care.

So, in this time of genuine mental health need, it becomes even more important that those with very serious needs – like Erica – can actually get the care they need, the care that *we* should provide.

It's very hard to imagine that in other areas of medicine (cancer, heart disease, severe arthritis, diabetes, multiple sclerosis) that the response to obvious failures in health care would be, 'Well, treatments aren't perfect, so let's focus on prevention instead.' Abandon the needs of those who present in life-threatening situations today in favour of the long-term illusion of illness eradication by prevention. By the way, there is no one-shot vaccine for clinical depression, and it's unclear what specific strategies actually work to prevent it.

In mental health – and particularly for our most costly condition, namely major depression – we now need to re-learn a basic lesson. We will always need both a high-quality health care system, which is readily available (preferably early in the illness course), *and* a sophisticated prevention system – one that's not just for prevention of the illness but also for secondary prevention of recurrence.

In the context of Erica's abandonment by the health care system in 2021 (not 1956 or 1993), we spoke with a senior colleague at one of the hospitals involved. His comment: 'Ian and Liz, if you think it's just bad for young people, let me tell you, I recently sent an older man, with an agitated depression and alcohol abuse, to the ED for acute admission. He was sent home without anyone consulting me. He suicided the following weekend.'

When I was younger, I spent my academic career investigating the neurobiological basis of clinical depression in older people. Basically, their needs and the misattribution of their illness to 'normal ageing' was catastrophic. As I've got older, I've shifted my focus to earlier intervention for young people. Basically, because their needs and the misattribution of their illness to 'normal adolescence' is catastrophic.

4

What Does the Perspective of a Clinician-Researcher Bring to the Table?

JESS'S STORY

My mum says I was an anxious child since birth, but you could have just said I was shy – or a little bit different to my three siblings. When I was 14, I started experiencing severe depression and self-harm. There was no trigger – I'm from a close and loving family and nothing major in my life had happened. There was no divorce, no financial problems, no trauma. I really struggled with the concept of not having a valid reason for my suffering.

Over the next couple of years, there were doctors and psychiatrists and hospital visits and about 22 different medications, none of which provided any relief. I'd be clinically depressed and majorly suicidal for at least seven months at a time. Then it would randomly lift and I'd be able to study, see friends, party, engage in risky behaviour and be completely proud to be alive – before going back down again.

I had to leave school because I missed out on so much of it. It was probably more of a big deal for my parents than it was for me. I'd completely checked out. Ruminating on the depression just made me feel like I was nothing more than a chunk of space, making problems for everyone.

A lifechanging encounter

At a charity dinner nine years ago, Mum met respected psychiatrist Elizabeth Scott. Liz's partner is Ian Hickie, who runs the Brain and Mind Centre, and together they've made a huge difference to my life.

Ian took me under his wing, assessed me, explained all the science – and advised I go into hospital. I had a massive fear of hospitals, because they hadn't helped in the past and I hate being away from home. He persisted: Liz would work with me as my psychiatrist three days a week, assess my medications, and, most importantly, my sleep and re-evaluate my diagnosis – really she did everything and anything.

Two days later, I was admitted to hospital and diagnosed with bipolar spectrum disorder. What does that even mean? Bipolar is a whole spectrum of symptoms and I suffer way more with my depression. I don't like labels, but it helped to be able to understand my mood cycles and know it was more than just medication. Lifestyle, getting enough sleep, exercise, sun exposure and also sufficient self-care – simple things – are very important too and crucial in gaining some control over my condition.

A lesson in perspective

If I had a choice I wouldn't get rid of my mental illness, or any of the things I've been through. I wouldn't change it for the world. Having experienced what I have, you feel for people more; you want to help people more. You really want to sit with someone and understand them and not just see them as whatever it is they're going through. You realise there's more to people than their issues or illness, because you've been there.

My life now is looking good. I've moved in with my fiancé and I'm three weeks away from completing my master's in social work. My own struggles reinforced that I want to help others, and my illness has taught me to be a better person. It's brought my family closer together. I'm a better daughter and granddaughter – my parents and grandparents have been with me through thick and thin and learned so much about mental health on my journey. My sister is about to have her third child, and I'm enjoying being an aunty to my niece and nephew. I can teach them to be proud of who they are and that they can get through anything.

It may seem like a very odd time for someone as traditional as me (old, psychiatrist, clinician, researcher, advocate) to wish to share his perspectives on clinical depression. But that's where I'm headed.

I am hoping that readers with a genuine interest may benefit from the combination of:

1. Useful messages, reported directly, from the very deep and thoughtful reflections of those individuals, and families and carers, who have lived experience of depression;
2. The insights of a clinician who has journeyed with many of these people, of all ages and from many backgrounds, over long periods and challenging terrains;
3. The constantly changing 'knowledge' of an active researcher – and one who is also well aware that there is much that still remains in that marvellous Donald Rumsfeld class of 'unknown unknowns';

4. The experiences of a long-serving advocate for improved access to high-quality mental health services.

Drawing on personal accounts

I'm often asked by people living with depression and their families, 'Should I read so-and-so's account of their own depression?' My answer is usually delivered in five parts:

1. 'Definitely, yes!' The more people share first-person accounts, experiences and lessons learnt, the better!
2. 'And, here's a few more that I strongly recommend.' (See Recommended Reading at the end of the book.)
3. 'But remember, it's one story – and your own will be quite different.'
4. 'You also might like to start reading some of the research literature that supports my own views – and some of that which also strongly disagrees.'
5. 'Also, you might think about writing your own account as we go along – for yourself and potentially to share with others in the future.'

There is no doubt that many of those who have lived with major mental illnesses like clinical depression have been subject to active discrimination, social exclusion and loss of major economic, education or other opportunities. For centuries, their capacity to participate fully in our wider society has been compromised. In many parts of the world, this is still the reality.

Some of this discrimination can be explained by society's fundamental misunderstandings of the nature of the illness. Its behavioural and emotional effects are often attributed to defects in character, lack of willpower, low personal motivation, absence of individual resilience or the presence of strong religious or political beliefs.

Some historical perspectives

However, other important factors include ongoing lack of access to effective treatments. The only really specific treatments first emerged in the 1930s (largely, in relation to physical interventions like convulsive therapies). Before that, a large number of people died prematurely or did not recover, while others had spontaneous remissions. Sadly, large numbers received various experimental forms of medical treatment, sedation, hospitalisation, brain surgery or talking therapies that not only did little good, but made the situation worse.

In the late 1950s came the first effective medicines. But neither the first round of physical or medication-based treatments was widely prescribed. They were too complex and medically dangerous. The great majority of people with depression never received effective care. Historically those illnesses that were debilitating or life-threatening, but not readily treated, have evoked fear, stigma and discrimination (for example, tuberculosis, epilepsy, leprosy, cancer). It's been a reality for many medical conditions that stigma and discrimination don't really decline until effective treatments are widely available.

Only with the advent of the second generation of antidepressant medicines in the 1980s were treatments widely provided in the community. These treatments were not actually more effective but they had key advantages – far fewer side-effects, less toxicity in overdose and a broader scope for use. They were moderately effective for common and less severe forms of both anxiety and depression.

Two further factors still strongly influence the personal narratives of those who lived through earlier periods. One was the negative response to the style of top-down, paternalistic medical care that characterised not only the management style of clinical psychiatry but also most medical disciplines until the early 1980s. The second, which applied more uniquely to psychiatry, was the history of abuse and neglect associated with the worst phases of mass institutionalisation of those with severe and ongoing illnesses. This phase has largely passed, but it is still presented, often disingenuously, as the dominant paradigm of mental health care.

Although this phase began to decline from the late 1950s, various aspects continued well into the 1980s in most Western countries. The decline was driven by improved treatments – not by changes in the socio-political aspects of mental health care or the community's largely negative views. In parts of the world where access to effective treatments remains highly restricted, such practices continue to this day.

The value of the stories of those with lived experiences of clinical depression

The detailing of personal accounts of clinical depression has a very long and rich history. Those depictions provide unique insights not only about the true nature of the disorder and its debilitating effects on both the body and mind, but also the rich and deep humanity of those affected. As with personal accounts of many other illness journeys, these individual narratives provide us all with more direct links to the fundamental challenge of being better humans in a harsh external world.

As highlighted so eloquently by Susan Sontag in her 1978 classic *Illness As Metaphor*, the thoughtless language, myths and metaphors that surround certain illnesses can have many negative impacts, including discouraging those affected from seeking optimal care (in her personal case, cancer). The process of simply telling it as it is, and hopefully presenting the experience for what it is – an illness, and 'not a curse, not a punishment' – helps understanding.

The therapeutic capacity of this style of high-quality and informed storytelling, unfiltered by other professional perspectives, cannot be underestimated. As a source of fundamental and genuine hope, in the face of real turmoil, these personal accounts are invaluable.

Over recent years, we have seen an explosion in these very important personal stories occupying considerable space in traditional and new media forms. In terms of increasing wider public understanding, they are important for all of us.

At least twice a month, we see some new personal (or celebrity) account of a cancer journey that inspires genuine hope, new perspectives that resonate strongly not only with those affected but also the wider world. In Australia, Julia Baird's 2020 book *Phosphoresence* is a great example. In the same way, we desperately need as many personal accounts of clinical depression, and other major mental disorders. We need them written in many different styles, so that they can connect with the widest possible audience.

Given the extent to which those with major mental disorders were often marginalised and disempowered in previous generations, this explosion in personal narratives has been a very positive move forward. The many different accounts have provided a very rich set of resources, and the wisdom of lived expertise to others. The fact that those who write include both the rich, powerful and famous, as well as those who have never been in the public eye, is most encouraging.

Some like Alastair Campbell, the former political advisor to UK Prime Minister Tony Blair, have written a whole series of very useful and brutally honest accounts. Many have then linked their narratives to other multimedia and highly accessible media platforms. The best describe their own personal pursuit of much better sources of knowledge. These stories provide the depth and authenticity that only first-person accounts can truly reach.

For example, how's this for a personal account of what clinical depression really feels like (from *Living Better* by Alastair Campbell):

> I have a sense of a dark grey cloud, oval, about five times the size of a rugby ball, which fills me with dread. It has a colour, a texture, and it has a feel, a kind of really unpleasant sort of jelly feel. I might talk to it: 'Please, no, go away. Just fuck off.'
>
> In my mind's eye there is now a smile on this cloud, and it is moving in, and I am trying to push it away, but I can't. Its smile is growing because it knows I am about to give up the struggle and let it in. Reluctantly, I say: 'Come on then, let's get it over with,' and then it is inside me, and it feels like a heavy liquid is being poured through my veins, and my body starts to join my mind in feeling heavy. The cloud has evaporated, but its smile is still there, and it is saying, 'Gotcha . . . again . . . you thought you were rid of me . . . no chance . . . I'm back, and this time I'm never going away.'

The more varied the stories, and the more diverse the identities of those telling them, the better! Currently, as society begins to engage much more seriously with the impacts of clinical depression on young people, we are fortunate to have access to their unique experiences. It makes a lot of what was written in the 20th century seem very quaint indeed!

Those personal narratives have also appeared alongside more detailed critiques of past and current clinical practices. We all have much to learn from this very active commentary on the treatments we provide, the way that we organise and deliver mental health care, and the experiences of living with these conditions in the 21st century. The process of holding medicine to account for its past failures, and its current systems, remains an important socio-political and cultural process.

The limitations of single personal perspectives

The most obvious limitation of such accounts arises from the fact that each person's journey is truly unique. And each is essentially a story – meaning that the person's specific explanation for what they believe to be the factors that most influenced the onset of their illness, its course or their recovery is not contestable. They are simply stated as experienced realities.

Key questions may never be asked. Critical information can be covertly or overtly omitted. Qualifying statements are often not pursued. Large gaps in knowledge are rarely conceded. Strong conclusions are not challenged. The extent to which the 'facts' are true, or the conclusions are warranted is, therefore, unclear. How readily the derived wisdom can be transferred to others is open to question.

Such personal accounts are very powerful – and if they fit well with our own preconceived ideas about the way the world really is, then we are very likely to be strongly influenced by them. If someone we trust or care for deeply says taking antidepressants or, alternatively, stopping antidepressants, made them more ill or made them attempt suicide we are likely to take their account at face value.

When someone reports that they only recovered by stopping their medication (which had bad side-effects) and actively pursued alternative therapies we may be impressed by their 'bravery,' 'courage' or their stated 'resilience'. This is often portrayed as a great personal victory over the twin evils of the 'medical model' and the 'illness' itself.

For those who have continued to take conventional medical therapies, and stayed well, there is often a level of condescension or disappointment expressed towards them.

Statements like: 'I suppose if you have to take treatment, that's sad but maybe necessary – at least for you.' 'Maybe some day you'll be able to get by without that stuff – it's only relieving the symptoms, it's not fixing the underlying cause.' 'I hope you'll be strong enough soon to stop the drugs.' 'It's such a shame that you're still dependent on those things.'

These themes are still commonly heard.

Given the breadth of lived experiences, there have also been incidences where the focus has been deliberately negative – directed against 'the medical model' or 'the clinical establishment', their power structures or the treatments they provide. Sometimes they come with an attack on the role of the 'evil, profit-driven' pharmaceutical industry.

While these are legitimate areas for public debate, I do find it insincere when I read personal accounts that start with statements like: 'I did take antidepressants and got well, but I wish I hadn't. I know now that they don't really work. If you need to take them, you probably should, but most other people don't need them. They do well with no help or get psychological therapy to sort out the real cause.'

These personal accounts are often accompanied by declarations of health professionals of their own road-to-Damascus experiences. That is, although they once provided conventional treatments that restored or saved many lives, they now regret their own role. Instead they advocate strongly against the wider public acceptance of depression as a clinical entity – 'it's not a disease' – and recommend strongly that effective treatments should not be more widely provided ('Pull up the ladder, I'm on board!').

Given the reality that public controversy sells, a series of false opposing views are often promoted. These include: public health initiatives versus individual clinical medicine; illness prevention versus active treatment; medicines against psychology; psychologists against psychiatrists; non-clinicians and community supports against trained clinicians; psychological versus biological theories of causation; and the value of 'diagnostic' systems (like DSM, the *Diagnostic and Statistical Manual of Mental Disorders*) vs unique individual experiences.

My goal in this book is not to get lost in these straw man debates (though they do often appear in the media, academic literature, online and TEDx worlds). Instead, it is to highlight where the insights from clinical medicine and genuine research may add real value to the insights provided by those who have directly experienced these disorders.

What do doctors do when they get sick?

When I get sick or when someone who is close to me looks like they may be in trouble with their health, I don't muck around with half-baked common-sense, intuitive, natural or other lay explanations. I go ask someone who really knows – an expert. My experience with real medical experts is that, whenever they are in trouble, they are the first to seek new and additional knowledge from their trusted friends, like other highly specialised experts.

Among my colleagues, we all share the phone numbers or private email addresses of the best clinicians we know, here in Australia and globally. Why do we do this? Because we want the best options now! We treat the art and science of clinical medicine, and its leading practitioners, with great respect. With new ways of sharing information and access, it's time for everyone else to get in on this process.

Our own lives depend on it, along with those we love and care for.

In medicine, there is one golden rule: 'First, make sure you stay alive – so that when the real cure arrives you'll be the first to know!'

An unexpected emergency response

Last week a close colleague rang and asked me to see an older male friend, Mark, who had rapidly descended into a very depressed state. His family were terrified that he was on the precipice. He was inconsolable, believing a recent error in judgement had cost him not only his reputation, but all future hope of living a productive life. While those close to him recognised this was a gross distortion of reality, there was no persuading Mark otherwise. He was losing weight, unable to sleep and to stay still.

I agreed to see him urgently. Accompanied by distressed family members, he arrived downcast, somewhat dishevelled, pacing, ruminating and lost in regrets. Diagnostically, it was very straightforward: severe clinical depression.

For a psychiatrist, this is the equivalent of a cardiologist watching someone have a heart attack right in front of your eyes. But then he said something rather unexpected: 'I understand that treatments take at least six weeks to work, so what hope do I have?'

'Stop right there,' I interrupted. 'We are taking actions right now. The goal is to make sure you stay alive tonight and through to tomorrow. We have many effective therapies, and short and long-term options. We can act like all other areas of medicine: save lives first, then work through the longer road to recovery.'

The value of clinical medicine

Basically, clinical medicine is about taking all that we know from the collective experiences of many others, alongside that which is supported by science, and applying that distilled knowledge directly to the person (and family) affected. As in Mark's case, many of those options, short or long-term, are not widely known. That combination can be uniquely designed – it's not a cookbook recipe – so that the individual can make the best possible choices in their very personal journey.

This concept of trying to maximise what it is about an individual's particular situation that indicates genuine illness, and is similar enough to some (but not all others) with that same pathological condition, lies at the core of the clinical process. It includes the initial diagnostic part, then treatment selection and then revising those treatments on the basis of whether or not you respond well. This is as true in clinical psychiatry as it is in cardiology or cancer care.

One of my favourite aspects of providing clinical care in the modern, technology-rich era, is the way people can come back and show me on their smartphones detailed records of physical activity, sleep patterns and body functions. Some have proclaimed, 'Look, Doctor Hickie, I did exactly what you recommended and it didn't work for me! So, what's your next best option?'

My reply is, 'Well, now that we know what doesn't work, we can explore other options with more confidence!'

Of course there are many individuals who reject any collective groupings of experience. They believe they are so unique that they have nothing to learn from health professionals or the experiences of others. They strongly believe they must find their own way. Think of Steve Jobs, the founder of Apple, and his initial belief that he could manage his own pancreatic cancer via alternative medicine and survive without professional help! Eventually, he did have surgery several months after the diagnosis and went on to live another seven years.

Trained clinicians spend years listening, observing, caring and partnering with many unique illness journeys and trials of treatment. They are observing the gap between what might be expected in the average situation and what actually happens in each case. The most important advances in medicine have derived from this capacity to observe and be challenged to reconsider previously strongly held ideas.

A great example is Australia's most significant contribution to modern therapeutics in clinical psychiatry (and perhaps in the whole of medicine) – namely Dr John Cade's description, in Melbourne in the late 1940s, of the therapeutic potential of lithium carbonate for manic-depressive illness (now called bipolar disorder). This unexpected and fortuitous breakthrough was based on the very astute observation that lithium salts induced calmness, first in guinea pigs, and then in humans.

The clinician is well represented in Peter Kramer's best-selling book *Listening to Prozac*. Despite Kramer's competency in delivering complex psychological therapies, he observed something intriguing in the mental life of people who in the 1990s were taking the new selective serotonin reuptake inhibitors (SSRIs). It was not what he (or they) were expecting – but he was open to actually hearing their experiences. He was prepared to challenge his own assumptions about the limited utility of medical therapies for common forms of anxiety and depression.

The pursuit of highly informed, but also highly personalised approaches, to care

In the modern age, clinical medicine is striving to make each treatment selection much more personalised, be it for cancer or heart disease or clinical depression. And that personalisation is not just a medical concept, such as that which is best suited to your genetic profile, metabolism or brain scan. It is also about finding the options best suited to your own cultural, demographic and personal situation.

So that the final informed choice about treatment selection is not one that is simply top-down, imposed by the medical system, or generic clinical guidelines. Instead, it is arrived at through active partnership and high-level information sharing.

For example, I might suggest that you are likely to have a form of clinical depression that I call 'circadian depression' (being driven by your dysfunctional body clock) and that one realistic option focuses on behavioural approaches that try to maximise morning sunlight, daily exercise and regular sleep routines. But, another option is to use melatonin-focused antidepressants or melatonin itself to recalibrate and stabilise your clock. After sharing much more of the new science about all of this, and the potential risks and benefits, you express a strong desire not to start any medicines now. We then agree to monitor your response closely and review our options depending on your response.

Much of this book is devoted to achieving this goal. What is the information that a person (or their family and carers) with clinical depression needs to have in order to be a fully engaged partner in high-quality care? What are the questions that need to be asked (of professionals, of families and carers, of the person experiencing depression, of the health system), particularly those that you just can't guess without access to more specialised knowledge. There is lots of evidence in clinical medicine, that those who ask the most relevant questions of their health carers – get the best care!

Depression as just one end of the normal dimension of sadness

On the other hand, clinical depression has become so commonplace in public discourse that everyone assumes they have some relevant personal experiences to contribute or that they already know both the questions to ask, *and the answers.* This can be amplified by the view that anxiety and depressive disorders are simply at one end of the normal range of emotions – just more severe or enduring, but not fundamentally different in terms of the underlying brain and body processes.

In other words, as clinical depression is just a more extreme presentation of a normal emotional state, it doesn't require the application of any particular or expert knowledge. This is like saying that asthma is a more severe form of the breathlessness that we experience when running up stairs, or that abnormal rhythms of the heart are a more extreme form of the rapid pulse we get when we work out at the gym.

These approaches can also encourage people to believe they can control all these things by just being mentally and physically healthy. Basically, you may well be helped by a personal trainer but you certainly don't need a skilled psychologist or a medical specialist!

So the role of a skilled clinician (psychiatrist, clinical psychologist, mental health nurse, highly experienced and trained family doctor, trained mental health social worker or occupational therapist) lies in recognising those phenomena (symptoms the person describes, physical signs that can be observed and test results that throw light on possible underlying causes) that indicate a break from normal functioning.

A personal diversion into clinical care

I was reminded of these key aspects of clinical practice some years ago when I admitted myself to the emergency department, feeling quite unwell, and knowing that I had suddenly developed an irregular heartbeat.

A very experienced triage nurse picked up my wrist and after 30 seconds stated quietly, but firmly: 'Doctor Hickie, you do know that you are in slow atrial fibrillation and although you have avoided us for the last 36 hours you will now be going nowhere till you're safe!'

I noted that this nurse performed this very accurate diagnostic task without reference to any specific technical instruments, modern machines or artificial intelligence – as experienced clinicians have done for centuries. Accurate diagnoses were not invented by machines.

At the point of presenting myself to ED, everyone else's common-sense explanations as to why I was unwell ('overworked', 'just tired', 'got the flu', 'too much alcohol the weekend before') were no longer relevant. Also their subsequent diagnoses – like you've got coronary heart disease due to your 'bad diet', 'high cholesterol', 'lack of physical fitness' – were wrong.

It turned out the abnormal heart beat is something I share with several siblings – something we are all likely to have inherited (i.e a genetic vulnerability). So, my atrial fibrillation was not a normal extension of a fast pulse due to any clear environmental factors. It was not a result of the more common pathologies seen in men of my generation (coronary heart disease). And, it did respond marvellously well to a conventional if rather dramatic intervention, namely cardioversion (a sudden electrical shock to the heart). End result, I walked out of the hospital 36 hours later – very well, life no longer in danger and very grateful for expert medical assessment and skilled interventions.

What happens to me next is likely to resemble some but not others of the many people who have been in this situation. I'm most interested to learn from my cardiologist what he thinks will work for me, based on the best research and his extensive specialist knowledge. In my clinical work in psychiatry I'm trying to provide a similar experience; high-quality care that provides the most effective treatments available, particularly to those who are at risk of harm.

The importance of active research-based knowledge

Beyond a clinician's knowledge, gained by thousands of hours spent in active partnership along the many unique journeys with those affected, research knowledge is another quite distinct dimension.

If you want to live longer after being diagnosed with a serious medical condition – take yourself to a clinical research centre (like the Mayo Clinic equivalent). People live longer and have better experiences of care in clinical research centres, no matter what treatment (experimental or conventional) they receive.

Why is this so? The clinicians who do a lot of research know a great deal more about what they don't know. So, what do they do when the evidence changes, or more commonly, just evolves? They quickly change what they think and what they do!

That means they don't just keep doing what they have been trained to do, what they get paid to do or do what they believe is right. Essentially, they are pragmatic and not ideological.

They are also not simply methodologists, meaning those trained only in the relevant disciplines of statistics, brain-imaging, genetics, pharmacology, animal behaviour, clinical trial designs or psychological theories. They are constantly trying to reconcile the results of new science with the crisis that each unique person presents.

Sadly, providing recommendations for the average patient is just not that useful. In fact, I'm happy to say that I've never met the average patient, that mythical person who is the assumed target of many of the consensus guidelines for best practice.

By contrast, most clinician-researchers would say that what they strive to deliver is 'evidence-informed' clinical practice. This is a world in which there are no absolutes. The evidence is always incomplete. Occasionally, it will be just wrong. But, most importantly, it is being developed continuously by those who are most committed to delivering the best possible care.

Choosing science or non-science (nonsense)

In the modern world, we are confronted by the outcomes of doing things in a variety of scientific and non-scientific ways. The variable impact of COVID-19 worldwide is obvious. If you act on the best available scientific evidence, and are fortunate in its deployment, you end up with the situation we have seen in Australia and New Zealand – major social and economic impacts, but many lives saved.

If you simply reject unacceptable truths and promote 'alternative facts', 'truthiness' or 'fake news' you end up with the Trump-induced disaster we saw in the US. The experience of COVID-19 has once again not only highlighted the true social value of medical expertise, but also its social, political and personal limitations.

For mental health, we face similar choices. We can value expertise and scientific methods and continue to push for increased access to effective care. Or, we can just leave all those in need to their own preferred remedies.

The perspective of a public mental health advocate

It's that last set of considerations that (at least in part) got me into mental health in the first place. Not only is it the most fascinating and least understood major discipline within medical science, but it is also the one in which the experience of illness, and access to great care, is most strongly embedded within the specific cultural and social circumstances in which we live our lives. Where great care is delivered, lives are transformed. When ignored or marginalised, great suffering and neglect are common.

So, in the years that I have spent arguing for improved mental health services, and increased investment in developing the mental wealth of our nations, it has become very clear to me that that this will not be possible unless we all share a much deeper understanding of the true nature of these illnesses, and their dramatic impact on our lives.

So, hopefully this book is most valuable to those who need to know that real clinical care is out there, and the more you (and your family) know, the better the chance that you'll be able to access the specific care you need.

5

Take the Journey to Recovery

Taking the personal journey of discovery for many people with depression can feel frustrating and challenging. Take the experience of Professor Otto Lidenbrock, the central character in Jules Verne's 1864 classic science fiction novel *Journey to the Centre of the Earth*. He is accompanied on his obsessive quest by his nephew Axel, and a skilled guide Hans.

Lidenbrock pursues his belief that it is possible to reach the Earth's centre by following lava tubes down a volcano in Iceland. For many of those with clinical depression, this journey to the centre could be seen as the very dangerous (and very personal) adventure towards the 'real cause' of their depressive illness. Those causes could include commonly discussed risk factors such as adverse childhood experiences, past traumas, other recent life disruptions, or more biological explanations, such as inherited genetics or chemical brain changes.

This journey is often commenced while the illness – the volcano – is still in its destructive phase. Just like Lidenbrock's exploration, this journey is typically not just across place but also across time – back to past experiences and real dangers. As the journey continues, the central characters are frequently disconnected from each other and become disorientated. The expedition also encounters various signs that while this is a unique and challenging experience for them, others have travelled these paths before.

After surviving many threats, the central characters are swallowed up in a bottomless pit that, just as all hope seems lost, fills rapidly with seawater. They are then thrown up through a volcanic chimney and cast out into the open air. Naturally, the key lesson is contained within the journey, not the failure to arrive at the mythical destination.

It is very tempting to advise those with clinical depression *not* to take this journey. But, by the time people come to care, they are often already operating within that underworld, and family members and practitioners are along for the journey, whether they like it or not!

For many, this becomes an endless journey through the labyrinth of past experiences; dead-end, pseudo-psychological explanations; futile changes in diagnostic labels and poorly monitored self-help or recommended treatment options. It's not surprising that many lose hope along the way.

The real challenge is to gain those insights that are derived from the journey – that is, coming to understand one's own and others' experiences, and to translate those quickly into a more productive life *above* the surface.

In my work, it is not uncommon to meet people who have been wandering below the surface for months or years, with little relief. They've often developed a sense of permanent detachment from the world above.

Those who reach out frequently to emergency departments, especially those who are young and express their emotionality, can be viewed harshly. Others are informed that there is little more that can be done. Simplistic recreations of their journey are offered as explanations: 'It's all trauma'. The clear implication is that there is no real hope of exiting this dark and threatening underworld.

I'm reminded of the many people I've known who, just at some of the worst points on that journey, are presented with a new treatment option – electroconvulsive therapy (ECT), combination pharmacotherapy, repetitive transcranial magnetic stimulation (rTMS), hormonal therapy, immunotherapy, ketamine or lithium, or some external factor (say, the onset of spring), or a dramatic change in illness course (maybe the onset of mania in someone who has never had bipolar disorder) or some process that remains largely unknown. Suddenly this new treatment rockets them out of their subterranean prison.

I love the volcano analogy. The forces at work are not controlled by simple cognitive or rational processes. We know these forces exist, but we also know we have little control over their strength, their timing or their place of most impact. The emotional and physiological world in which human behaviour resides is well captured by such stories.

Others rush to provide more narrative explanations, since the personal story just can't tolerate large blank pages. By contrast, those who have often experienced the greatest sense of relief remain truly mystified as to how their suffering ended.

Accepting the focus on the ladder out of the hole

Having experienced the equivalent of the volcanic chimney, surprisingly, some people have an overwhelming sense of failure. Yes, they are better and back in the 'real' world – but they failed to find the true cause. Some are even actively encouraged by their family, friends or health professionals to dive right back in!

Perhaps this relates to the way popular culture can make people feel bad for having 'found an easy way out' or 'just supressed the symptoms'. This is especially the case if the volcanic chimney engaged medical treatments (medications or physical treatments like ECT or rTMS).

Sadly, people often abandon effective treatments as soon as the crisis has passed. Many feel that they can only declare publically that they are better once they have stopped taking medications.

Let's hear again from Lewis Wolpert:

> I take my antidepressant every morning and I think it's a lifesaver. All the hostility and media about the dangers of antidepressants totally misses the positive effect. My joke is that if Prozac grew on trees people would be much happier with it – but it is very serious when the media tries to frighten people about antidepressants. Many more people would commit suicide if there weren't antidepressants.

This is a unique aspect of mental ill-health. We don't say to those with asthma, diabetes or heart failure, 'Stop taking your life-saving medicines, then we'll know you're normal and ready to resume your life roles!'

For others, the disappointment appears to come from a sense of failure to control their illness. Since disorders like depression undermine our capacity to control our mental wellbeing, the re-establishment of that self-control is a very high priority.

There is a key difference between being able to exercise control over the 'cause' of your illness (which, like the centre of the Earth is entirely unreal) and, by contrast, being the master of your own future – which includes a more profound understanding of both the uncertainties involved and the options available.

For instance, if you live in Hawaii, Sicily or Japan, you can't just pretend that volcanos don't exist. For those who live in San Francisco or Christchurch, New Zealand, you can't just pretend that earthquakes don't exist. For those who have experienced clinical depression, you can't pretend that the underlying vulnerability, or the forces that release its destructive powers, just don't exist.

Working out how to live best with these realities, and prevent what can be prevented in the future, are the real goals.

Another key insight is to try to differentiate known science from science fiction. The reality in brain-related science is that there is much we don't know, no matter how much we wish we did. A key prerequisite for health professionals who guide such journeys is to admit upfront that while they are aware of the many possible paths (and many of the common pitfalls), there is no guaranteed destination.

A recurring theme of my own clinical practice is: 'We may never really know how you got into the hole, but that does not stop us from finding the best ladder out!'

Whenever I encounter professionals who claim they know the cause, I seriously wonder about their honesty (after all, it's a very popular message to sell to those afflicted), their lack of awareness or understanding of the complexity of human behaviour, and their lack of empathy for those affected.

At this point in medical history, and the science associated with it, much greater humility is required. Coming to understand what can be understood, and what else remains outside of current understanding, is more likely to provide a safer direction for future life plans, treatment selection and living every day with a challenging illness.

The (active) pursuit of happiness

For those who framed the Declaration of Independence in America, life was all about 'the preservation of life and liberty and the pursuit of happiness'. One could infer it was far less the destination and much more our capacity to take the journey that really mattered.

It is often asserted that the emergence of the centrality of our emotional lives, not just individually but also at the centre of our collective aspirations, was a critical turning point in human history.

More cynical commentators contend that such an emotional and personal focus simply distracts from our responsibility as a society to provide basic needs (food, shelter, health, education) or somehow justifies wider social inequities.

By contrast, in my own personal conversations with a range of Indigenous leaders and people on the ground in various Indigenous communities, who commonly experience the most profound socio-economic and physical disadvantage, they have expressed the view that a society that fails to promote the social and emotional wellbeing of all is an empty vessel.

Most biographies of Thomas Jefferson, one of the authors of the Declaration of Independence, present him as a very emotional and passionate character, highly engaged with life, relationships, national and international politics and the natural world. (He also exhibited many of the limitations of the times and was an owner of enslaved people, as were most prominent US politicians of the day.)

Jefferson's 'happiness' was not a quiet state of non-confrontation, non-activity, retreat from the traumatic world or some sort of substance-induced mental numbness. It was certainly not a retreat from the ever-challenging, argumentative and threatening world in which he lived. It could be viewed as the relentless pursuit of a better future, socially engaged, always inquisitive and confrontational – but also informed by the hard lessons of earlier life experiences.

In my experience, accompanying those who make this journey to genuine recovery from depression is very personal, active, uncertain and ever-challenging. While the things that might assist can include the known (medication, psychological therapies, physical activity, other physical and novel treatments), it's highly likely other relevant factors will become apparent along the way!

JACK'S STORY

I first met Jack soon after his recovery from a self-inflicted gunshot wound to his stomach. Only due to good fortune, the rapid actions of his loving wife and the skill of an on-call surgeon were we ever able to have a conversation. I'm often drawn to reflect on the reality that many men like Jack never had that good fortune – no such conversation ever took place.

Jack was in his 60s, a grandfather, and his serious suicide attempt completely shocked his family.

They didn't see it coming. He'd never said a word.

They assumed that after his retirement he had retreated more into his own world – more time alone, on his own, in his shed. He'd lost contact with workmates, but he still showed up to family events.

My time with Jack was not about, 'Why did you do it?', but rather, 'Can you tell me how you were feeling?'

'Just couldn't go on,' he replied. 'Had to put a stop to things. Hard to say how I was feeling. I don't really know. It's not something I've ever talked about much. Most people I mix with don't talk that way.'

This is not uncommon – I'm asking a man to talk about feelings.

I'm assuming that we will have some common language, some shared way of putting words on feelings, and that those feelings (emotions) underpin or explain the actions (social withdrawal, disconnect from loved ones, suicide attempts).

But I spend my professional life taking about such things. Many others just don't have those same experiences, and they certainly haven't been surrounded by the modern age of mental health awareness and consciousness raising.

So, Jack and I started a really interesting journey: For him, to be able to name those feelings that, if unrecognised or ignored, might end his life; for me, not to assume that just because we both speak English that we understand each other or that we are operating on the same emotional plane.

Jack was not embarrassed by his feelings, or talking with me about them – he just hadn't really had the opportunity before.

Some months later (after a successful trial of medication), he arrived in my office with a broad smile on his face, and in his most laconic style announced, 'I've just told the kids. I wasn't pissed with myself. I was the problem, but now it's great to feel warm again.'

6

The Birth of Major Depression

In the 1970s, most people with clinical depression never attended a clinic and never received care, which meant there was an urgent need to develop a more standardised set of criteria for what the illness actually was. Clearer definitions are essential to the conduct of better and more systematic research.

As the concept was meant to cover the more severe forms of depression, the title 'clinical' was replaced by 'major' – with the clear implication that other 'minor', transient, non-impactful forms of distress were not relevant to the discourse.

Defining major depression as a tool to estimate the true 'costs' of the illness

The first modern attempts were driven by US-based research groups in the late 1970s. They developed the Research Diagnostic Criteria for major mental disorders. Very quickly, this approach was included in large community surveys to identify the prevalence of specific diagnostic categories, such as major depression.

This massive effort was driven by the publicly funded National Institutes of Mental Health (NIMH). It was not a construction of the international pharmaceutical industry or a mindless or socially blind branch of basic neuroscience.

For the first time, it highlighted the extent to which major mental disorders, particularly major depression, were leading causes of disability and premature death in the wider population. These surveys put mental health on the public agenda in the US, then globally.

Similar surveys were conducted in most developed countries, demonstrating the universal significance of these disorders. They are even more relevant in developing countries where various combinations of other external factors (poverty, disadvantage, poor maternal and childhood health, exposure to violence, the exclusion of women from education or employment, war, conflict, discrimination, lack of access to mental health care) are especially obvious.

The disease burden of major depression

From the 1990s onwards, every major disease area has been in the game of estimating its so-called 'disease burden'. It's an effective way of highlighting not just individual areas of neglect, but also whether public health or health services investment actually matches overall community need. It's a global industry, and one that produces regular updates to guide public policy decisions.

It is done by assigning various social or economic values to each condition – for example, how likely it is that you wouldn't be able to go to school or work; whether you're likely to die prematurely from the condition and, if so, at what age? So, if the condition starts in early childhood or adolescence, and is disabling, but you're still likely to lead a moderately long life, the cost, or disease burden, is very high.

In the 1990s, major depression was one of the big winners from this exercise. Clinical depression was used as the template for assigning the critical values. It often starts in adolescence or early life, it is very disabling, it leads to other medical and social problems and it recurs. Although it does shorten life expectancy (by about ten years on average), most people will live with the impacts of the condition for 40 or 50 years.

Major depression became front-page news. Major economic bodies, like the World Economic Forum and the World Health Organization, suddenly saw mental ill-health, and major depression, as a health and economic priority for the 21st century. Our own national depression initiatives, like Beyond Blue, were a direct consequence.

Mental ill-health, and most importantly, major depression, were no longer the concern of just a few unfortunate individuals with severe psychotic disorders (the traditional territory of specialist psychiatry and mental hospitals). This was now a case of 'every family', 'every community', 'every economy'. To be progressive was to be on the front foot on these issues – despite the objections of those who labelled such efforts as 'disease mongering' or evidence of the silent hand of the global pharmaceutical industry.

The late 1990s and early 2000s were also the major growth period in the marketing and distribution of the new Prozac-style antidepressants. The surveys demonstrated that the majority of people in need never received medical or psychological care. The newer drugs did not require close supervision by specialist psychiatrists. This was undoubtedly a massive commercial opportunity. Across the developed world, prescriptions of these compounds increased exponentially.

Depending on your sociopolitical perspective, this was either great progress or a major disaster. My own view is clear. Providing evidence-based, effective treatments to people who have never received care, and when deprived of treatments led impaired and shortened lives, was a very welcome advance! It would be hard to imagine that providing real treatments for people with cancer, asthma or heart disease, who had never previously accessed such treatments, would be met with such hostility and active pushback.

Research that I was party to at this time in Australia, and which was consistent with elsewhere in the world, indicated that increased treatment of depression, either medically or psychologically, saved lives – by reducing suicide in those who were most at risk. That's quite an achievement.

Despite the cynicism expressed by some, this explosion in medical treatments, linked with the economic and social burden of the disease, had other unexpected benefits. Along with surveys of the prevalence of depression, and limited psychological management options for common anxiety and depressive disorders in the waiting rooms of family practitioners, it was one of the major drivers for inclusion of psychological therapies under Medicare, in Australia, in 2001.

When I was young and starting in psychiatry, mental health was rarely mentioned as a national or international health priority. By the early 2000s, while CEO of Beyond Blue, I received my first ever invitation to join a federal taskforce on national health priorities. Major depression was given a seat at the table with cancer, heart disease, diabetes, asthma and arthritis.

In the COVID era, despite the huge impacts of the pandemic on the health care system, the potential mental health consequences and suicide prevention initiatives have been prioritised in many countries, including Australia. This dramatic change over the past 30 years can be accredited largely to the marketing success of major depression.

The other side of the coin – why 'major depression' is problematic

So, given those huge public gains, what could possibly be the downside of the change from 'clinical depression(s)' to the one highly standardised, standalone entity 'major depression'? Unfortunately, quite a few.

It is all derived from the proposition that major depression is a single, discrete entity. That is an illusion. By comparison, we know that things like headache, back pain, fever, insomnia and fatigue are not just one thing, and we know that treatments for such problems are not one size fits all. So too with major depression.

The clinical entity that preceded major depression was always much more complicated.

Proving efficacy – one discrete illness at a time

When I find myself in vigorous debates with pharmaceutical company scientists (that is, the ones who are interested in developing better treatments), they quickly raise the challenges they face on a daily basis. For a new compound to achieve regulatory approval and then be advanced into clinical care, it must show that it effectively treats a specific category of illness (at least that was the case before the recent rebirth of medicinal cannabis and psychedelics). For the past two decades, the category that has mattered most for serious pharmacology is major depression.

In most of these important proof-of-efficacy trials, middle-aged people with long-standing illness are enrolled. Key groups are often left out. They include those with suicidal ideas or behaviour, substance misuse, other medical problems or features of bipolar disorder or psychotic depression. Typically, they do not focus on younger age groups (or early intervention) or older people (who are often more sensitive to side-effects).

Concurrently, a whole set of trials – of medicines and psychological therapies – focus on those with single anxiety disorders (generalised anxiety, social anxiety, PTSD), as if these disorders exist in isolation. Most people with recurrent or persistent forms of these disorders experience depressive disorders at some point in their journey.

This significant problem for new drug development is the same for new psychological treatments. Hence, claims that psychological therapies are equally effective as medical treatments for major depression are based on studies that have also deliberately narrowed the range of participants.

That is, the refusal to engage with the complexity of the clinical picture of major depression encouraged the pursuit (and very active marketing) of magical one-size-fits-all cures – either medical or psychological. It also encouraged the notion that simplistic single-entity disorders are being linked to complex brain or biological research. It fired up the pursuit of one specific test for diagnosis or one typical brain picture that could characterise the illness.

The end result is an ongoing perpetuation of the myths that antidepressants don't work, that major depression is a marketing ploy of the global pharmaceutical companies and that all treatments – medical or psychological – are equally good (or bad) for everyone with the illness.

These difficulties are not simply perpetuated by those with an axe to grind. Major public health figures in the field are often led to conclude that only a minority of people currently receiving treatments are deriving a benefit from them. These sophisticated critiques all rest on the adoption of major depression as the single illness entity we have promoted. So we end up creating individual victims of the public health success.

This overwhelming scepticism about the utility of active

treatments leads to very serious proposals to further delay, downgrade or restrict access to any specialist care. The inherent risks that arise – like not caring for those who are at considerable risk when they present for care, or recognising that suicidal behaviour is one of the most important reasons people seek care, or appreciating the extent to which people with clinical depression die prematurely from all health causes – are just not highlighted.

If everyone has depression, everyone can take their own actions to beat it

In the 21st century we have grown to believe that major depression is everywhere – and rapidly increasing in developed societies. The true epidemiology is much more complex. It is probably headed up in young people (particularly post-COVID) but continuing to go down in older people.

The marketing success of major depression also draws more investment – not just from governments but from the private sector, and not just from the pharmaceutical industry. The marketing of diet, exercise, yoga, meditation and a whole world of wellbeing products is a clear outcome. Much of this public promotion makes unfounded claims about our capacity to self-manage or prevent major mood disorders.

For those with more serious forms of clinical depression, there is now very little differentiation in the public commentary from the general psychological ups and downs of everyday life. The thinking goes that everybody gets depressed and most people really should be able to handle it on their own – or, perhaps with some help from the right self-help products or lifestyle coaches. Nobody needs *real* medical care, as depression is not really an illness – it's 'tough times' or a 'life predicament'. Just get your head straight, eat well and exercise.

If depression is simple, and able to be self-managed, it can also be prevented by simple interventions

Another implication of the widespread adoption of a simplistic model of depression, and one that is often managed well by straightforward psychological techniques or lifestyle adjustments, is that it should be relatively easy to prevent.

Such beliefs have underpinned some of the drive towards teaching universal self-help strategies to children and young people ('sleep hygiene', physical activity, meditation and mindfulness and simple cognitive techniques). While these have considerable benefits across the spectrum of psychological distress, their genuine capacity to prevent the onset of clinical depression, or alter its longitudinal course, remains highly contestable.

An unintended effect of such universal movements is to discourage investment in upscaling high-quality treatment services. Many advocates of primary prevention make the argument that large-scale investments in these approaches will result in a reduced need for treatment services. Some go so far as to say that treatment doesn't really work anyway, so prevention is the only real way forward.

This is just wrong.

A real effect of expanded prevention programs for children and younger people is an increased recognition of those who need care. The same is true of many new digital health (e-health and apps) initiatives. Rather than decreasing the need for care, they actually result in more people coming into care. Which is a very good thing, as long as you have planned for it and intend to provide that care!

So, we are still light-years away from reducing the overall burden of depressive disorders, or being sure which strategies will be useful for those with the more severe and life-threatening forms.

Back to the future

So, throughout this book, while accepting the public health success of major depression, I'm re-stating a much longer historical perspective of clinical depression(s) – that is, those disorders where there is no real debate about their:

- existence as illness entities;
- adverse impacts on people's daily lives;
- true response to various medical and psychological treatments;
- association with premature death due to suicide, accidents and injuries and other medical conditions (most notably heart disease);
- risk to later onset of other medical, substance misuse and psychological disorders; and,
- close links with physiological disturbance of both brain and body, as demonstrated by brain imaging, blood markers and various other tests.

7

20 Great Myths About Clinical Depression

Myth: 'a widely held but false belief or idea'

To put it another way, just because we keep telling (yelling, repeating, advertising) certain ideas about clinical depression, doesn't make them any more true . . .

Myth: 'a traditional story, often used to explain a natural or social phenomenon'

Mental health lives and breathes deeply human stories. They are anchored in traditional beliefs ('free will', 'original sin', 'suffering is noble'), unique personal circumstances or shared beliefs.

One of the great things about living in Australia is that the vast majority of people I speak to are incredibly interested in mental health, and particularly the experience of depression. The public is almost universally sympathetic to the devastating impacts on those who live with the illness, along with the consequences for their families and carers.

When it comes to lifting our national depression awareness, we have been gold-medal winners. We certainly have left the UK, North America, Europe and most parts of Asia behind. There is some anxiety these days that we have slipped behind the Jacinda Ardern-inspired New Zealand. When she was prime minister she responded to overwhelming tragedies with genuine human kindness and compassion. One should not underestimate the positive impact of an empathetic and emotionally intelligent leader on the national psyche.

But one of the most frustrating aspects of spending a great deal of my professional life talking about depression is the continuing need to confront commonly believed 'facts'.

There is a long list of things that many people, notably socio-political critics of the medical model of clinical depression, would like you to believe. If they were true, many politicians, decision-makers and health-care providers could better justify our inadequate responses to this critical area of social policy and health care.

One of my main motivations for writing this book was to confront destructive myths about depression – with specific emphasis on debunking just-plain-wrong ideas about 'known' causes, 'useless' treatments, 'resilience', 'self-help' and 'universal' prevention.

Every day, I hear various versions of these myths, often presented by well-meaning media, relatives of those affected and even some health professionals.

The hurt and confusion caused to those who live with the condition is considerable.

So here's a list of my top 20 myths about clinical depression.

1. Clinical depression results from acute traumatic events.

While acute traumatic events often result in great distress, grief, sleep disturbance, fear or tears, they have little to do with the onset of clinical depression. Clinical depression didn't start yesterday when you lost your job or your partner walked out. Chronic unresolved stressors, like prolonged unemployment, abusive intimate relationships or poor physical health are important risk factors (see Chapter 11). In reality, many episodes of clinical depression occur without any clear life event or chronic stressor.

Given the unrelenting public belief that traumatic life events cause depression, and the insatiable human drive to wrap our feelings and experiences within our own personal narrative, someone – usually a poorly informed relative, friend or health professional – will come up with a story that 'explains' all we need to know about the onset and course of your illness.

2. Bad childhood experiences are the main cause of clinical depression.

Adversity in childhood explains very few cases of clinical depression. Population-level genetic studies indicate that only about 10 per cent of depression in the community can be attributed directly to early childhood circumstances. This compares with about 30 to 40 per cent due to genetic factors and 50 per cent due to other factors in your own unique environment, leaving up to 10 per cent unexplained. In fact, as childhood adversity goes down in developed countries (better maternal health, less child abuse, quality education and supports), the explanatory power of childhood adversity will continue to fall.

So, in most cases, we can quit blaming your mother, your siblings or your boarding school.

Trawling the past for traumatic events that you can't remember or simply did not happen is not helpful.

3. Antidepressants are massively overprescribed.

> Depression is overdiagnosed in the US, but for some people it really is a brain chemistry issue. But zombifying people with SSRIs for sure happens way too much. From what I've seen with friends, ketamine taken occasionally is a better option.
>
> Elon Musk, Twitter post, 27 June 2023

Actually, the majority of people with clinical depression never get access to *any* treatment, be it effective medications or high-quality psychological care. Despite the number of community surveys that confirm this, many commentators start from this 'fact'. It's very interesting that this perspective is rarely applied to medical treatments for asthma, heart disease, infection, cancer or diabetes. Its origins lie in the false belief that most clinical depression is not physiological (meaning of the brain and body), but rather a psychological disorder (meaning of the rational and emotional 'self'). Therefore, it can be prevented and best treated by rational thinking.

It's this line of flawed, 'cognitive-only' argument that makes life so tough for those who need, and benefit greatly, from appropriate medicines or other brain-stimulation therapies.

It's also what makes people who have benefited quickly give up effective medicines prematurely – and then run the considerable risk of relapse.

4. You must find the real cause of depression to get effective treatment.

People with depression are driven to complete distraction by everyone else's explanation for their condition. 'It's just your job', 'It's just your marriage.' 'It's just your poor diet.' 'It's just your hormones.'

And then: 'It must be trauma' (past, current, perceived or expected).

The reality for many of those who experience clinical depression is that you may never really know how you landed in this gaping, and ever-deepening, black hole. Our understanding of how those brain processes that control emotion, thinking, behaviours and other body processes go astray in clinical depression remains limited.

Most studies reveal the incredible complexity of these processes, right across the life cycle. Different sets of genetic, environmental, brain and other factors combine in very different ways at different life stages.

The real goal is not to find the cause – but rather to find the right ladder out of the hole, and as quickly as possible. And then the best ways to stay well into the future.

To do that, you need to work out (often over time and different experiences) what makes you particularly vulnerable to relapse and what other actions you can take to stay well.

All this effort is very much in the here and now – it's not a journey back into some past world that may or may not underpin your vulnerability.

For instance, once you have cancer it doesn't matter whether you were exposed to a known risk factor (e.g. smoking for lung cancer), or you don't have a clue what caused it (breast cancer in healthy young women and blood cancers in young children). By that point, the only thing that matters is whether your own unique cancer is responsive to treatment.

The more we learn about cancer, the more we realise that each one is very different. The more we learn about something much more complex, namely clinical depression, the clearer it becomes that individual differences are huge.

Effective treatments in medicine often have no specific links to those risk factors that 'caused' the illness – but they do work best when they target the underlying and continuing process that still drives the disorder.

They work best when given early in the illness – just like for cancer, severe arthritis or diabetes. Late intervention is never a good idea.

For example, for arthritis due to inflammation of the tissues surrounding a joint (e.g. rheumatoid arthritis in young people), we often don't know what caused the inflammation. But if it's turned off completely by highly targeted anti-inflammatory agents, then the acute suffering is relieved, the progression of the illness is delayed and, most importantly, the joint is not eaten away by the destructive inflammatory process. That prevents joint degeneration and, hopefully, joint replacement.

5. You must find the real cause of depression to prevent recurrence.

Understanding the depth of your own personal vulnerability, and not searching for alternative real causes, is the most effective strategy for preventing recurrence.

Some aspects may be apparent when you first get sick – like a very strong family history of clinical depression or suicide. Those are indicative of inherited, and often genetic, factors. Some may emerge by careful reconstruction of relevant timelines – particularly as they related to early stages of brain and body development. For women who first became depressed in adolescence in association with their monthly hormonal cycles, and then experienced postnatal depression, and then became depressed again in the early phases of menopause – consideration of the role of fluctuating estrogen levels is critical. For those with strong changes in mood, energy and sleep cycles in association with the changes in the seasons, body-clock related factors may be critical.

Finding out what works uniquely to improve your daily mood – like physical exercise, sunlight exposure, social connection, productive work, reducing alcohol intake, regular sleep–wake times, better or different diet – is a critical insight.

Figuring out the extent to which long-term dysfunctional thought patterns put you at risk of depression may well indicate the need to pursue those psychological therapies that focus on changing unhelpful thought patterns.

As many people with depression know, they do not have dysfunctional thoughts, bad intimate relationships or a dissatisfying job when they are well – these conclusions are a consequence of, and are not a cause of, their depressive illness.

Some psychological colleagues are distressed when a person reports that the best cognitive therapy (the one that focuses on changing unhelpful thought patterns) they received was a course of antidepressant medication!

Taking active steps to know what works best when you start to slip is critical for preventing recurrence. For many, this may include restarting effective medicines or pursuing psychological therapies early – getting in before you really sink back into that black hole.

6. When you are depressed you are not physically sick – you are simply psychologically distressed.

Clinical depression is a whole-body (brain included) experience, not a detached cognitive process in some separate 'mind' space. When most people with depression report that they feel physically sick and overwhelmingly tired with a complete lack of energy unrelieved by sleep or rest, they are reporting accurately the essential physiological elements of the disorder.

Prolonged, unrelenting and unexplained jet lag would be a better description of the depressive experience, rather than a sad mood.

The medical evidence for pathological changes in brain function, along with major disruptions to hormonal, immune, metabolic, heart and gut function, are overwhelming.

7. Clinical depression is a disorder largely characterised by prolonged sadness.

Sadness is the normal emotional response to major loss, disruptions to our significant intimate relationships and other personally disturbing events. It's often prolonged when those losses are big and ongoing. But sadness is not the main emotional feature of clinical depression.

By contrast, loss of pleasure in those things that normally keep us going on a daily basis – great food, sex, being out in nature, social connection, purposeful work – is the key emotional feature.

8. Suicide is an inevitable part of the human condition.

Suicide rates have been highly variable across different historical, cultural, demographic and geographical settings. It's true that most are strongly linked to treatable mental disorders, like clinical depression. The most effective suicide prevention strategy in those with clinical depression is high-quality treatment. Suicide rates fall quickly and dramatically in those receiving effective treatments. But suicide rates remain high in those who do not receive medical or psychological treatment and in those who stop those treatments that were actually working for them.

9. Psychiatrists, doctors and their medicines, create many more problems (including suicide) than they ever solve.

People with clinical depression who do receive effective care have high rates of recovery and far less chance of premature death from suicide, accidents, overdoses, heart disease and other medical conditions. While there is much media reporting (particularly in the US and UK) of the potential adverse effects of antidepressant medications, there is far less reporting of the benefits – on brain health, physical health and personal recovery.

It's much easier to sell a book devoted to how someone was harmed by evil doctors and their partners in crime, the pharmaceutical industry, than to report accurately the benefits that have stemmed from widespread use of effective treatments since the 1990s. It's even better if you are one of those practitioners who has suddenly seen the light and now appear regularly as a major critic of the treatments they once prescribed.

Science, however, is a funny thing – it doesn't do opinion polls or track TedX downloads. The weight of evidence continues to grow strongly in favour of earlier and more effective medical and psychological treatments – to deliver longer and more productive lives for those affected.

10. If we simply build more resilient children, (or turn more vulnerable adults into resilient ones) we will prevent clinical depression.

While the resilience industry (and other wellness packages) continues to thrive, it has little impact on the onset or prevention of recurrent clinical depression. In my view, the true meaning of psychological resilience (the capacity to recover quickly from emotional destabilisation) is best applied to groups of people (families, small social units) rather than individuals.

We all cope best when we are in social groups that protect and support us during periods when we are least able to help ourselves.

Depressive illness is not due to a lack of resilience – that is, if you interpret resilience to mean being emotionally and personally bulletproof in the face of adversity. We actually need people to be more sensitive to their emotional circumstances, their own temperament and the best ways to manage their own risks.

11. If we exercise more, lose weight, eat special diets, stop alcohol, think rationally and get a good job or education, then we will prevent clinical depression.

Ah, if only depression prevention were so simple! And, of course, those people who are clinically depressed must have failed to do one or more of these essential prevention strategies. After all, someone must be to blame. The historical record of blaming those who are sick for their own demise is long.

Of course, we all love the idea that we can be so easily in control of our emotional life and that such simple strategies will prevent us from ever falling headlong into the pit of clinical depression.

When people who have engaged in a lot of self-improvement strategies do find themselves lost in the depths of depression, they can be particularly hard to assist. The 'why me?' syndrome kicks in hard.

'I did all the things I've been told to do – I've read all the books, I've listened to all the gurus, I've downloaded all the podcasts.' For others, 'I'm wealthy, I have a great partner, I have a great job. I have supportive family and friends.'

The harsh reality of the onset of many life-threatening illnesses is that despite our best efforts at reducing risk, there are many other processes at work. An interesting paradox is that as we improve the environment to reduce risk factors, including mental disorders, those with high inherited risks will be *more* evident among those coming into care.

12. If we institute widespread depression prevention programs, then we won't need high-quality treatment programs for those who are clinically unwell.

Elsewhere in medicine, we have learned to walk and chew gum at the same time! The more we institute widespread public health programs, the more we also invest in high-end, and highly personalised, interventions for those who do become ill.

Consequently, for many other health areas (and my personal favourite – middle-aged and older men with heart disease) the optimal combination of health promotion, specific illness prevention, early detection and specialised interventions has yielded large and continuing falls in premature death rates.

Sadly, in mental health, many ideologues and social critics argue for a zero sum-game. Take money away from health services, don't invest in early intervention, stop investing in medical research, only support psychological services, don't fund more specialised services, or only put new money into universal (for everyone) or selective (those groups known to be at risk) prevention programs. Worst of all, just fund more community awareness campaigns.

Of course, for more cynical governments or other vested interests who have never invested in the provision of high quality, or early, intervention programs, this is music to their ears!

It's very hard to imagine that we would not continue to invest in world's-best treatment or research programs for those with cancer, heart disease or infection just because we are lifting up our broader health promotion and illness-prevention efforts.

13. Older people get depressed as they age.

Leonard Cohen – there he was, aged in his mid-70s, touring the world with perhaps his most successful artistic collaboration ever. He was full of life, energy, creativity and empathy, and attracting both public and critical acclaim. This was all despite many darker periods of 'melancholy' earlier in his life. At a concert in July 2008 he said:

> It's been a long time since I stood on this stage in London. It was about 14 or 15 years ago. I was 60 years old, just a kid with a crazy dream. Since then I've taken a lot of Prozac, Paxil, Wellbutrin, Effexor, (antidepressants); Ritalin, Focalin (stimulants). I've also studied deeply in the philosophies and the religions, but cheerfulness kept breaking through!

In fact, physically healthy older people are much more content than younger people and have falling rates of clinical depression – probably as a result of improved brain health, social participation, longer work lives and improved general health care. As you get older, your mental health improves and you react less dramatically to life's difficulties – as long as you are able to do those things physically and socially that keep you well.

When clinical depression does occur in older people, it is often a signal that something has changed in their physical health (e.g. small brain strokes, Parkinson's disease, thyroid disease, musculoskeletal changes and pain). It is also commonly associated with memory, attention and other cognitive difficulties. Sadly, it is often mistakenly attributed to ageing or dementia.

Clinical depression in older people is highly treatable, but it requires additional care and effort due to the increased rates of complications (confusion, loss of balance, falls, gut changes) from medicines and other physical treatments.

14. Social media is the cause of rising depression rates in young people.

Evidence from large community studies across the developed world indicate rising rates of depressive symptoms and suicidal ideas and behaviours in young people. However, the proportion of these young people who actually have clinical depression remains unclear.

So, while we are identifying more young people with clinical depression – and initiating psychological and medical interventions at younger ages – mostly this is a result of younger people and their families coming for help before they develop other medical, social, educational and psychological complications.

The rush to attribute these changes in the number of young people with depression directly to the harmful impacts of new forms of social media has not yet been clearly supported by data. The real story is likely to be far more complex.

Suicide rates in young people were much higher in the late 1990s – that was before Facebook was invented! Of course, the success of Facebook (and many other forms of social media since) was based on its capacity to increase social connections between young people.

It is likely that what is of greatest relevance to the mental health of young people is the decline in social connection within our communities, and between generations.

15. There are no diagnostic tests for clinical depression because the condition doesn't really exist.

We actually do have many useful tests – many of which could be more widely used by practitioners – for people with clinical depression. Some are used to exclude medical conditions that mimic clinical depression (like anaemia or low thyroid hormone function), some signal a likely precipitating factor (like a small or silent stroke on a brain scan) and some indicate a process that may be perpetuating the condition (like evidence of an ongoing inflammatory or immune process attacking the body or brain).

From a research perspective, we have lots of evidence from modern brain scanning techniques (fMRI, structural MRI, PET) of both structural and functional brain changes in people with depression. When compared with people who have never been depressed, these clearly indicate a range of changes that possibly precede the onset of depression, get worse during the course of the illness or recover following the provision of effective treatments.

Unfortunately, we can't yet jump from these clear signs of the biological reality of clinical depression in larger groups of people to using any one of them right now in individual people.

16. Depression is simply caused by a chemical imbalance.

Importantly, the whole chemical imbalance debate was not really initiated by psychiatrists! In the 1990s the arrival of the Prozac-like drugs (selective serotonin reuptake inhibitors or SSRIs), which increase brain levels of serotonin, brought this idea to popular attention. The imbalance concept (and it was never simply a serotonin 'deficiency' model) does have its origins in attempts to develop common media and public explanations for the effectiveness of these biochemical interventions.

Most effective antidepressant medications increase brain levels of serotonin, dopamine or noradrenaline. These are the major monoamines that support biochemical signalling within brain circuits that regulate mood, cognition and movement. For example, dopamine is the agent that when depleted in the brain results in Parkinson's disease.

Psychiatrists have not argued that there is a lack of monoamines in the brains of people with clinical depression, but simply stated that they constitute effective treatments for many (but not nearly all) people with clinical depression. By analogy, even though aspirin or other non-steroidal anti-inflammatory agents do provide effective pain relief for many musculoskeletal conditions, doctors promote their clinical value without ever claiming that those disorders were caused by a lack of those same substances.

17. So you've done exercise, improved your diet, sleep hygiene, done meditation, yoga, therapy, mindfulness and medications, but you're still depressed. There's nowhere else to go!

Just wrong. By the time people with depression reach specialist care, we're only just starting to get it right.

Every individual with depression is on their own unique journey. But it's a journey of discovery best not taken alone. You need team-based clinical care and lots of support from family and friends – which is fine, as you'd do the same for them if they were in trouble. When you are not thinking straight, those who know you best can take on the health system or work or social security. Just when you think you are really lost is often the best time to engage with specialist mental health care.

Keeping accurate records of what doesn't work, or what only works a bit, is critical.

There are a lot of new tests, treatments and different options open to you – just accepting low-level, non-specialised and previously ineffective care is not your best option.

18. I need time off work to get well.

We don't get well to go to work, we go to work to get well. Purposeful participation is essential for good mental health and wellbeing – and recovery from clinical depression.

Whenever I hear that someone is about to retire and head to the beach to recover, I suggest that that's the quickest way to get more depressed and then die. While it may be necessary for those in very responsible positions to step back from the frontline until they benefit from effective care – and to postpone other critical life decisions (quit job, leave marriage, move away) – these are short-term options.

To get well, and stay well, those with clinical depression need to be focused on regaining the maximal emotional, social and cognitive engagement with our surrounding worlds.

19. Recurrent depression does no harm to the body or brain. So, there's no hurry to treat it early or prevent recurrence.

One of the principles of clinical medicine is that you treat an illness early to prevent further damage to the organ of interest. We prevent recurrent heart attacks to stop damage to our heart muscle – which, if severe enough, results in heart failure. Similarly, we prevent recurrent kidney infections to stop progression to kidney failure and prevent recurrent chest infections to preserve the lungs.

Commonly, approaches to treatment of depression promote the idea that each new episode is as treatable as past episodes, as there is no underlying process causing damage to brain tissue.

We are now certain that active processes are underway during depressive episodes and that some of these, notably involving inflammation or linked immune processes, can cause the destruction of connections between brain cells and, eventually, the death of brain cells. Brain imaging studies have indicated the extent to which persistence and recurrence of clinical depression is associated with loss of brain cell connections and possibly brain cells within critical brain structures, such as the hippocampus (which is essential to memory function) and the frontal lobes.

So, one of the major downsides of both simplistic psychological and biochemical explanations of clinical depression is that they have failed to promote active and ongoing neuroprotection – meaning ongoing protection of the brain tissue responsible for regulating emotions, thought and complex behaviours. The provision of antidepressant medications appears to be associated with preservation of brain cells and their connections – and may constitute an important reason to continue treatment between episodes.

A novel approach to depression suggests that true antidepressant therapies share a common element, namely that they are neurogenerative – meaning they provoke new brain cell connections. Other medications, like metformin, which is used normally to treat diabetes, may also be in this category.

These same brain neuroprotection or neurogenerative actions may also be true for other psychological and behavioural treatments – with the strongest evidence being present for increased physical exercise, improved sleep–wake cycles, reduced alcohol intake and increased participation in social and work (mentally hard) activities.

20. Mindfulness is compulsory. It should be recommended to all those with anxiety or depression.

Mindfulness is just one popular psychological activity – and particularly appealing to those who normally respond to environmental stressors with high levels of anxiety and distress. But, there are many other ways to relax and focus on everyday pleasures and moderation of your internal distress.

Being active and engaged may be your best form of meditation or relaxation. Doing things with other people, particularly those who care for you, is often more relaxing and much more pleasurable!

In my view, if we all dispensed with these very unhelpful myths and simply shared the known facts, we could make the journey to recovery a whole lot easier for those with clinical depression.

JAN'S STORY

'I don't have any reason to be depressed – I'm wealthy, I'm successful, my partner loves me. And, no, my dad didn't abuse me as a child. So, what am I doing here? What do I tell my family and friends?'

Jan is one of my favourite patients – not only because she isn't blaming anyone else for her troubles; she is genuinely interested in trying to figure out what has made her vulnerable to this debilitating illness at various stages of her life.

And there have been no easy answers – no clear family history, no typical precipitants, no past trauma, no recent medical illness, no big life transitions (pregnancy, post-natal life, menopause, retirement).

So, where do we go now?

Let's assume Jan has got risky genetics, even though we don't know what those specific genes are or what brain systems they regulate. But, the things we've asked of her history of recurrent depression are:

1. What symptoms come on first?
2. What symptoms *doesn't* she have?

3. What treatments don't work or make her worse?
4. What treatments and self-help strategies have helped?

For Jan, when an episode starts, it is signalled by waking up tired, despite being asleep for seven to eight hours; gaining weight and losing interest in sex. When depressed, she doesn't really feel sad but more empty, sort of dead inside. She doesn't get particularly self-critical, but she does withdraw from those around her. Every time a doctor has prescribed a Prozac-like (SSRI) medication, it's made her feel worse, not better. The medications that have worked best have been more stimulating types (increasing levels of dopamine or noradrenaline) and the self-strategies that have helped emphasise daily physical exercise, diet regulation, cutting down on alcohol and getting more regular sleep.

So, while we can't simply request a brain scan or blood test to prove it, I've reached an agreement with Jan that it's her genetics that have made her vulnerable to depression. And those genetics are probably acting through her sleep–wake cycle (body clock) rather than her stress-response system. So, we need to focus on:

1. Self-strategies to keep her sleep–wake cycle stable (morning light, daily exercise, a regular sleep cycle).
2. Medications that target the body clock and not the stress-response system, and enhance daytime energy or promote better sleep.
3. Using new wearable devices to monitor mood, sleep, weight and physical activity, so that we can react early and effectively to each new episode.

8

Social Connection for Wellbeing

I've had the chance in a number of public settings (most unexpectedly with the Dalai Lama) to express my view that: 'It's all in, you can't really be well on your own. For our most precious groups, like marital and family relationships, I'm often saying, "You've all got to be well, if you want to be well individually."'

So, as part of the personal journey to recovery, and the prevention of recurrence, there is quite a complex process to be navigated. When unwell, people are very dependent on those who are close relatives or friends to provide practical support, stick with them through different treatment options and provide intimacy, empathy and physical care. That's the case even when the person with depression is rejecting them or just not responding.

For those without such personal supports, the clinical care team needs to take on these roles – in appropriate ways. There is also a role for the wider community and non-professional people. We could all go out of our way a lot more for those who are not our own kin.

None of us survives alone. Humans are social animals, in sickness and health. Perhaps the most destructive influence, economically, socially and psychologically, over the last three decades has been the fierce individualisation of goals. *Personal* wealth, housing, career success, retirement funds, access to quality health care are all more highly prized than those things we share with our local community (like the health of the natural environment, protecting everyone's health or our collective contribution to social welfare and supports).

Not only has this process corroded social cohesion, at the level of nations but, from a mental health perspective, it has led to far weaker local communities. These are the actual small worlds in which we transact our daily lives. They are held together by common values of kinship, support and mutual care.

The practical consequences of strong local communities include their willingness to volunteer, take care of the young, the elderly and the disabled, donate to local charities and protect their natural environments. While those things are not counted towards our national Gross Domestic Product (GDP), they constitute our collective 'mental wealth'. When faced with national challenges like the pandemic, or regional disasters like the bushfires and floods, their real value becomes apparent.

While there is a discussion to be had about the wider socio-political context of good mental health and wellbeing, it's not the main target of this book. Here, the main focus is getting individuals to survive episodes of illness, and getting those who are vulnerable to dodge the iceberg. In that context, what factors are really protective in local communities?

The limitations of personally focused psychology

Much modern psychological practice has too often retreated within the head of each individual – as if our thoughts and emotions exist in a unique space, uninfluenced by other social and personal interactions. Along the way, key strands of modern psychology have also dropped much of their previous emphasis on changing behaviour, not just thoughts. For behaviourists (which is my bias), it's a case of 'get out in the world and do different – only then will you feel and think differently.'

This does come back in new forms, such as a focus on individual fitness regimes to treat clinical depression. (Personally I hate gyms where everybody has their earpieces in place and interacts only with themselves.) Relationship-based therapies are particularly effective for preventing relapse of depressive disorders, and group therapies are particularly effective for moderating social anxiety.

The limitations of personally focused medical research

From a medical research perspective, some other unfortunate trends have also been present since the late 1970s. With an explosion in the technologies (genetic, brain imaging, biochemical) that can take us further inside our heads, there has been an even greater tendency to treat each person as a 'brain in a bottle' – isolated from wider environmental and social realities.

One of the most eloquent, and perhaps saddest, examples of this in recent times has been the opioid crisis in North America. We have extensive evidence on the circuitry that drives addictive behaviour in rats but none of this elaborate scientific work has any real implications for how best to respond to that current health crisis.

Significant improvements in our collective mental health and wellbeing will not be achieved without parallel and complementary societal and health-care movements. Prevention and higher-quality services need to be large scale, structural, commencing early in life, enhanced in high-risk groups, socially embedded and rigorously evaluated.

SAMANTHA'S STORY

Sometimes in my consulting room I think there are two people talking, but there are actually three: me, the person opposite and the other voice they have in their head. To be clear, I don't mean that the other person is hallucinating – the other voice is their own, but it's very self-critical much of the time, and most people are reluctant to concede that these critical experiences are driving their behaviour.

Samantha is vivacious, full of life and seems least likely to be critical of anyone, let alone her herself.

She's warm and engaging, the sort of person who picks up injured animals off the street and takes them to a refuge. She loves kids and loves playing with them. She is the first to rush over to help friends in any kind of crisis. She's not a drama queen; it's not about her. She is there to help.

So, why do all her own intimate relationships end in a massive train wreck? Why does she get so down, so much that sometimes she just can't see any reason to carry on? Why does she get stuck on some minor comment that a workmate made three weeks ago? Why do those people she helped sometimes just not return her call?

Well, the answer is that third person in her own head – the one that is the cause of so much of this distress. It's at her – sometimes softly, sometimes howling – and it never really goes away. She's never good enough. She's never really done enough for others. She always messes it up or lets other people down. It's not really them; it's her own fault.

That's the argument going on endlessly in her head – everyone else (even those she is intimate with) is an outsider. They can't hear the same conversation. The whole thing makes no sense to them. They often get blamed, but they weren't even in on the argument, so they withdraw and move on.

I find myself asking Samantha at rather random points in our conversation what the other voice had to say – not so much *literally*, but what's the alternative, negative thought she is not sharing with me. If we can out it, we can challenge it. If it's hidden or just denied, it remains powerful.

We could debate endlessly where it came from – her dad; her elder sister, maybe? We could postulate about who should have protected her – her mum, her aunts?

But, at this stage, it is so internalised that it doesn't really matter. Moving on requires an active play to kill it off, disown it and engage with those who are more external and genuinely value Samantha's place in their world!

PART 2

THE CAUSES OF DEPRESSION

9

The Sources of Individual Differences

When I'm giving my yearly lecture to medical students on the genetics of major depression and other psychiatric disorders (which as a 'social' psychiatrist is always fun), I usually start by asking, 'To what extent do you think any aspect of your own behaviour is strongly influenced by your genetic profile?'

The response is, 'Not much . . .'

I then ask whether there are any twins in the class – preferably identical twins who have exactly the same genes – or whether each student can think of a set of identical twins they know. 'So, have you ever noticed any behavioural or emotional similarities between those twins? And, what about significant differences?'

Typically, quite a long list of shared characteristics, as well as some key differences are noted.

While this discussion is going on, I flash up on the screen my favourite photo of 90-year-old twins, since everybody expects to see infants or children. In part, this is to challenge the common idea that genetic effects are only relevant to childhood development, including those early physical, cognitive and emotional processes, but also to remind me to explain the fact that different genetic factors are relevant at different stages of life.

I then go on to ask the students, 'Does anyone have children of their own?'

If the answer is no, I suggest that the following discussion of genetics, temperament and genetic-environmental interactions may well go right over their heads. On a good day, there are at least a few parents in the class.

'Great, so how many children do you have?' If the answer is one, I ask, 'How much do you think you are determining the behavioural characteristics of you child?'

Usually, response is 'overwhelmingly so' – for better or worse!

If anyone answers two or more children, then the discussion gets really interesting: 'How similar or different are your children in terms of their basic dispositions, their temperament – things like being easy to settle, leave with other people, feed or get to sleep?'

Typically, the answer is 'quite different!'

So, I ask, 'Given that they have the same parents, have grown up in the same environment, how do you explain those differences? And by the way, have those differences been evident since the day they were born?'

For those who have two or more children, I go on to say, 'Do you really believe you are driving your child's behavioural development or do you feel that you are mainly reacting, as best you can, to the temperamental characteristics of the child you have created?'

Here, the inverse rule often applies: the more children a parent has, the less they believe they are causing anything!

I'm one of seven children. I'm the father of six children – the outcomes of a poorly planned life. At last count, I have three grandchildren. What is most striking about my children (and my observations of my brothers and sisters, and now grandchildren), is that despite the shared childhood settings, they each have markedly different temperaments – meaning those most basic behavioural characteristics that were evident from the day they were born. Most of which has largely stayed with them throughout their development.

Individual differences matter – they assist our species to survive!

Do you ever look at those really big group photos, like family weddings, a grandparent's 90th birthday, workplace teams or, one of my personal favourites, international scientific conferences (which are very diverse by place and cultural background)?

Does it ever occur to you that humans have survived and thrived not only as a consequence of the tight emotional bonds between generations, but also because of the diversity of skills we have access to? Together these two factors make us very effective when we act as social groups.

In modern terms, the 'mental wealth' of those groups, meaning their common emotional, cognitive and social strengths, depends on two factors: the capacity to maintain diversity (and capitalise on our individual differences), as well as the capacity to function coherently as a social group.

The following three chapters are devoted to the three big topics about causation: genes, environments and gene–environment interactions.

1. Human genetics: although we are all very similar, actually we're quite unique

First, the role of genetics in causation – meaning what we inherit directly from our parents via the mixing of their DNA (50 per cent from each parent). This incorporates the mixing of the DNA of their respective parents (25 per cent from each grandparent), and then back to the many generations who preceded them. Along the way, parts of that genetic code have changed as a result of errors in the underlying biology of replication, or as a consequence of exposure to toxic elements in the environment (like radiation).

While all humans share a common genetic makeup (about 30,000 genes), we do vary in our own genetic makeup – as a consequence of single nucleotide polymorphisms (SNPs). SNPs are caused by a single substitution of one element of one base pair in our genetic code. In the end, these substitutions make each of us the unique person we are. Humans have a remarkable 3.2 billion of these base pairs, acting as the links of a zipper across our 23 pairs of chromosomes. Every human is estimated to have about 4–5 million SNPs, with one of these 'substitutions' occurring in about 1 in 1000 base pairs.

The proportions of these differences vary widely between different ethnic groups. But their real significance is the extent to which these variations in SNPs occur in association with specific diseases like type 2 diabetes and Alzheimer's dementia and, now, the major psychiatric disorders like schizophrenia, bipolar disorder and major depression.

2. Human environments: we all need the social group, but we all live our own lives

Second, the role of environmental factors in causation includes factors that are shared with many others (family homes, physical places) and those that are unique experiences for each of us. None of us live identical lives. Consequently, the many and varied environmental exposures that occur to each of us, particularly during the long period of brain and physical development (minus nine months to 25 years), really drive us to many different places along the continuum of risk. Some types of environments are clearly toxic (sexual abuse, personal violence) at any age, particularly where they are chronic, prolonged or repeated. They substantially increase the risk of developing clinical depression. Others are more subtle, like social disconnection, but they may still be important.

3. Gene–environment interactions: how the world really is

These first two sections on causation might be thought of as the classic nature versus nurture debate with regards to how we come to think, feel and act (that is, how we come to have our adult personality or self), as well as being the most important causes of physical and mental illness.

Third, however, is the more fascinating and much more 21st-century discourse about the ways in which genes and lived experiences actually come together, and possibly drive each other, to create the true risk a person faces. Of great interest is how both these factors combine to drive the brain and bodily changes that characterise clinical depression.

Population-level considerations – and public health policy

Throughout, I've touched briefly on genetic or environmental things that are most relevant to large groups of people (so-called population-level insights) and are, therefore, central to the development of public health policy. That is, those things that are relevant to all of us and best actioned in a universal, everybody-in, way.

At least, in theory, that's how public health works. Fix the sewerage system to prevent cholera, remove asbestos to prevent lung diseases like asbestosis and cancers like mesothelioma. As we've experienced with the pandemic, we promote mass vaccination not only to prevent individual infections but also to promote herd immunity. Reduce the smoking rate to prevent smoking-related heart disease or lung disease. One doesn't need to know each person's individual characteristics to save many lives – you simply provide the potential benefit to all. For clinical depression, reducing the rate of childhood physical or sexual abuse is an obvious candidate for this type of all-in approach.

Individual differences persist and we need them to survive

Despite our noble public health efforts, individual differences will still exist – and strongly influence the types of illnesses that people develop. Despite the massive efforts to reduce tobacco smoking, most people still die of heart disease, cancer or lung diseases. Sadly, there are many other types of heart and lung conditions, and common cancers (bowel, breast, ovarian, thyroid, melanoma) that are not due to exposure to cigarettes.

Individual differences are very apparent across our behavioural repertoire. While we have the collective capacity to care for and nurture our infants, our ill and our disabled, we also display great variation in our capacity to respond to the needs of others, take risks, overcome fear, display empathy or battle various forms of physical or social adversity.

We need those who are very sensitive to the emotional expression of others, that is, those who are highly empathetic, to promote the nurturing and safekeeping of children from minus nine months to about 25 years of age. These temperamental characteristics protect the young and keep our social groups together to function effectively. Unfortunately, that high degree of personal sensitivity can also be a major risk factor to clinical depression.

We also need those who confront danger, physically battle the world and, at times, can be seen to be little affected by others' distress (think first responders, emergency room doctors, surgeons, soldiers) to take on really hard challenges. Further, we need those who get lost in thought, the dreamers and the genuinely creative thinkers (even when they are somewhat detached from daily realities), to imagine new and innovative ways to solve complex problems.

This diversity of temperaments results in the group behaving appropriately, and in many different ways, in the face of a harsh, ever-challenging and frequently changing world. A clear evolutionary advantage for humankind!

So, while many social policies aim to respect fundamental human rights, promote inclusion and treat people equitably, their goal is not to try to make us all more alike. In fact, from a genetic and evolutionary perspective, those groups that are too similar or identical (like clones) die out very quickly, particularly when the environment changes in some new or unexpected way.

Effective social policies do not result in us all achieving the same outcomes; rather, they foster the capacity for all of us to reach our various potentials and, hopefully, not be held back (or made ill) by an unnecessary social or environmental barrier.

In the following sections, I've used physical health analogies such as: providing good nutrition to all children does not make all adults taller. But my point is really behavioural and emotional. Minimising toxic or traumatic emotional experiences, or promoting more positive early and highly sociable environments, will not make everyone more empathetic and sensitive.

The challenge of clinical medicine is an 'n=1' experiment

In clinical medicine, every person is unique. Every patient journey is its own (n=1) natural experiment. This means that the sample size for the experiences is just one – that is, you. To navigate that journey more effectively, the detailed study of individual differences (and their genetic and environmental underpinnings) is critical.

Individual differences are not individual stories. Stories are stories – we tell them to each other, we repeat them across generations. Stories help to maintain our cultural and collective heritage. They promote social cohesion. They don't have to be true.

We often don't know the real source of our differences or that those differences are causing any particular problem. Our understanding of the human genome at great depth is a very recent (early 21st century) phenomenon. Simply mapping your genetic code (much of which you can now purchase commercially) does not tell you what your genome, or the functions it regulates, is actually doing at any particular time. Just like other codes (think computer software), it simply sets some of the rules of the game. What the operator does with that prewritten code is a whole other story! To know what is really going on, we need much more sophisticated measures of the outputs of the system. In clinical psychiatry, we need to see what is happening at many levels – individual cells, brain circuits and a wide range of other hormonal, immune or metabolic measures.

The ways in which the environment changes those functions every day is radical – just think about what you are doing in the daytime, and what your body and brain are doing, as compared to when you are asleep at night. Like other animals, humans respond differently to the same environments – like the light–dark cycle, the changing of seasons or interpersonal relationships – on the basis of their own intrinsic characteristics. In the face of a big sugary meal, we don't all generate the same blood glucose level. It's actually a function of our individual capacity to generate, in response, the right dose of insulin.

So, basically, when I'm in my clinic, I'm not asking what is best for everyone. Instead, I'm only asking, given your current situation (age, sex, patterns of other illness, social context):

1. What will work best for you?
2. How quickly can we work that out?
3. Can we choose interventions that are most appropriate, meaning highly personalised, to you?
4. What combinations of treatments for you – not for the 'average' person with the illness – will result in a longer and more productive life?

TAKE-OUT TIPS

- Parents aren't really in charge of development: they spend most of their time reacting to the temperament of the child.
- The more difficult the temperament of the child, the greater the parenting challenge!
- Our collective survival has been fostered by the diversity of our individual emotional, cognitive and behavioural characteristics.

10

The Genetic Architecture of Clinical Depression

Jackie Crowe, former Australian National Mental Health commissioner (2012–17), lived with a severe and recurring mood disorder. She once said to me, 'Ian, I want to get my own genetic profile now. Then I want you to tell me what it really means, as distinct from the company I'm paying to do the lab work, and then I want you to tell me whether I should be taking different treatments.'

Genes are the architect's rather incomplete drawings. They are not the built house. And has anyone ever known the builder to stick to the plans? There are always contingencies, unexpected gaps and stuff the architect never really considered (at least not for this house, in this street, somewhere in the 21st century).

Similarly, the genes for clinical depression are not the illness itself and, for many, despite the fact they're at increased genetic risk, they will never develop the illness. The real risk may well depend on what other things happen along the way.

So many times I've heard parents, partners or children exclaim, 'Depression doesn't run in our family, we've never seen anything like this before!'

I respond benignly, 'Does anything run in your family, like eye colour, height, skin tones, or maybe other medical conditions – like asthma, epilepsy, diabetes?'

If we are then headed down the path of it's okay to talk about those things that we so obviously share with prior generations, I start to branch out a bit: 'So, any other emotional or behavioural characteristics – like anxiety, emotional sensitivity, attentional problems?'

And finally: 'What about other serious problems like depression, alcoholism or suicide?'

Of course, the other question I get asked, typically after it's become clear that the person has a serious mood disorder, and so did their uncle and their grandmother, is, 'What's the chance that I will pass this on to my children?'

Do we believe that risks of illness, not just temperaments, are also inherited?

After hopefully convincing medical students (see Chapter 9) that genetics plays some significant part in the way temperaments and other behavioural characteristics, like obsessionality, sensitivity to criticism, sleep–wake cycles and daily patterns of physical activity, pass from one generation to the next, I finally get to the point: 'To what extent do you think the risk of any common disorders, like anxiety or depression, has a significant genetic component?'

In decades past, the typical reply was, 'Very small, if any, as those things are largely explained by early life circumstances.'

In recent years, as we are now in the modern genomics era and the discussion of personalised medicine, based on an individual's genetic code, is part of every student's basic medical education, the more common reply is, 'Yes, genetics plays an important role, but not the major part – environments still matter much more.'

That last student reply is correct, at least on average. If we ask what proportion of the total risk of common forms of anxiety or depression is explained by genetic versus other environmental factors, then genetics only explains about one-third. It's also basically true that the onset of clinical depression at any age is, in part, due to the environmental stressors that are operative at the time. Genetic influences for disorders like clinical depression determine an underlying vulnerability. That vulnerability does not often become a manifest illness without exposure to some individually relevant circumstances.

I say all of this upfront, as we now disappear into a longer discussion about the genetic architecture of clinical depression – or at least the best we understand it in the early 21st century.

Genes and environments are the left and right hands of the same organism, not competing or mutually exclusive factors. The big wide world we live in is constantly changing – see climate change, global security, financial uncertainty, new forms of social media, social disconnection or the COVID-19 pandemic. Our own smaller worlds, our interpersonal, social and health circumstances (and our responses to them) are also in flux.

Advanced understanding of the role of both genes and personal environments is essential for better public health. It drives big social initiatives that can reduce risk for all of us and help to prevent illness or reduce its impacts. It can also drive better clinical care, resulting in earlier, more effective and high quality interventions for those who develop clinical depression.

So what does run in families (and how does that happen)?

I've always been intrigued by what exactly runs in families and how normal behaviours, and risk of mental illness, pass from one

ROBYN'S STORY

One of the saddest episodes of my professional career occurred when I met a young mother, Robyn, who had been hospitalised for severe postnatal depression, immediately after attempting to kill herself and her child. Due only to good fortune, both survived.

Robyn was distraught, guilt-ridden and inconsolable. She still wanted to be dead. The very sad part of the story was that Robyn's own mother, Sally, had had postnatal depression that was so severe she'd been hospitalised for two years after Robyn's birth.

For the first time, and only as a consequence of this near catastrophe, Sally shared this family secret with Robyn. While Robyn had been exposed to the same risk as her mother, she (and her medical and nursing supports) had no prior knowledge of the extent to which she too may be in danger of one of the most serious and life-threatening complications of normal childbirth.

generation to the next. Although the answers are complex, and still the subject of much high-tech research, the first place to start is that behaviours and vulnerabilities to mental illness do repeat across generations.

Having recently become a grandparent, I'm fascinated not only by the physical characteristics, but also behavioural styles that I recognise as having been present in at least two generations before me, and now seem to be reappearing one or two generations below me.

In other words, right alongside eye colour, skin tones and risk of physical illnesses, there are discrete behavioural, cognitive and emotional characteristics that are shared by individuals who are joined by DNA – even though they have never lived together or ever met.

If I were to describe my own family in terms of its physical characteristics – pale Celtic skin, fair hair, blue eyes and variably tall and thin or shorter and stockier – most people would accept that those characteristics had come via my very recent ancestors from the West Coast of Ireland. From then on, they have been passed genetically down the generations to my grandchildren.

These things are so striking that a very old photo of my grandfather at age 19 could easily be interchanged with my teenage nephews. One of my daughters, who has red hair and blue eyes, on arriving to study in London, was constantly annoyed by being told she was obviously Irish (and not Australian).

Unfortunately, some of those desirable genetically acquired characteristics, when combined with environmental exposures like prolonged exposure to bright sunshine in childhood, have resulted in a higher risk of skin cancer in my generation. Sadly, one of my brothers died before the age of 50 from melanoma, and then my father developed the same unusual type of nodular melanoma in his late 80s. Dad's cancer actually turned out to be a genetic twin of the one that killed my brother.

In these all-too-common stories, there is no argument, medically or socially, about the relationship between the transmitted genetic characteristics from our Celtic heritage and their very active interactions with early childhood sun exposure. To date, my brother is the only one of seven children to have had active melanoma – and, physically (skin colour, hair type), he was the one most like Dad.

But what of our behavioural characteristics? It is often said, only partially in jest, that the Irish migrants to Australia brought with them not only warmth, song, friendship and a fierce independent streak, but also high rates of alcoholism, mania and depressive disorders.

A few years ago I had the opportunity to travel with my two youngest children to Western Ireland. While engaging in a very animated, edgy conversation with a middle-aged woman in a rural café, both my kids broke into laughter. They couldn't believe we'd travelled halfway around the world for me to have almost the same style of animated, edgy, but well-natured and humorous conversation that I have most weekends with my beloved sister!

Although we'd obviously never met before, many interpersonal signals, communications and emotional transactions were simply shared in common: speed of speech (I'm known to speak quickly), lack of concern for interpersonal niceties (without being deliberately rude or offensive), preference to not take the whole thing too seriously, and a broad smile and laughter to conclude – as the woman I'd never met before made great fun of me.

My point is, despite the fact we'd never met, we physically looked like family, spoke like siblings and laughed like cousins. Undoubtedly, we still shared many genetic factors for both physical appearance and interpersonal behaviour (and probably risk to illness) in common.

TAIMANI'S STORY

While working as a young psychiatrist in an acute-care hospital, I was intrigued by the journey of a young woman and her family. That particular facility provided care to many young people from culturally diverse backgrounds.

Taimani was the eldest daughter in a large family of South Pacific origin. She was brought to our emergency department by her parents and her grandfather. They were all terrified by the sudden onset of self-harming behaviour, lack of sleep, and chaotic physical activity with periods of intense agitation. These were interspersed with periods of dream-like states and outbursts of shouting at imagined figures. On the night she came to care, Taimani had attempted to jump from the third floor of her parents' apartment block.

The parents, along with other members of the extended family, believed that their daughter had been possessed by the spirit of her long-dead great aunt Kaneli. More importantly, they'd been very reluctant to bring Taimani to care earlier, as they were certain we would reject their understanding of the problem. They feared that our Western-scientific medical approach would label them as uneducated, or that we would be dismissive of their explanation.

However, as they were also very protective, and afraid that without immediate help Taimani would come to great harm, they brought her to care. Taimani was not able to describe the events that had led to her extreme and dangerous actions or give any coherent explanation for her behaviour.

Taimani was clearly scared, sweating profusely and jumping chaotically from one very odd posture to another. She appeared to be responding to external things, like voices or visions, that were not apparent to anyone else. Our Western view was that she was experiencing an episode of acute mania.

But, I was still intrigued to hear much more about Kaneli, the great aunt, and her normal behavioural and emotional characteristics – if the great aunt was thought to be responsible for this possession, what was she actually like?

Kaneli had been much feared by many members of the family due to her fiery temperament, boundless energy, mistrust of authority, rejection of formal religion and her lifetime determination to disrupt her father's well-ordered plans for her. That energy and disruptiveness was also tempered by periods of low energy and melancholy.

Following the birth of her first child, Kaneli had descended into a period of confusion, sleeplessness and talking with spirits. Although she eventually recovered, she continued to have episodes of very high and low energy throughout her adult life.

As the family had migrated to Australia before Taimani was born, and Kaneli had died in her late 50s, the two had never met. Despite no shared experiences, the family were certain of a direct link between them because they shared physical characteristics, the aunt had had a very similar and life-threatening episode at about the same age, and they displayed very similar emotional styles (warm but short-tempered, well liked but easily provoked to interpersonal conflict, exquisitely sensitive to personal criticism). Within this cultural tradition, the passing of emotional characteristic from one generation to another is well recognised, though described in more culturally specific ways.

Very quickly, we were able to reassure the family that within our biomedical models, we too recognised that behavioural and emotional characteristics, including risk of mental illness, can pass from one generation to the next. Although we argue a lot about how much is genetically versus behaviourally transmitted, we still accept the basic proposition.

We also recognise that many families live in great fear that past shames or other tragedies, notably suicidal behaviour, may reappear in later generations. While our explanations may differ, our different cultural traditions simply recognise the importance of knowing a great deal more about those who have come before us.

SHARON'S STORY

Some years ago I was asked by a centre specialising in the management of clinical depression to participate in a case discussion involving three generations of one family.

The young mum, Sharon, was being treated for postnatal depression and was accompanied by her mother, Vera, and her nine-month old daughter, Toby. What was immediately striking to me was the similarity in physical appearance between them: blonde, sparkling blue eyes and engaging faces. They were warm and sensitive, and shared an obvious closeness.

The discussion moved to Sharon's key symptoms, including her anxious preoccupation with the health of her daughter, suicidal thoughts and the poor sleep patterns and physical exhaustion she had experienced following Toby's birth.

As an aside, it was noted that Vera had a long history of anxious preoccupation with the health of her own children and that she was also a very poor sleeper. The infant, Toby, had not yet settled into any regular sleep–wake cycle.

My colleagues deduced that Vera's anxious behaviour had clearly been copied by Sharon, and that this was now driving her to parent Toby in a similar way. Sharon was terrified to put Toby down to sleep, could not leave the room while she was sleeping, and could not institute any regular feeding or sleeping routine.

It was assumed that all this turmoil promoted more chaotic daily rhythms (like sleep and feeding times) in the young child. Additionally, whenever she was not in physical contact with Sharon, Toby was often very distressed, crying uncontrollably and hitting out at other caregivers.

For those who are familiar with anxious attachment, this

was a classic case. Some theories of the cause of anxious attachment place emphasis on the disturbed nature of the parenting style ('mother-blaming'), emphasising its inconsistencies, lack of routine, intrusive presence and very high levels of arousal and distress.

In Sharon's case, it was immediately assumed that she was simply repeating (consciously or unconsciously) the behaviours that had characterised her own early relationship with Vera. Given the striking similarities in physical appearance, posture, facial expression, voice tones, speech pattern and emotional tones, I couldn't help asking: 'Do you think that it's possible that the striking similarities in anxious behaviour across all three generations, just like the striking similarities in physical appearance, are just as likely to reflect shared genetic factors as much as shared exposure to early childhood environments?'

You might ask, 'Well, who cares what causes transmission across generations – surely, it's bad for the child, no matter how it happens?'

I'd suggest it matters a lot – to those affected, to those trying to provide the best treatments, and to our capacity to prevent transmission across future generations.

First, when people come to understand that key aspects of their behaviour are not simply under their personal control, have not simply been learnt through earlier childhood exposures and were not simply caused by their wayward parents, a whole lot less blame gets sprayed about.

Time to wonder whether your parents may have faced very similar difficulties.

In this case, it's not all Vera's fault, or Sharon's fault or, in the future, Toby's fault. In truth, they are all living with a shared and, in part, genetically determined vulnerability. The last thing Sharon needed was to be blamed for Toby's difficulties, and to be blaming Vera for having put her in this situation in the first place.

Second, it makes a big difference to thinking not only about causation but, more importantly, to long-term treatment and secondary prevention. The challenge for all of us is to acquire the best set of skills, supports and treatments to deal with this challenge – as it plays out in parenting and many other aspects of our interpersonal lives.

Sharon does not need to spend a lifetime in prolonged counselling focused on the past. She does not need to reconstruct her own early childhood experiences and, most likely, feel more alienated from her own mother – just when she most needs Vera's practical and emotional support.

So, how did my question about the possibility of shared genetic risk across three generations in this fascinating family go down with my professional colleagues?

Actually, a cold silence followed . . .

In the simplistic world of nature versus nurture, it is still as unacceptable as ever to suggest that nature plays a strong role.

For many, the emphasis on nature – genetics, neurobiological patterns, medical science – seems to lack empathy and promote an old-style genetic determinism where what you inherit rules your life chances. Worst of all it seems to say that such things cannot be changed by any interventions, be they medical or psychological.

While that last bit is the one often most expressed by health professionals, it is also the most wrong, but more of that later.

BELLA'S STORY

Bella, who lives in a regional town in Australia, many hours away from any specialist treatment centre, came to our attention at age 13. She had gone from being a well-socialised primary school student with some anxiety and learning difficulties to being almost mute, frequently banging her head against a wall and being entirely non-responsive to her parents. She was now out of school, and unable to socialise with anybody outside the family. She drew pictures of monsters, violence and threats to herself and others – without being able to give any explanation.

Bella's mother, Clara (who also has bipolar disorder and thyroid disease), was extremely distressed by the sudden onset of this very confronting behaviour, so she had taken Bella to local health services. The team there quickly decided that this bizarre behaviour was due to Clara's anxiety, that she was too over-responsive to these violent outbursts. They recommended leaving Bella alone in her own room, and just letting her bash her head against the wall. Bella's problem was described as being 'behavioural' in origin and, thereby, not worthy of further medical or specialist investigation.

Fortunately for Bella, Clara didn't follow that most unhelpful advice. She was, as a consequence of her own experiences, more informed than the average parent. Specifically, she had benefited greatly from treatment with lithium carbonate – a mainstay medication for bipolar disorder. Further, her own mother had also had bipolar disorder – so, there were two previous generations in her family.

Due to her mother's efforts, Bella did eventually get more specialised neurological and psychiatric care. She has a periodic and epileptic-like electrical discharge from the part of the brain that regulates memory and emotions (the temporal lobe). However, her young age and very unusual presentation still led most professionals to focus on family therapy to reduce both Clara's anxiety and Bella's reliance on her parents.

Clara remarked again on her own and her mother's good response to lithium. A psychiatrist responsible for her care, who was actually listening to Clara, was persuaded to trial lithium as a treatment for Bella. From that point on, although still complex and very challenging, Bella's illness dramatically improved.

Positive assortative mating: the complication of when like breeds with like

Most studies aimed at finding the genetic underpinnings of risk of illness are a whole lot easier if the DNA of each parent is not more similar than what you would expect by chance. For many rare, and strongly genetically inherited conditions, only one parent is responsible for transmitting the risk to their children.

Unfortunately, in behavioural medicine, life isn't like that. Many people choose partners on the basis of shared characteristics – and not just physical (height, hair colour) or cultural (same religion, ethnic background) factors. It turns out that emotional characteristics – things like sensitivity, empathy or shyness – are just as relevant. Other behavioural characteristics that are relevant to the risk of developing clinical depression, like the degree of physical activity and exercise or the way we arrange our 24-hour sleep–wake cycles, may also be shared by both parents.

Jasper is a man in his 30s who I first met after he left hospital with a presumed diagnosis of bipolar disorder. He'd had his first episode of illness – a depressive episode some years before – in winter, during which he stayed in bed all day, gained weight, avoided light and generally hibernated. A few years later, at Easter, during the period of rapid change in daylight in early autumn, he had become psychotic, believing he was the Messiah. After recovering, he'd quickly descended back into a severe depressive episode. The 'on–off' characteristics of his mood disorder were clearly linked to the changes in season, and strongly affected by light exposure (a circadian-type depression).

Interestingly, Jasper always described his family as 'very interesting and diverse'. Given his clinical history, I expected to hear a lot about possible bipolar disorder or related syndromes. A rich family history can be very useful – for explaining where the illness vulnerability comes from, but also where it may go! It turned out that although Jasper's dad was very successful and high-functioning, he also had a recurrent mood disorder and a major alcohol problem. Jasper's mother had a major anxiety and depressive disorder with frequent 'nervous breakdowns' and his maternal aunt had lived with a major opiate addiction. And that was just for starters. Across the broader family, on both the paternal and maternal side, various forms of mental illness and alcohol and drug abuse were rife.

My summary to Jasper: 'Well, collectively, they've certainly left no stone unturned! We won't focus on the specifics anymore. Suffice to say, they've certainly passed on a full house of risk to you . . .'

It's not simply your fault, or your family's, even though we keep saying so!

For many of those affected, it is often a great relief to know that there are factors way beyond their conscious control (or that of their parents, or their grandparents) that have played a large role in disrupting their life course.

Clinical psychiatry has a bad track record of blaming mothers (and, and more recently, fathers) for a whole range of mental health problems in the decades before more specific genetic or other biological elements were identified). Most notably those with a more Freudian or psychoanalytic bent, have attributed:

- autism in children to cold and unemotional mothers;
- schizophrenia in young people to 'schizophrenogenic' mothers – accusing them of providing chaotic and inconsistent parental responses;
- anxiety in children either to deficient (abandoning) or overly responsive (controlling) patterns of mothering;
- shyness in children to overprotective parents; and,
- depression in youth and adults to failures of parents (mostly mothers) to provide warm and secure attachments for their infant children.

In these causal models, at birth, (while ignoring its inherited eye colour, hair colour, skin tone, facial features) the child's emotional and behavioural features are a blank canvas – on which the parents (mostly mums) imprint their own neuroses and other emotional deficiencies.

All those things that attract attention or cause distress, and are observed by parents, other family members and grandparents – such as inability to separate from the primary parent, emotional non-responsiveness, irritability, poor sleep and feeding patterns – are chalked up to the child's response to the primary cause – namely, poor or abusive parenting.

Back to the future

In 1987, based on findings across generations of Amish families living in Pennsylvania, the first report of a specific gene linked to bipolar disorder (or manic-depressive illness) was published in *Nature,* one of the world's leading scientific journals. I was living in Sydney at the time and vividly recall the CNN newsflash that followed: 'Discovery of gene for manic-depression spells end to clinical psychiatry.'

For someone just leaping into specialist psychiatry training, this was rather confronting! Perhaps my mother was right – a career in cardiology *was* preferable. Heart disease is never going out of fashion – and certainly not on the basis of an important scientific discovery. (As is often the case in science, the discovery turned out not to be correct, and the whole genetic story got much more complicated.)

Perhaps what was even more distressing was the media conclusion that progress in unravelling the genetic architecture of bipolar disorder would lead to the demise of clinical psychiatry. By comparison, in the early 1990s, the genetic defect that gives rise to Huntington's disease was discovered, but CNN did not suddenly predict the end of clinical neurology.

Of course, what this media perspective did reflect was the huge gap between community understanding of how genes work and more common beliefs that major mood disorders like clinical depression are principally caused by psychological and environmental factors. Additionally, these external factors are assumed to operate independently of any inherent or intrinsic vulnerability in the affected individual.

In other words, the common environmental view is that when exposed to certain stressors, we are all equally likely to develop severe anxiety or clinical depression. Individual differences in risk don't really exist, just the random chance of being exposed to specific environmental toxins.

Importantly, certain psychiatric disorders appear to make this assumption quite explicitly – like post-traumatic stress disorder

(PTSD). It's the trauma that causes the disorder, and the very specific symptoms presented by individuals who have been exposed to overwhelming threat. There's no role for individual vulnerability, genetically determined or otherwise.

The facts, however, are contrary to these views. Even for really terrible examples of exposure to life-threatening or other demonstrably traumatic events, the majority of people do not develop PTSD, clinical depression or any other psychiatric disorder. Many other personal and social factors are known to be relevant: number of prior exposures, temperamental characteristics of the individual, cognitive and other neurobiological characteristics, whether the event was experienced alone or as part of a functioning social group, and the social and personal management immediately after the event. For depressive disorders, it is now clear that the degree of underlying genetic risk plays a big role.

In the US, the huge gap between these various explanatory models – psychological-environmental versus genetic-neurobiological – was not simply a case of 'lost in translation'. The proponents of these alternative views may well have lived in separate universes. Sadly, it is still very common to hear baseless repetition of these extreme views.

To unravel this rather messed-up view of the role of genetic architecture, meaning that which is coded in your DNA, we need to take a brief historical detour through some challenging terrain. Stick with me – by the time we arrive back in the third decade of the 21st century, the picture should be a whole lot clearer!

So what exactly is inherited from one generation to the next?

The basic questions of the degree of heritability of normal behaviours, risk of various forms of mental illness, suicidal behaviour and chances of full recovery when receiving treatment, are very active areas of mental health research.

Heritability is basically a statistical concept that measures the extent to which an observed feature in a population (say height, weight, eye colour, IQ), at a particular time in history, can be attributed to variations in the genetics of that same population. As environmental influences vary over time and place, heritability estimates also vary.

Importantly, heritability also varies across the lifespan. For many common features it is lowest in childhood, as the environment plays such a large role. Nutrition, education, health status (like infectious diseases), family and social structures have very big effects during intra-uterine development and early chidlhood. Heritability then increases throughout adolescence and becomes relatively stable in adult life.

Classically, in well-nourished Western populations with good maternal and child health care, the height of adults is said to have a heritability of approximately 0.8, meaning that genetic factors explain about 80 per cent of the variation in height in the population. By contrast, for Body Mass Index (BMI) the heritability index is estimated to be 0.4, meaning that 40 per cent of the variation is due to genetic factors – leaving 60 per cent explained by differences in individual environments, such as food availability, consumption and dietary composition.

If we are all malnourished, as in famines and wars, then the proportion of variation in weight explained by the environment goes up and the heritability goes down – even though there has been no change in the underlying genetic architecture. More likely in Western countries now, as food consumption rapidly increases, the heritability of height is likely to remain high, while the heritability of BMI goes down. Sadly, now, we all tend to over-consume, under-exercise and fail to attend to the metabolic implications of disturbed circadian rhythms.

For something like general intelligence in adults, measured historically as Intelligence Quotient (IQ), heritability estimates are classically in the 50–75 per cent range, though more recent estimates go as high as 80. If none of us received any decent education, then the heritability estimates would be much lower. So, contrary to what you might imagine, as we improve the early educational environment for most children, variations in adult IQ are increasingly likely to be explained by underlying genetic factors.

To cut to those things I really care about, it has been estimated that the heritability of suicidal behaviour is in the range of 25–50 per cent, for clinical depression in the range of 40–50 per cent, and for the most severe forms of depression associated with bipolar disorder above 80 per cent.

Twins are a great natural experiment

A somewhat different way of looking at the genetics of psychiatric disorders is to look at the rates of illness in identical versus non-identical twins. Twins are one of nature's great experimental conditions. They have enabled serious scientific studies of genetics. As identical twins share all of their genes in common, if an illness is entirely due to genetic factors alone then they will both inevitably develop the condition – that is, 100 per cent of the time. The variations in environments that they've experienced pre-birth and throughout their childhood and adult lives will have no effect on their chance of developing a specific illness.

For most illnesses, identical twins do not develop the same illness 100 per cent of the time. But, if an illness has a strong genetic basis, then the rate of the illness in identical twins (the concordance rate) is typically twice as high as it is in non-identical twins. This is because non-identical twins (just like other brothers and sisters) only have about half their genetic code in common with their co-twin. For an illness like bipolar disorder, the concordance rate in identical twins is 40–50 per cent. For clinical depression it is lower, more like 25–40 per cent and for suicidal behaviour, it is generally about 25 per cent. However, the concordance rate for non-identical twins in all these conditions is much lower (often single digits), indicating that genetic factors play a significant, but not overwhelming, role in determining the prevalence of these conditions in our community.

As an aside, I'm fortunate to be the father of a glorious set of non-identical twins – a boy and a girl. She has bright blue eyes, red hair and a fiery temperament – clearly her great-grandfather's Irish heritage and her grandfather's energetic nature. He has brown eyes, brown hair and a quiet, reflective nature – clearly his mother's French heritage – and is a physical and emotional copy of his mother's brother. My great friend and colleague, and Chief of the Genetic Epidemiology Research Branch at the US National Institutes of Mental Health, Dr Kathleen Merikangas, on first meeting these twins as small children, remarked, 'My hunch is that these twins don't have a single gene in common.' Even though they have shared the same family environment, educational and social opportunities, and extended family relationships, they remain as different – physically and emotionally – thirty-something years later as the day they were born!

Twin studies are not only a marvellous source of information about the role of genetic effects but they can also tell us a great deal about specific environmental risk factors. As the genes of identical twins are exactly the same, any differences in risk of illness, or response to treatments, must be explained by non-genetic, environmental factors. If one then compares male and female identical twins, one can start to look not only at sex differences due to genetic effects but also differences driven by their unique and gender-dependent environmental experiences.

Individual-level estimates of risk

Unfortunately, all these population-based or 'average' estimates tell us absolutely nothing about how much genetic risk of illness is active in any individual. For some it may be very large, while for others it may be very small. We often try to guess this genetic dose by asking about family history. Sadly, this is notoriously unreliable, often because families don't have access to the real history of past generations. On the other side of the coin, for some the influence of environments, past or present, may be very small. For others, like those exposed to childhood sexual abuse, it may be very large.

This person-level genetics, as distinct from population-level, is a whole new ball game, one that is alive and well, and rapidly expanding. Right now, we know that clinical depression is polygenic in origin, meaning many different genes, and a large number of biological processes that they underpin – like brain development, connections between nerve cells, biochemical signals between nerve cells and immune processes that regulate and reorganise the connections between cells – are involved. However, every individual can have quite different combinations of these many genes and biological pathways. So, each person has their own unique, genetically determined smorgasboard of risks.

In 2019, 102 independent genetic variations, 269 genes and 15 gene-sets specifically associated with depression were identified, on the basis of Genome-Wide Association Studies (GWAS) that combined data from 807,553 individuals. In 2023, the number of genetic variants identified was over 400, and links with specific areas of the brain that regulate emotion and thought, such as the frontal cortex, or processes that regulate nervous cell structure and signal transmission are much clearer. For the closely related condition of bipolar disorder, the number of genetic variations initially identified by GWAS was about 40. That number has rapidly increased as more people have contributed their DNA to these studies. It now stands at over 100, with considerable overlap with genes that give rise to clinical depression or schizophrenia.

For some individuals with clinical depression, both their genetic risk and their history of exposure to toxic environmental factors may both be very high. Is this simply very bad luck? Just to send our heads really spinning, these two big risk factors may not be entirely independent. As genes influence behaviours (like risk-taking, shyness or negative responses to criticism), and as behaviours lead individuals into different environmental exposures (like drug-taking or abusive personal relationships), any particular individual may have had a life journey where genetic characteristics have strongly influenced their chance of being exposed to toxic environments.

Genetics may also strongly influence the chance that a person perceives, and then reports to others, an environmental event as being aversive or traumatic. That is, even when people are exposed to the same event, only some people report of being distressed and go on to list it among the negative things that have happened to them in their lifetime. It turns out that those who are at higher genetic risk of developing depression (as determined by their polygenic risk score), report more early life and more recent traumatic events than those at lower genetic risk.

These recent discoveries blow a large hole in many traditional models of the respective roles of genetic and environmental risk factors. Historically, it was believed that many people had high genetic risk but low environmental exposures, while others had low genetic risk but, sadly, had experienced a very large number of adverse events. Turns out, those with higher genetic risk also report more, not less, exposure to adverse environments. These bad things probably happened both before, and following, the onset of their illness.

Now, to make things really complicated, it turns out that environmental factors can turn some gene functions on and off. That is, they result in changes to the physical structure of the DNA code. These processes are termed 'epigenetic'. Just to make Charles Darwin turn in his grave, it appears that some of these impacts may even be passed from one generation to the next.

So, genes are driving illness, genes are driving environmental exposures (including to major personal traumas), and environments are changing gene expression. Some of these environmentally induced genetic changes may then be passed onto the next generation biologically, not just psychologically or socially. Bad environmental influences can be inherited!

At the moment, neither the individual person nor their treating clinician, can actually know the true answer to the degree of genetic or environmental risk a person is carrying. The methods to work out the degree of polygenic risk, for each individual, are now well-developed. They are called polygenic risk scores (or PRS) and we may see them coming into the clinic fairly soon.

Modern genetic scientists are now employing really fancy statistical techniques (such as Mendelian randomisation – see below) to help unravel the true causal sequence between different genetic and environmental factors. Which came first? Are the influences bi-directional? Are the observations we're making of associations between various factors due to other common factors that we have not yet discovered?

As the general environment gets better, so does the importance of (genetically and environmentally determined) individual differences

As a social progressive, my hope is that as we improve the standards of living, health, education and social inclusiveness, particularly as they relate to child development and lifetime opportunities, then the rate of very poor outcomes will decline. At the public health level, this is largely true. It is certainly true not only for those things that impact on physical health but also those things that impact on brain development – and its behavioural, emotional and cognitive outcomes.

That is, the rates of very obvious risk factors like poor maternal health, maternal smoking, prenatal infection (diseases like rubella and measles), prenatal alcohol exposure, obstetric complications, nutritional deficiencies and exposure to other toxins (like lead and other heavy metals) continue to decline. Consequently, in most developed countries infant and child development, including brain health, continues to improve.

Other really important risk factors, prenatally and in childhood, also continue to decline. Things like exposure of the mother or child to domestic violence, neglect, childhood sexual or physical abuse and other forms of emotional trauma. Additionally, developed societies continue to put more emphasis on enriching the environment of small children, physically, and emotionally, through actions such as supported early childhood care, family support and linked child welfare structures, plus enhanced early childhood education.

So, as we make such important collective moves, what is the result for illness outcomes? Are they becoming less common? And, are the potential benefits shared equally? For problems that were a direct result of a specific risk factor that has been markedly reduced, such as the impact of vaccination against rubella to prevent infection during pregnancy, there has been a marked fall in birth defects due to this virus. Where there was a more general risk factor, such as an improvement in maternal health and access to better quality prenatal and obstetric care, there have certainly been benefits to all.

However, as we reduce environmental risk factors and promote better environments for all, for individuals, their own (often genetically determined) risk becomes even more relevant.

For example, when most adult men smoked tobacco, the rates of tobacco-related heart disease or lung disease strongly reflected the degree of exposure to that toxin. Now that we have reduced that exposure, we have not seen the end of heart or lung disease, but rather a change in the types of diseases that commonly present. These forms now reflect much greater individual variation in the age of onset, course of illness and outcomes.

When I was a young doctor, hospital emergency departments were full of 60-year-old men, often daily smokers, having heart attacks due to blocked coronary arteries. Sadly, many dropped dead before they reached the hospital. These days, there are far fewer of those men – and there are also many more healthy 70, 80 and 90-year-olds!

But, I'm a non-smoking 60-year-old male, so when I find myself in an emergency department with a major heart problem there's no point lecturing me about the importance of reducing smoking rates, changing diets and increasing exercise to extend my life. Something else – quite specific to me (and as it turns several of my siblings – see Chapter 4) is the underlying problem!

For my 65-year-old colleague who has never smoked, has exercised all his life, stayed trim and focused heavily on reducing his high cholesterol, but suddenly had a complete block in just one of his major coronary arteries – there was no point in suggesting that his lifestyle was to blame for his life-threatening event. Worse, he almost died because his medical care team didn't believe that he could have a blocked artery – because he just didn't look at all like those 60-year-old men of years gone by.

Similarly, when one of my very fit, non-smoking 60-year-old classmates came staggering out of the surf with excruciating pain in his chest and down his left arm, saying that he thought he was having a heart attack, the local lifesavers didn't really believe him. When he then had a cardiac arrest, fortunately in the back of an ambulance, there was far less scepticism. He was given fast-acting anti–blood clotting agents, preventing more extensive damage to his heart. Turns out, he does not have coronary artery disease. After removing the clots he's alive and back in the water surfing again!

I'm dwelling on all these heart disease examples not just because I'm the son of a cardiologist. The bottom line here is when we are all exposed to something toxic – smoking, malnutrition, childhood infections – we become more like each other, despite our actual individual differences. The population rate of that form of illness is high and a common understanding of the main cause is widely accepted. When mothers are starved, all of their children are shorter, their later growth is stunted and everyone knows what caused it.

When the environment improves, we become more different and the explanations for illness onsets become much more variable. Have you ever noticed how as maternal health continues to improve, your children (and grandchildren) are more variable in height? (Mine are mostly much taller!) The adverse effects of maternal malnutrition on a child's height, which were common in my Irish relatives in the late 19th and early 20th century, take two generations to recover. This is because of the impacts of nutritional deficits on their daughters when they were still in-utero, which causes them to also be shorter than their own children.

Same with many mental health problems like major depression. There are complex intergenerational (genetic and epigenetic) processes at work. Some adverse environmental effects don't simply wash out in one generation. Consequently, we may still be living with the negative impacts of those environmental factors that affected our parents and grandparents. But the more general movement over time has been towards the rapid and dramatic reduction in catastrophic environmental effects, accompanied by an increased commitment to protecting children, removing barriers that prevented women reaching their full social potential, reducing life-long violence against women and children, and reducing social barriers to full participation experienced by many other marginalised or disadvantaged groups.

While personal and historical accounts of very adverse environmental factors are common in our broader cultural life, and dramatically depicted in literature, film and other creative arts, there tends to be less reporting of the remarkable social changes that have taken place over the course of the latter 20th and earlier 21st century.

While much of this progress would be expected to lead to better population-level mental health, it doesn't necessarily lead to a dramatic reduction in disorders, like clinical depression and bipolar disorder, that are still underpinned by strong genetic vulnerability.

The population-level averages of genetic, shared family and individual environmental risks

At the population level, we have had the methods for a very long time (twin, family and adoption studies linked with complex statistical models) to determine the relative contributions of genetics, early shared family environments and unique past and current environmental factors on the liability to develop common mental disorders like anxiety and depression.

The bottom line, which may surprise many since it is rarely reported in the wider media, is that 30–40 per cent of the risk of those disorders that develop before age 25 years is genetic, 40–50 per cent is due to unique environmental experiences and only

10–20 per cent is from shared early childhood experiences (that is, the environment that is shared at home by brothers and sisters).

When we say something is genetic in these large population-based studies, we don't mean very specific or individual genes or groups of genes (say, of the type that cause Down syndrome or haemophilia or Huntington's disease). In these studies, it is a composite measure of all the genetic factors, which are actually extremely variable from one individual to another and are likely to be influencing a very wide variety of brain development and brain signalling processes.

As the age of people studied increases, the ongoing contribution of shared childhood experiences continues to fall. In other words, we were all more alike when we lived at home together as children, but our own unique genetic makeup and our own specific lifetime experiences become much more important to our risk of illness as we move from adolescence to adulthood.

In fact, by the time you reach mid-life or later years, we start to detect the impact of new and different genetic influences that are not linked to adolescent-onset types of anxiety and depression. They are actually more closely linked with risks of things like vascular (blood vessel) disease. In other words, your risk of developing vascular disease is much more relevant to your chances of becoming depressed in old age than what happened to you in childhood or adolescence.

So, the things that have happened uniquely to an individual (in childhood or currently) do explain more of the difference between individuals than genetic factors. But that is all of the possible environmental risk factors over the course of a lifetime, which are many! Actually measuring the contribution of specific factors (childhood sexual abuse, unemployment, alcohol and drug exposure, domestic violence, conflictual interpersonal relationships) is a very challenging process.

With regard to the genetic factors, long before any specific genetic factors were detected, it looked like the genetic risks were shared across a variety of common mental health problems like anxiety and depression. By contrast, the highly variable environmental exposures we all report may provide more of the explanation as to why different clinical conditions present with different symptoms. As summarised in a classic scientific paper of the time, it looked like 'same genes, different environments' gave the best explanation of different underlying causes.

Like the moon mission of the 1960s, the birth of the Human Genome Project in the late 1980s was seen as the next great step forward in global medical science. From then onwards, scientists were able to use new molecular methods to move from broad population estimates of genetic risk to determining which specific genetic mechanisms were responsible for major diseases, and whether as a result we could predict which individuals were actually at risk of which illnesses. Much of the work focused on cancer risk and determining who was most likely to respond to which specific treatments.

Alongside these efforts, mental health researchers went hunting for very specific or 'candidate' genes that could be linked uniquely with different clinical disorders – like schizophrenia, anxiety, major depression or bipolar disorder. That is, it was hoped that just like Huntington's disease or some rare forms of epilepsy, major mental health problems would have a simple genetic explanation. In the end, those hopes were dashed. They have now been replaced by studies that focus on polygenic risk – meaning the cumulative impact of very many genes on the illness outcome of interest, including clinical depression. But, remember those combinations are highly variable from one person to the next.

For clinical psychiatry, the concurrent development of new methods in brain imaging (most notably magnetic resonance imaging – MRI) in the 1990s precipitated great scientific excitement, leading US President George H. W. Bush to declare it as the decade of the brain!

A long list of scientific advances can be attributed to the combined international efforts of the US-based and European science and medical research agencies that aggressively pursued brain and genetic research. These have included major advances in structural and functional brain imaging techniques, developments of new therapeutic medicines for psychiatric disorders (antidepressants and antipsychotics), development of new brain stimulation techniques, most notably through the use of relatively safe magnetic fields (transcranial magnetic stimulation – TMS), and an emphasis on the extent to which brain cells and their connections are actively changing during childhood, adolescence and adult life ('neuroplasticity').

However, their respective failures to deliver much greater societal benefits, or lead to more personalised and high-quality care for many of those living with major disorders has also attracted considerable criticism. While brain imaging and genetic research studies continue globally, and now link data from many thousands of people living with these conditions, there is also a much bigger emphasis on searching for novel ways to prevent these disorders or deliver much better short- and long-term health outcomes.

So what is it about genetic risk factors that scares people?

Like many medical professionals, it's always been apparent to me that mental disorders like clinical depression are serious illnesses, and that a large chunk of the possible causes must be genetically determined.

For cancer specialists, cardiologists and neurologists – and the patients they treat and the families they advise about active prevention – these are just basic and commonsense ideas.

For psychiatrists, any discussion of possible genetic factors is still highly likely to arouse fear, suspicion and concern. Often, it elicits two main concerns:

1. the historical record of the misuse of psychiatric genetics to do harm; and
2. the mistaken belief that genetics equals an unalterable destiny – an illness course that is beyond the personal control of the individual, and beyond the capacity of medicine to alter that course.

So where did it all go so wrong (historically) for clinical psychiatry?

One of clinical psychiatry's most challenging realities is that it has always been tightly engaged with both the best and the worst of the sociopolitical circumstances of the day. On the one hand it is very socially progressive, trying to reduce social harm and support those with illnesses that have often been very poorly understood and associated with alienation or active social exclusion. For example, the asylum movement had its origins in trying to provide a safe place for people with mental illness, after they had been totally abandoned during the urbanisation and social dislocation of the industrial revolution.

On the other hand, psychiatric institutions have been misused by many totalitarian and authoritarian regimes, and other regressive social movements, to persecute those who are not aligned with the dominant power structures. Further, when people or nation states have wanted to express racist ideas, justify active discrimination, do harm to those who did not look like them or behave differently or express quite different social values, they have often invoked pseudogenetic or pseudoevolutionary concepts of superiority (for things like intelligence, sociability, spirituality, virtue, cultural development or sexual preference) to support their position.

The notions that such undesirable cognitive, emotional, ideological or behavioural states were inherited, or built-in from birth and unchanging, came to underpin many of these repressive movements. The ultimate culmination was in the eugenics movement of the early 20th century (notably, in the United Kingdom, Central Europe, and North America). Eugenics is typically defined as the set of beliefs and practices that deliberately aim to improve the genetic quality of the population. Historically, this has resulted in excluding less 'desirable', typically dark-skinned, non-European, less 'educated' people from breeding, and is most commonly known for its associations with Nazi Germany and the Holocaust. It has promoted forced sterilisation, or extermination, of the 'lesser' people, while actively supporting the preferential reproduction of the more 'superior' groups (white-skinned, European, upper class and highly educated).

Many leading academic institutions, including those deeply engaged with the study of the genetic mechanisms that underpinned evolutionary biology, and the Darwinian concept of natural selection, were active supporters of eugenics. This disastrous movement came to its zenith during the Nazi period in Europe in the 1940s – resulting in the extermination of millions of 'undesirables' (including the Jewish people alongside those with mental illness, intellectual disability and other forms of cognitive or brain impairment). It is estimated that more than 200,000 psychiatric patients were murdered between 1939 and 1945.

I remember attending the first meeting of the World Psychiatric Association to be held in Germany after the Nazi period (in 1999), more than 50 years after the end of World War II! This only took place after it was agreed that there would be a formal recognition of the previous atrocities, and that the event would include a memorial detailing the unconscionable actions of those involved and the specific role played by many eminent psychiatrists. It was a very sobering lesson for any young psychiatrist like me, and particularly one with a keen interest in psychiatric genetics.

Unfortunately, for the later development of psychiatric genetics, the concepts of eugenics and genetic determinism – whereby common human behavioural characteristics including the liability to mental illness are held to be caused almost entirely by genes, and have no capacity for change throughout life – became intertwined with any later or independent genetic studies. So, discussions of psychiatric genetics, and their relevance to public health or clinical medicine, even now, still occur in the dark shadows of these previous sociopolitical and ideological disasters.

Sadly, the re-emergence of genetic or biological determinism to disenfranchise, discriminate against or withhold treatment from those with severe mental disorders is, a real and constant fear.

An unalterable destiny?

Like other medical professionals, I've always thought that as scientific knowledge about the biological and genetic underpinnings of depression developed – particularly through new brain imaging and molecular genetic technologies – this would greatly help to improve prevention and treatment options *and* to reduce the stigma and discrimination experienced by those living with the conditions.

That is, depression would be treated just like asthma, diabetes, cancer or heart disease. In fact, when I was the inaugural CEO of Beyond Blue, this was a central element of our public awareness campaigns and health system advocacy. We promoted key concepts such as 'It's just another illness', 'It's not your fault', 'Go see your family doctor for help'.

In the wider society, it's just not that simple. Most people do think genetics and neurobiology are predictive of their destiny.

These fixed beliefs then work against the notion of treatable or curable disorders. By contrast, if the condition is instead caused by your environment, most people believe they can fix the environment to prevent it or treat it effectively.

The discovery of new genetic mechanisms still runs the risk of undermining the social messaging about the value of environmental enhancements, self-care or the provision of more effective treatments. I assume that is the reason so many still rail against the discipline of psychiatric genetics, particularly when applied to common disorders like clinical depression.

The Australian Genetics of Depression Study

So, now we live and work in the 21st century, what are the attitudes of people living with severe depression on the role of genetics? What are their experiences of taking antidepressant medications?

In 2018, more than 20,000 Australians volunteered to take part in a national collaborative study (see Chapter 22) that aimed to:

- detect the likely genetic factors that put you at risk of clinical depression;
- predict a poor illness course;
- guide individual selection of the treatment (including class of medicine) that might deliver the best results; and,
- predict which treatments to avoid because of the likelihood of developing severe side-effects.

In this study individuals with depression and other family members filled in detailed online questionnaires about their experiences of treatments, specific benefits and common side-effects. They then provided a spit sample, which was analysed to determine the DNA code of each participant. They did this as volunteers and did not expect to derive any personal benefit.

More than 5000 individuals have now participated in a parallel study of bipolar disorder and several thousand in a study of anorexia nervosa and other eating disorders. Either Australians love to volunteer or they have a greater appreciation of the potential gains, personally and collectively, from advancing scientific knowledge about the genetic underpinnings of major psychiatric disorders.

The potential benefits of genetic testing in clinical depression

We need to ask what are the potential benefits of widespread genetic characterisation, of whole populations, for those who are potentially at high risk, and for those who actually develop an illness like clinical depression. While some families may turn out to have very rare genetic mutations that explain the transmission in their own family (as has happened with epilepsy) these are likely to be uncommon for disorders like clinical depression.

Now, it is much more likely that we will move to using general risk estimates derived from Polygenic Risk Scores (PRS), rather than the identification of any very specific genetic abnormalities. While this work is only just starting to move from the laboratory, and the statistical computer program, to the clinic, the potential benefits are already being promoted by a wider range of commercial interests.

For mental health, the genetic picture is getting more complex each year. We are trying to understand how thousands of genes, which are collected together in many different ways in many people, can give rise to a much smaller number of often overlapping neuropsychiatric syndromes. There are no simple or discrete syndromes, and certainly no simple genetic disorders.

What is becoming clear are the ways many genetic combinations drive common mechanisms – like altered patterns of brain development, the architecture of nerve cells and their connections (synapses) – or the immune response to external stimuli. Identification of these main pathways has implications not just for one disorder, say clinical depression, but potentially for preventing or optimising treatment for several disorders.

Alternatively, determining whether any combinations are unique to specific conditions – like autism, schizophrenia, bipolar disorder or clinical depression – and, if so, which systems they are preferentially affecting is the complementary task – like circadian ('body clock') systems in bipolar disorder and atypical depression, or stress-sensitivity and hypothalamic-pituitary adrenal (HPA) axis function in anxious depression. Such basic science has the potential to point to those brain mechanisms which are most salient for both enhanced prevention and better treatments of more specific disorders.

When such major genetic paths are identified, then it is also possible to search for those environmental factors which promote best development or protect against disruption. That is, prevention programs are potentially greatly enhanced if we know much more exactly which paths are at risk and which environmental elements (when encountered during which developmental periods – in utero, childhood, adolescence) have the largest impact.

From a public policy perspective, the more we know about the specifics for preventing all major mental disorders, and how better to prevent each specific syndrome, the more likely we are to move from very broad generalisations to more targeted interventions. This has been the case elsewhere in medicine. Think about the use of folate supplementation by women in pregnancy to reduce the risk of neural tube (spina bifida) defects, or limiting alcohol intake in pregnancy to reduce the risk of foetal alcohol syndrome. These specific examples sit alongside big preventive programs like reducing smoking or reducing blood pressure to prevent a whole range of diseases (in this generation and the next).

Knowing your own risk can be empowering

If you come from a family with a high risk of a major mood or psychotic disorder, you are at higher risk (maybe one in five or one in ten). Theoretically, you could be the focus of more intensive or targeted prevention or early intervention programs.

But, on the basis of such general estimates, we don't actually know specifically whether *you* are at risk. That is, while we say you are statistically at higher risk, you may not actually be at any increased risk. Once individual genomic sequencing becomes more common, and the PRS for the major disorders are validated, we will be able to give you a much more specific estimate of how high your own real risk is. Unlike current probability estimates, which assume that you and your other family members are all at the same risk, you will get an answer that specifically applies to you, and not your parents, siblings or children.

Different people respond quite differently to highly personalised knowledge. Many want to know their risks and take active steps to minimise their chances of illness-onset or bad outcomes. This very positive approach is only really justified if we have effective strategies to modify those risks. Earlier intervention for those with symptoms, using existing treatments, is certainly one of those ethically justified approaches. It seeks to minimise the secondary harm that accumulates from the duration and intensity of untreated clinical depression.

Other preventive strategies are increasingly being investigated and promoted, with positive outcomes in selected populations for sleep–wake cycle management, physical activity, cognitive therapy (and other brief psychological strategies), and reduction of alcohol and other substance misuse. The extent to which these general strategies are actually effective in those with very high genetic (PRS-rated) estimates of risk to clinical depression requires more research.

Where individuals have also been known to be exposed to high environmental risk (e.g. impaired foetal development; childhood sexual or physical abuse; childhood brain infection; adult sexual or physical violence; physical illnesses like severe viral infection or immune-based chemotherapies for cancer) and they are also known to have a high PRS estimate for clinical depression, then it may be argued that a strong case exists for more intensive interventions to prevent the onset of the illness.

Is perinatal depression a good place to deploy PRS scores for clinical depression?

There are some very specific population groups where these tests may also become a viable tool. One of these is in pregnant women, who have high rates of both prenatal and postnatal depression. Initially, this may be those with a known family history (specifically postnatal depression in their own mother or female siblings), so that preventive interventions and close surveillance during the risk period (prior to and for at least six months following the birth) can be employed.

Given that at least 15 per cent of women are at risk of significant perinatal depression, it could be argued that such screening tools should be used more widely – since many women will not know their own family history (see 'Robyn's story' on page 125), or will not have a clear family history. The ethical principle here, however, is that you don't screen unless it is clear that taking actions will reduce the risk *and* that you do intend to provide those interventions to those who are identified. It's that latter bit that is so hard in mental health. We really need to lift our game in active service provision for those in genuine need.

Interestingly, during my time as CEO of Beyond Blue, the establishment of a national screening framework, based on self-reported symptoms and not genetics, for perinatal depression was one of our highest priorities. It flourished for some years, due to the cooperation of those individuals and families affected, and the support and ongoing commitment to clinical care provided by the leading psychiatrists and clinical psychologists. All of this sat alongside a very active program of ongoing research and development. Sadly, that national focus gradually subsided, and we still have only a limited capacity to identify and assist those women, and families, in the greatest need for care.

Of course, pregnancy and childbirth are not the only increased risk periods in a woman's life. The menopausal years are another, when mood disturbance is common. A significant proportion of those who are affected may progress to clinical depression. So this may prove to be another time in life where having access to this personalised genetic information could lead to proactive prevention and early intervention strategies.

Other high-risk groups where PRS may be used, including following COVID-19 infection

We are well aware of the fact there are other groups who come into medical care as a consequence of developing a specific illness, where PRS scores could be deployed. These are situations where we know statistically there is a significantly increased chance of developing clinical depression in the following six months, but we have little indication of who is actually at risk. At the moment, we just wait and then respond. Important examples include post-stroke, post-heart attack and alongside chemotherapies or radiotherapy for cancer.

One of the most long-recognised but now potentially most important situations is post-viral infection. There is a long tradition of recognising the extent to which major infective episodes put individuals at risk of a whole range of neuropsychiatric syndromes, including clinical depression. In the COVID-19 era, with the sudden discovery of a new (but basically very similar condition) – 'long COVID' – the importance of this type of environmental factor is again evident. If we wished, we could be starting to look at whether PRS scores for neuropsychiatric conditions, or for other immune or circadian factors, are predictive of who is at most risk of the various ongoing and disabling disorders, including clinical depression, which may follow an acute COVID-19 illness.

Can PRS scores be used to guide more intensive interventions?

It may be the case that on the basis of PRS estimates, individuals start to make very specific choices about the styles of interventions (psychological therapies, specific medicines like SSRIs) they wish to pursue either as primary prevention strategies or in association with early intervention. This could mean choosing more intensive treatments much earlier in the illness course than would normally be the case.

This is also where the potential for combining genetic screening with other tools, like clinical staging, becomes really interesting. PRS scores can be derived not only for general or specific disorder risk, but also for risk of illness progression or recurrence. For example, the current PRS score for major depression appears to predict the likelihood of having more depressive episodes.

So, in those who have not yet had symptoms but are known to be at increased risk either because of family history or some known exposure to significant environmental risk, if they also have a high

PRS estimate, we might promote the use of as many low-risk strategies as possible – not only throughout childhood, but also during periods of very high additional risk (adolescence, young adults, childbirth, menopause).

For those who have actually developed early clinical symptoms, and who also have high PRS estimates for disorder onset or progression, would we then shift the goalposts towards greater use of treatments much earlier in the illness course? This is a very active clinical research question in the near future for two reasons. One is the power of PRS estimates – they are tools that we have never had before. They tell us critical things about the individuals that we (clinicians, families and the person themselves) are not able to know by just reporting, asking or observing.

Recently, I horrified some of my North American colleagues, by saying I was quite keen to work out when to prescribe lithium before a young person has ever had a manic episode. Manic episodes are dangerous, psychologically traumatic and socially damaging. Additionally, like first psychotic episodes, they are likely to be highly toxic to brain tissue and may initiate a whole series of secondary immune responses that do even more harm.

An Australian view is that lithium is one of the best tools we have for altering the course of major mood disorders, and preventing suicide in those with these conditions. But currently we wait till late in the course (after you have had a manic episode – our 'heart attack' equivalent) before we prescribe it. When discussing this with those affected, and their families, (see 'Bella's story' on page 133), this can seem a rather 'way too conservative' approach.

So, what would be the best clinical choice, or the choice you'd make, if you (as a young person):

- already had a clinical depressive episode, ongoing unstable mood, a perturbed circadian system (all of which put you at high risk of illness progression); *and,*

- you also had your own PRS estimate that suggested you were at significant increased risk of:
  - bipolar disorder (or psychosis); and/or
  - at increased likelihood of responding to lithium; and/or
  - at increased risk of developing side-effects or not responding to conventional antidepressant medicines?

In these situations, different people will make different decisions. But, as more useful personal information becomes available, we should be willing to share what we know (and also the limitations of that knowledge).

On their own, our current clinical tools have limited predictive capability

Our current clinical tools have their limits – while we can derive very general risk estimates, they have little capacity to advance the field of early intervention. Even when we've used our best clinical estimates, and combined them with our clinical staging models, we can't predict precisely who will benefit from specific treatments, who will have most side-effects or who will actually progress to more severe, persisting or recurrent illnesses. As a clinician, my general view is that the more objective evidence I have to share with you – that is really quite specific to you – the better!

To know more about the environment, we will make better use of genetics

Just finally, on genetics. As genetic tools become more sophisticated, we will learn much more about the ways in which the environment contributes to illness onset or course.

Specifically, this will occur as a consequence of:

1. More detailed examination of those at either end of the PRS spectrum who do or do not develop illness. Basically, this means looking at potential protective environmental factors in those who are at high genetic risk but don't develop clinical depression. And, conversely, looking for those adverse environmental factors in those who are at low genetic risk but did develop clinical depression. That is, by focusing attention on the most discordant cases, we may discover much more about how genuine protection can be enhanced (for those at various degrees of genetic risk), and, separately, are there very specific environmental circumstances that do put those at very low genetic risk in harm's way?
2. Mendelian randomisation being applied to large observational studies to determine which environmental effects are actually causal – and, therefore, justify much larger and targeted intervention trials (as compared to things which are simply non-causal associations and a waste of time and money – like many vitamin and dietary supplements!).

Mendelian randomisation: geneticists can now be really helpful!

Mendelian randomisation (MR) is a statistical method typically applied to large-scale datasets to test for potential causative (as distinct from simply associational) pathways. It pays homage to the father of modern genetics, Gregor Mendel, and his descriptions of the basic rules of genetic inheritance.

So much research from community surveys simply reports associations (like young people using technology and increased rate of mental health problems, or increased rates of prescribing of SSRIs and increased rates of self-harm in the community, or more physical activity and less depression, or eating fish diets and lower rates of depression) to imply, or outright claim, that one has *caused* the other. Worse still, much public policy commonly acts wrongly on such associations.

The technique uses a great trick of nature that we can now actually measure. The basic trick is that genetic polymorphisms (SNPs) are randomly distributed in the population. So genetics has created natural control groups of basically those with and without specified SNP variants. It then rests on the assumption that the genetic characteristic of interest is relevant to the disease of interest, but only indirectly. That is, it is dependent on exposure to a specific environmental factor. Given a few other assumptions (which we need to be careful about in mental health – like that the choice of reproductive partner is not also influenced by the genes of interest), it can then be used to disentangle causative from simple association paths.

It has been widely used in other areas of medicine to look at intriguing questions suggested by earlier observational studies – like the apparent protective effect of sunlight exposure generally, or vitamin D levels specifically, for risk of onset for multiple sclerosis. Here, it looks like vitamin D is a genuine protective agent – but only early rather than later in life. Almost as important, there is no evidence that vitamin D plays any causative role in any of the major psychiatric disorders, including clinical depression.

In other areas including the relationships between alcohol intake and oesophageal and head and neck cancers, and the different types of cholesterol and actual risks to cardiovascular disease, these techniques are increasingly employed. The areas of smoking and alcohol exposure are highly associated with major mental disorders and it will be intriguing to see how these MR studies play out in terms of causal associations with things like clinical depression. Recently, some evidence has suggested that smoking appears to *cause* mental disorders, while other evidence suggested the reverse, namely that depression causes smoking behaviour.

Of greatest interest, we are now seeing MR being applied to mental disorders, and notably depressive disorders. Recent reports confirmed one of our key findings from the late 1990s – the link between changes in white matter or cabling structures in the brain and depression. In general, it concluded that the experience of depression was doing damage to the brain. There was additional evidence that one specific type of structural deficit was actually causal, meaning it led to depression. Other findings include that there is a genuine interaction between childhood trauma, socio-economic deprivation and depression genetics, and the prevalence of sleep problems, pain, smoking and poor cardiovascular health.

Personal genetics is coming to a clinic near you

Psychiatric genetics has developed vastly in the past 30 years and we're now on the threshold of measuring personal genetic risk to the onset of clinical depression, its likely course and the probability that you will respond preferentially to one type of treatment or another coming to a clinic near you. When this happens, people will be able to make much more informed choices about how they wish to proceed on their own unique and long-term journey to recovery and sustained good health.

TAKE-OUT TIPS

- The amount of genetic risk in any individual person is highly variable. While some will have a relatively low risk, for others the risk will be much higher.
- Having an increased genetic risk for depression does *not* mean that you will develop the illness or pass it on to the next generation. It simply means that you are more vulnerable if other things go against you.
- Knowing your polygenic risk score for many different conditions – mental and physical – may be very important to managing your own health risks.

11

The Environmental Architecture of Depression

When I head to my waiting room to meet a new person, I'm always interested to see who else is sitting there.

Who is accompanying this person – let's call him James – on this very intimate and challenging journey?

Who else really cares about this person's mental health and wellbeing?

Is the accompanying person the one who got their friend or loved one, reluctantly, to my front door?

Are those other people looking afraid or relieved?

Often that accompanying person starts to apologise: 'I'm sorry, I'm just here with James. I'm happy to wait outside but if at some point, maybe after you've talked with James, you could just let me know . . .'

I'm quick to interrupt: 'On the contrary, would you prefer to come in too, as long as that's okay with you, James?'

I've got a large office with lots of chairs. Sometimes, on a really good day, I need to find a few more! Then a long and complicated story starts to unfold.

I think this all reflects my Irish heritage. The real story is usually more collective in nature, not just a personal journey. It's a small group narrative with many voices filling in the gaps, providing a much richer picture of what has been happening.

The reality is that at the height of clinical depression the nominated client may well be providing a perspective that is seriously distorted by their current mental state. The emphasis may be on their own failings, the state of the marital relationship, the lack of pleasure from their work or education. Usually, after the person has recovered, they go back and highlight which parts of the story they misrepresented at the time.

In other public settings, I'm often asked by families and carers, 'What should we do about the fact that James's psychiatrist/psychologist/doctor doesn't see families – or share information, or ask our opinion, or liaise with us at all?'

My reply: 'Get a new psychiatrist/psychologist/doctor!'

I say all of this at the start of this chapter, simply because while establishing a safe and trusted environment for the person seeking help is paramount, coming to grips with the realities of their intimate and family relationships is also critical. Yet it is often neglected.

So, despite the amount of time I've spent investigating genetics, brain structure and function, body clocks and immune function, at the end of the day my enduring interest is how do we best work with a person's circumstances. All of the intrinsic or biological factors that may be relevant are simply the background on which this very personal journey is being played out.

All illnesses have a social context

We talk passionately about the 'social determinants' of ill-health – big and broad social, economic and cultural factors that determine the rate of any illnesses in a population. Things that really matter like poverty, poor nutrition, lack of access to appropriate housing and sanitation, smoking, limited education, racism and active exclusion from opportunity or health care. This is as true for common mental disorders, like clinical depression and suicide, as it is for obesity, heart disease and cancer.

For individuals, I prefer to talk about the social context of their illness, things that need to be built into the planning of their unique care. Do you live alone? Do you have enough cash to buy medication? Are you about to lose your job? Are your kids still speaking to you? Who else might be recruited to provide you with additional care?

Social context is as relevant to the outcome of someone with clinical depression, as it is for any other physical health problem. The more positive the social context, the better the outcome.

Every personal experience of illness has its own narrative

Every person who has a serious physical or mental illness has a very specific story to tell. Their story is unique to them.

These personal accounts provide very rich documentation of the ways in which the attitudes and behaviours of the wider community, family and carers, health care practitioners and other social and welfare systems impact on people. Additionally, they often include practical tips for others entering this strange and different world.

Each person also has to adapt to this new illness role. The behavioural changes that can accompany adoption of this new role have generally been defined as the normal sick role or normal illness behaviour: stay at home and rest, follow medical directions, accept help, be grateful to others, follow prescribed treatment orders, welcome practical and social support.

But the sick role often implies a more passive self, with loss of control over aspects of individual decision-making and compliance with the expectations of family and health care professionals. It has long been recognised that normal illness behaviour varies widely between individuals, reflecting many other social, cultural, personal history, economic and educational factors.

Even more interesting, is the notion of *abnormal illness behaviour* whereby individuals are described as responding excessively or inadequately to the health challenges they now face. This creates much tension between the person (and family) and health care providers, but just like normal illness behaviour it is a response to the experience of illness and not a cause of illness itself. Unfortunately, for many of those with conditions like clinical depression, this key distinction gets lost – and the tense transactions involved become depicted as the major causes of the illness itself.

From an individual perspective, the environment doesn't exist in isolation

As I mentioned, we can't talk about the role of genetic vulnerability (what you inherit) without recognising the environmental context (age, social group membership, families, workplaces, neighbourhoods, historical and cultural factors). We also can't talk about environmental risk without recognising the reality that this plays out against the background of tremendous variation in individual differences that, at least in part, are genetically determined.

My colleagues who have devoted their careers to unravelling just exactly what we inherit often comment, 'Quit criticising genetics, it now gives you the best opportunity ever to sort out which parts of the environment do really matter, and when, in development, and how.' It's a fair call. This challenges those of us with a more social view to get past the restating of past myths or the retelling of personal stories.

The environment is dynamic (as is the brain and body itself)

It takes a long time to build our brain and ourselves – from minus nine months to 25 years of age. Throughout that very long and complex process, the environment not only needs to provide the basic building blocks – food, shelter, education, health care – but also the social structures that foster our cognitive and emotional development. Your parent(s) do not do it alone. A whole tribe of capable, diverse individuals and social groups contribute.

A great deal of human and animal research supports the notion that the richer the environment – socially, emotionally, educationally, physically – through infant, child and adolescent development, the broader the cognitive and emotional skills a child, and then a young person, develops.

When this is very seriously disrupted (a horrifying example was the emotionally deprived Romanian orphans abandoned in terrible conditions in the 1980s and early 1990s), long-term emotional and behavioural disruptions, and stunted development in thinking skills and emotional responses follow. In these terrible situations in children, modern brain imaging techniques have allowed us to document the lack of development of the brain itself.

But these are the extreme examples of deprivation. They are not the types of early childhood or other emotional environments described by those who experience common forms of anxiety or depression. Much more often people describe the things that they believed have gone wrong, in rather rigid, one-off, time-stamped ways. 'I was assaulted at school in the fifth grade.' 'I lost my job in the summer two years ago.' 'My wife left on Father's Day last year.' 'I had a car accident last Christmas.' It's the way we organise and explain our world. It's also the way we remember and recall our past.

Much psychological and life-event research is guilty of the same rigidity and focuses largely on logging single traumatic events, such as the death of a spouse, death of a child, divorce or separation. More research then tries to determine our perception of the impact or degree of resulting emotional stress following any major event.

But our environments are much more dynamic than that. Their true impacts vary depending on the age and developmental stage of the individual, but also in relation to the many other factors that were operating concurrently. We all tend to omit or just not recognise other critical information, including our own mental state at the time of these major life changes. If you were anxious, depressed, intoxicated, medicated or physically sick at the time, you are very likely to give a different account of the impact of those 'traumatic' events on your emotional state.

Take marital breakdown. Is it always bad? Is it equally bad for both parties? Did one or other partner actually benefit – emotionally, socially, financially – from the breakdown? Was it the first time or the second or third time around? In my early research, many women reported that while they were very depressed at the time of the relationship breakdown, afterwards, when living independently, they largely recovered.

Changes in the environment, and the challenges they cause (real life 'stress-tests') are very important to ascertain. Just as you don't know your roof has a leak until it rains, we all need to know how we function in a variety of different circumstances, especially when faced with sudden, dramatic or unexpected adversity.

In many clinical encounters I hear that the person who is now depressed coped perfectly well in the past with real stressors like changing jobs, leaving a relationship or dealing with financial difficulties, but is not coping now. So, we then need to consider that maybe the most recent event is not what really matters, and that some other intrinsic (like a physical change to the brain) or extrinsic (starting a new medical treatment) factor is really at the heart of their sudden decline.

Not all stress is bad. Many humans perform well under pressure, learn new skills from the experience, develop new social relationships and are, consequently, better placed to cope with future adversity.

Being as critical of the myth of environmental determinism

Previously, I've tried to discredit the myth of genetic determinism of disorders, like clinical depression. But there is another common myth that we need to treat with equal disdain – that exposure to environmental risks, such as deprived or abusive childhoods, domestic violence or unemployment, inevitably results in bad mental health outcomes.

While all these things do substantially increase your risk, the majority of people exposed to these experiences do not develop the illness. Traumatic experiences, just like smoking, are major risk factors – but they are not the illness itself. As the rate of these exposures go down, the proportion of people with clinical depression in which these risk factors occurred also decreases. Other factors (genetic or other unknown environmental risks) come to play a larger role.

A legacy of Freud's professional transition from neurology (and its brain-based illness models) to psychoanalysis was to abandon an emphasis on such physical and biological factors. Instead, he replaced them with psychological, child development and other experiential concepts that came to dominate much of the mid-20th century public discourse about anxiety and depression.

At the very top of that list was childhood trauma. Ever since, many people have assumed that psychiatrists believe that a developmental arrest or unresolved conflict, precipitated by poor parenting, causes all disorders like anxiety and depression. The assumption then is that a person cannot recover until these conflicts are revisited, and resolved. Freud was smart. He generated a whole new conceptual scheme to explain illness, and the method of treatment required to resolve it!

Sadly, late-20th century psychiatry made this much worse by deciding that traumatic events were not simply risk factors, but actually the illness itself. One we now call post-traumatic stress disorder – PTSD. The wrong assumption is that if you have been exposed, you will inevitably develop the disorder. Additionally, having been exposed, the symptoms are triggered by any re-exposure to the circumstances associated with the original traumatic event (a sight, sound, smell or word).

Much like the earlier and discredited theories of alcohol and substance addiction ('once an alcoholic, always an alcoholic' – even when you have been abstinent for years), many modern theories of traumatic disorders perpetuate the myth that once traumatised, there is no real cure. It's just suppressed, ready to jump out again and consume the life of the affected person.

The 21st-century scientific perspective

I would go one step further and articulate the issue as seen now by developmental neuroscientists, epidemiologists and social scientists. Environmental traumas or other adverse experiences are risk factors only. They increase statistically the chance of developing clinical depression. But, on their own, in most circumstances, they are not sufficient to cause the onset of clinical depression or other major mood disorders, like atypical depression, bipolar disorder or psychotic depression.

What we really need to know is how does the environment get in and change or influence those brain and body systems that drive clinical depression? How does the environment actually make you physically sick, keep you ill and then stop you recovering spontaneously? To what extent are those changes permanent, unless you get effective treatments?

That is, to what extent do they induce changes in key neurobiological systems? These include: the hypothalamic-pituitary-adrenal (HPA) axis, which controls the body's main stress hormone functions; the sympathetic nervous system (SNS), which controls our basic fight or flight response to acute stress and other aspects of heart function; the neuroimmune system, which controls our capacity to fight infections and prevent cancer; the circadian 24-hour 'body clock' system, which controls our daily patterns of sleep and physical activity; and our metabolic systems, which control our regulation of our energy production.

That environmental factors are driving the development of many of our critical neurobiological processes is taken up further in Chapter 12. For now, I'll focus on factors in the environment that are clearly associated with clinical depression, even if we still do not understand fully the physical mechanisms by which those links occur.

Learned helplessness

The concept of learned helplessness is a common feature of clinical depression. Typically, it's described as that state in which a person fails to take an appropriate action to avoid harm – even when that option is readily available. It is said to be due to the belief – based on prior experiences – that taking the action will not deliver relief from the harmful outcome. The person simply remains passive in the face of a clear threat of harm.

An important aspect of clinical depression is not simply what symptoms you report, but what you are observed to do, independent of the reason you give. Friends and family often observe this physical passivity in the face of threat, combined with an overwhelming lack of motivation to take actions that would otherwise be beneficial.

The concept was made very famous in the mid 1960s by the psychologist Martin Seligman and colleagues, and involved a series of experiments in which dogs were exposed to electric shocks. Basically, those dogs who were exposed to the shocks, but could do nothing active to avoid them, simply lay down and became passive and distressed.

Once this state had been learnt (noting that this behaviour is not characteristic of dogs) it could not be unlearnt. The dogs continued to behave this way even after the shocks were stopped and they could have escaped. That is, the stressors were painful, repeated, unavoidable and beyond the control of the exposed animal. (These kinds of experiments are no longer considered ethical.)

Almost of as much interest as to how certain kinds of environments could induce this very depressive behavioural response, was the fact that it was not easy to unlearn. It persisted long after the environment changed. To reverse the behaviour or unlearn, the dogs had to be repeatedly and physically picked up and retrained to jump away to escape the shocks. Once the physical movements were re-learnt, and frequently repeated, the affected dogs eventually returned to their normal ways of avoiding such harms.

The learned helplessness response is believed to be strongly linked to concentrations of serotonin in various brain regions, and medications that increase serotonin have a dramatic positive effect.

In modern depression research, the ways in which animals and humans are responding to positive rewards from the environment are closely studied. This research describes the roles of different brain circuits, and links those thought patterns and motor behaviours that seem to be mediated by the brain chemical dopamine. As with serotonin, many effective antidepressant strategies increase brain dopamine concentrations (just like in Parkinson's disease), and change these reward-based responses. They also share strong overlaps with the field of brain-based explanations of alcohol and drug addiction.

Attachment theories, evolutionary theories and passivity responses

The concept also has a longer history in terms of evolutionary theories of the origin of depressive (passive) behaviours. In the late 1950s, John Bowlby proposed that physically vulnerable and emotionally immature infants formed key attachments with their primary caregivers (typically mothers), and that these strong emotional bonds served to keep the mother and infant in close physical proximity.

These attachment and ongoing normal developmental processes were most successful when the caregiver was sensitive and emotionally responsive. Bowlby went on to posit that the successful development of this primary attachment formed the basis for the development of intimate relationships later on as an adult.

However, when separated from the primary caregiver during this early vulnerable period, when the infant would be more at risk, the normal response would be to express distress, anxiety or anger and move about to recapture the attention of the responsible adult.

When it works, the caregiver's attention is caught and they come running back. Consequently, the infant's anxiety and distress is quickly relieved.

This notion of appropriate care-eliciting behaviours is expanded to include tears, non-verbal facial expressions, slumped postures, vocal outcries and other various verbal expressions of distress and the need for emotional warmth.

But what if the caregiver did not come back or did not respond? In that situation, the infant would eventually become quiet and passive. From an evolutionary perspective, this was itself considered protective, as the infant would not then attract unwanted attention from predators. Of even more interest was that the infant sometimes did not take an interest in the primary caregiver when they did eventually return. This suggested that the primary attachment or emotional bond had been damaged and that the infant (human or primate) may be less trusting of the caregiver in the future.

So one can see that the persistence of this prolonged passivity response, *after* the caregiver returned, is somewhat akin to the state of clinical depression. That is, depression is viewed as the persistence of an abnormal care-eliciting response. This causes great frustration to caregivers, as it no longer matters what positive emotional signals are sent – the passive or non-passive behaviour of the depressed person just persists.

In human situations, we often witness a rapidly deteriorating vicious circle among the close connections of a person who is clinically depressed. An initial outburst of tears, anguish or despair elicits the expected caring responses from partners and close friends or family. But, unexpectedly, those emotionally warm responses have little or no impact on the depressed person. The person with depression continues to express the distress until they are exhausted, becoming increasingly passive and withdrawn.

As people from the person's close network are frustrated that their actions have no positive effect, they too start to withdraw and express less concern or warmth. Over time, they may become quite critical, commenting harshly on the 'selfish', 'childlike', 'self-preoccupied' or 'tantrum-like' behaviour of the person with depression.

Before long, although the bonds were originally very strong, they are quickly strained and both parties cease to engage in those supportive actions that worked in the past. The loss of physical intimacy, including sex, is a typical outcome – just at that time when actions not words may be of greatest benefit. When things deteriorate further, there may be a strong or overt element of punishing the depressed person for failing to mount appropriate responses.

I raise these two important examples (chronic, unresolved and unavoidable harm, and non-responsive or punishing intimate environments) as the types of environmental contingencies that are often beneath the stories of those who present with clinical depression.

Humans are not the only interesting primates!

As extensive studies of non-human primates in the wild and in captivity (and my personal favourites the free-loving and highly sociable bonobos, who share about 99 per cent of their DNA in common with us) have demonstrated, many things that we have previously claimed to be uniquely human, like empathy, kindness to strangers and social groups dominated by females, are shared by the great apes.

The great thing about the studies of primate colonies is that they do not simply mimic the preconceptions of the human research world. The way that parent–child interactions, emotional warmth, physical closeness, sexual behaviour or aggression or violence are transacted take place within their own natural and, most importantly, group settings.

Much larger kin and family networks, developed and sustained principally by the mature female members, function to promote the survival and optimal development of their highly vulnerable infants and children. And so it is with humans. There are many other important adult–child relationships than just the principal caregiver and infant model, despite the fact that that model has been the central preoccupation of most Western societies.

The adolescent period – the age of onset

One issue we need to sort out: what is really going on in the adolescent that explains the sudden onset of the major mood disorders, like clinical depression and bipolar disorder?

Any real explanatory model needs to provide substantive evidence as to how any proposed cause is having its major impact during this critical period of development. There are many environmental exposures (new intimate and sexual relationships outside the family, alcohol and drug exposure, new social media forms) happening. They may, or may not, be of great importance.

The personal narrative is a story. It may or may not be relevant.

Typically, any assessment of someone with clinical depression starts with me asking, 'Okay, just tell me how you got here.'

There is always a story. Humans tell stories. Humans impose a narrative structure on our chaotic and chance-ridden world. In Western cultures, that story is often very linear, rational and highly explanatory. It doesn't have many gaps. If there are gaps, we tend to fill them in. We impose explanations we believe to be true. We just don't handle uncertainty or ambiguity very well at all.

Relatives of those with clinical depression often ask me directly, 'Is he going to kill himself – yes or no?'

My real answer: 'Well, it's certainly possible, statistically unlikely, but rather unpredictable.'

Unfortunately, that's not what they are hoping to hear. Instead, they respond with something like, 'I know he won't do it because he is so devoted to his children.'

Many stories start with acute events – 'It was all fine till I lost my job' or 'I was fine till my wife left and took the kids with her' or 'I was fine until somebody was nasty to me on social media.'

The reality with acute events is that they rarely occur just out of the blue. Rather than being the actual cause, they are the reason the person is coming to care – as they are now in a crisis. But the underlying problem (the illness) often predates (sometimes by years) the 'acute' event.

I have met many wives who have left a husband with depression. Typically, this was after years of untreated illness, associated alcohol abuse, consequent financial stress and loss of intimacy. The depression came first, got worse and then everything else fell apart. Similarly, the job loss followed months or years of loss of function and productivity at work, but when it finally happens the whole situation is far worse.

Contemplating the 'unknowns' and the 'unknown unknowns'

So, when the story is being told I'm really listening for the longer-term threads, the pattern of interpersonal relationships, the recurring themes and, perhaps, crucially, missing links. The things that just don't add up.

Often there is a need to encourage all those present (the person with depression, family members, others with key information or other smart observations) to deconstruct the narrative, entertain other possible elements, suspend judgement or just reflect a little more deeply. Most importantly, don't assign blame (to other people, situations, workplaces, medicines or whatever) quite so quickly.

It's entirely possible that relevant environmental factors, although operative, are unknown.

One of my favourite knowns is unknown to many others – it's the effect of change in seasons. Every autumn, my waiting room is full of people with unstable moods, and poor sleep–wake cycles, who are just getting worse. They each have a different narrative as to why they are coming now – problems at work, financial difficulties, marital trouble, kids giving grief, etc.

I enquire gently, 'Did you notice how many other people were out there in the waiting room this morning?' And then I go on to suggest that many of these people share something else in common, namely seasonal sensitivity.

I love to review people's illness progress in spring, and also prescribe new treatments, as many people with the same seasonal sensitivity tend to get better at that time of year.

It's a clear external factor, with large effects, but one that is not often built into a personal narrative.

In most situations, there will still be many (with apologies to Donald Rumsfeld) 'unknown unknowns' – external things that are relevant but whose impact on this illness is not even suspected, until something else happens. Only then is its true relevance revealed. This happens with things like dietary deficiencies or unexpected reactions to a medication. For psychiatrists, living with such uncertainty is part of the job. For those in crisis, it's a very unpleasant and, at times, an entirely unacceptable proposition.

The (chronic, repetitive, unassailable) stressors that we know really do matter

In terms of life stressors that really do matter to the onset or course of clinical depression, there is a set of clear stand-out factors:

- chronic intimate relationship dysfunction
- prolonged unemployment
- chronic physical illness, particularly associated with pain, disability, infection or sleep disruption
- prolonged caring roles, including for disabled children, elderly or dementing parents or relatives
- extended financial distress
- chronic workplace-based conflict or disruption
- social isolation, after all we are mostly social animals who function best in groups
- physical inactivity
- chronic sleep disturbance
- prolonged disconnection from career, education or other social participation.

Recently I had one of those interesting experiences that you don't really want to have. I was swimming with a relative at a local beach, a place I know well. I've enjoyed it many previous occasions before, despite its occasionally challenging surf. Suddenly, I found myself being swept out to sea by a rip. I tried to swim back towards the shore, but I was still being swept away seaward. Then a very big set of waves started to roll in. Normally, I would swim further out and just go underneath the waves – but as I was already out of my depth and tired, that didn't seem like a great idea. Thinking rationally, I began heading back to shore, which proved to be the wrong thing to do!

It wasn't the first wave, or the second that did the damage.

Though I was already tiring and thinking about calling for help (thank God for volunteer lifeguards who patrol our beaches). It was the third, most powerful wave that picked me up, turned me upside down, and dumped me face-first into the sandbank. When you're seeing stars under water and not sure which way is up, you know you're disorientated. A fourth large wave was then washing over when I was already exhausted.

Any more waves, and I was in serious danger of not popping up again. On my own, there wasn't a lot I could really do. No good choices were obvious. Fortunately, I was coherent enough to stick my arm straight up to signal for help. Two very fit, young guys (who had watched me get unceremoniously dumped a few minutes earlier) were already headed out to drag me in. Once I realised they were on the way, I felt a whole lot better about the likely outcome.

When I was safely back on the beach, my partner in life, dearest Elizabeth, was very surprised to hear that I'd actually called for help. She thought that wasn't much like me and that the surf life-savers must have just realised that the silly old bloke 'out the back' was in more trouble than he realised!

As I've got older, and as a consequence of prior experiences and personal knowledge of other bad outcomes, I've realised that there are many situations I can't fix on my own. Calling for professional help earlier rather than later is a much smarter idea! And, just because I've been in these types of situations before, doesn't mean that this time around I've got it in under control. We just never know, at what point, life may present a series of challenges that overwhelms our own capacity to cope.

My point: it's chronic, repetitive, unassailable stressors – things we just can't control – that lead to exhaustion or fatigue and put us at greater risk. That exhaustion is both biological, psychological ('learned helplessness') and often social. The otherwise supportive environment may fall away or we fail to ask for help. That endless attempt to find our own way out, or do it on our own, often fails. In fact, it may make the whole situation a whole lot worse. One bad decision after another puts us at more, not less, risk.

Other physical factors in the environment

Exposure to other factors in the physical environment that we know matter include seasonality, daily light exposure (don't live in the dark!), alcohol and drug misuse, serious (mostly viral) infections, and some medications.

Injuries to the brain itself, during development or later in life, increase the risk of depressive disorders. These include blunt traumas – concussion, car accidents and other serious head injuries – as well as specific illnesses, most notably strokes that damage key parts of the cortical and subcortical circuits that regulate emotions, feelings and our motor behaviours (see Chapter 14).

Once again, there is great interest in the role diet may play. Although rare, some specific nutritional deficiencies (folate, B12) can occur. There is more specific evidence about the potential role not only of relative reductions in B-group vitamins, but also vitamin D, omega-3 fatty acids and other factors. Generally, there is much ongoing debate about how important dietary factors really are in either the onset or course of depressive disorders. Unfortunately, our own most recent clinical trial of giving young people supplements of omega-3 fatty acids for youth depression had no benefit.

'To begin at the beginning: Is God?' (Or in our case, is it always a traumatic childhood?)

As a teenager, I was very fortunate to be dragged by my father to the theatre. Somewhere in that period, I was exposed to the very clever productions of the playwright Tom Stoppard and his key line (from *Jumpers*) 'To begin at the beginning: Is God?' The deconstruction of the whole intellectual and theological argument to a two-word question has remained firmly with me.

What intrigues me is the challenge humans face when they try to reconcile their most intimate beliefs and experiences with the conflicting realities of the world they inhabit. This Stoppard production also highlighted another key aspect of the human condition, namely, our unwillingness to tolerate uncertainty. A childhood friend, who to my great surprise jumped from shameless hedonism to fundamentalist Christianity, is prone to badgering me with the question, 'But, Ian, aren't you compelled to answer the question "Does God exist?" Why yes or no?'

Whether God (whoever you perceived her to be) exists doesn't occupy much space in my emotional or cognitive life. That's not to say that the related concepts of spirituality and connectedness are not central to mental health and wellbeing. In fact, I'd suggest you can't be mentally healthy without a strong and reciprocal set of emotional attachments.

By contrast, what has continued to intrigue me is why people find it so necessary to have a definitive answer to these questions. To me, questions of faith (what we believe, but can't prove) are quite distinct from the empirical questions that are central to the scientific foundations of clinical medicine.

From a belief versus empirically sound perspective, the recurring question in my field starts with the inevitable: 'What's the cause of my illness?' Often this rapidly descends into, 'What's the precipitating event?', followed by, 'No, not that – I want the "real" reason', and then finally, 'Is it trauma?' or even more specifically, '*Is it childhood trauma?*'

So, as we head down this very contentious path, I'd suggest we all need to strive to understand better in what ways trauma, and particularly childhood trauma, really determine the onset or course of clinical depression.

But doesn't everything start in childhood?

There is a great disconnect between the evidence and public beliefs concerning the relevance of things that happened in childhood or the quality of parenting provided. Most parents, and certainly most mothers, didn't cause the onset of clinical depression in their adult children. In fact, in the famous words of Donald Winnicott, a paediatrician and psychoanalyst from the 1950s, most of us will have received perfectly 'good enough' mothering (or parenting).

With regard to parental styles, it's the belief that you were raised by an uncaring parent – one who did not respond warmly and empathetically – that is reported more frequently by depressed adults. I say belief because this is the retrospective account by an adult with depression of the parenting style of their mother or father.

Other parenting styles, notably of being overly controlling or uninterested or being abandoned, don't seem to be so toxic. They are also subject to a great deal of cultural interpretation and misrepresentation.

For adult depression, the home and family environment shared by siblings in childhood appears to account for only a relatively small proportion of the variation in the population of risk of depressive illness. However, this doesn't mean that when very severe neglect or abuse occurs that it isn't toxic for that individual. It is. The clearest examples are things like prolonged and extensive sexual or physical abuse, particularly when this has been perpetrated by a trusted caregiver.

Sadly, parent-blaming has a long and rich tradition in psychiatry (note previous references to the autism and schizophrenia-causing maternal styles). To my great frustration, nearly every media interview with someone who has had depression opens with, 'So what happened in your childhood?' In truth, for many people with clinical depression, the real answer is 'not much . . .'

But what about trauma?

Significant trauma, such as sexual assault or domestic violence, particularly when it occurs in the context of other trusted or intimate relationships really does matter. Particularly if it is prolonged and unrelenting. This is not controversial.

The real controversies are:

1. How common was this type of abuse in the past, and how common is it now?
2. How significant are less severe or less persistent forms of hostile or aggressive interpersonal interactions?
3. Which individual differences account for the fact that most people exposed to significant trauma do not go on to develop clinical depression?
4. In those who are affected, how are the negative impacts of trauma encoded within our brain and body systems?
5. What are the interventions – psychological, behavioural, interpersonal, medical – that are most effective in extinguishing the negative impacts of past traumatic experiences?
6. How do traumatic experiences and risks of major disorders act over generations? Can we really disentangle the major genetic and environmental interactions that are at play?

Unfortunately, many who work in this field are convinced that trauma is *the* major cause of all depression, emotional instability, suicidal behaviour, alcohol and drug addiction and most other ongoing interpersonal dysfunction. So, if the person themselves cannot describe it, or can't recall it from their past, then we must help them to uncover it.

We've been down this very dangerous path many times before. Although certain patterns of behaviour, such as self-harm, very unstable mood, suicidal ideation, multiple suicide attempts and unstable interpersonal relationships, are increased in those who have experienced serious or repeated traumatic experiences, this does not mean that all of these people with these behaviours have experienced traumatic events. There are many alternative explanations.

The perpetuation of traumatic determinism – meaning you are permanently damaged and will not ever recover – is as destructive as the genetic determinism that many others fear. Basically, we need to deal with the impacts of trauma when they are apparent – by fostering those supportive and therapeutic environments where we can provide appropriate care, alongside family and community support, for those who have been hurt.

The trauma is clear, but (sometimes) the explanation is more complicated

As a young psychiatrist many years ago, I was often asked by older colleagues to take on short-term psychotherapy with young people who were in trouble. Elsewhere, I'll relate some important stories of young men I've known who have come crashing into emergency mental health care. By contrast, many young women I've assisted presented with depressive episodes and marked sleep–wake cycle disturbances (due to my clinical interest in chronic fatigue). These episodes were accompanied by transient or more persistent self-harm, low self-esteem, unstable mood, body image disturbances, anxious preoccupation, obsessional ideas or disturbed eating behaviour.

While they nearly always presented during a situational crisis (school exams, bullying at school, relationship breakup at university) and as a result had been dismissed as having an 'adjustment disorder' (meaning a brief depressive reaction to a defined life stressor), I have continued to look after a small number of these young women for the next 20 to 35 years.

Meet Susie, Sally, Sarah, Samantha, Sadie, Sofia and Stella

Rather than relating any specific account, I'm keen to describe a composite of these 'Susie, Sally, Sarah, Samantha, Sadie, Sofia and Stella' stories. I do this not only to disguise the identity of particular persons but also to highlight common elements and insights. It is also to accentuate what differentiates this group from many other young people who only had transient difficulties.

By any definition, these young women were all exposed to prolonged traumatic experiences at key points in their childhood or adolescence. Variously these experiences consisted of physical or sexual abuse by a family member (fathers, mothers, grandfathers, brothers), harsh or unusual punishments by parental figures, or repeated verbal abuse and emotional neglect.

Not all of these prior experiences were clear, or certainly had not yet been revealed, at the time of seeking professional help. The more immediate and perhaps more universal factor was the history of a lack of warmth or emotional care from any significant parental figure during childhood and adolescence.

While the focus at the time I first encountered these young women was on providing individual psychotherapy, I often took the opportunity to meet with those family members (partners, siblings, parents) who were most engaged with their care. Importantly, this did not include any person who had been responsible for any physical or sexual abuse. These meetings provided me with a unique opportunity to compare the young person's perspective of their family with my own observations of the family members' emotional styles.

I was most interested in how dysfunctional intimate relationships precipitated or prolonged clinical depression. A key insight was that people with depressive disorders often provided a more accurate picture of the nature of their intimate relationships than their non-depressed partner. The implication was that most of us operate with an overly optimistic view of the quality of our close relationships.

During the course of these long-term therapies, I concluded that these young women often *underestimated* the degree of psychological dysfunction that had operated in their family environments. The level of overt hostility, emotional abuse, neglect and distorted thinking to which they had been exposed was not evident to the world outside their tight family units.

Having met many such families, who were often led by highly respected professionals, church leaders, community spokesperson, media celebrities, business owners and ordinary mums and dads, I have been astonished by what they say about themselves, and the way they behave when asked to provide their perspective. There is an immediate rush to self-justification, accompanied by criticism of the young person and a long listing of their child's supposed failings, oversensitivity or lack of resilience.

Overall, I would say that these parents shared being emotionally cold, self-righteous and fiercely opinionated. All were only too ready to espouse alternative facts, while simultaneously rejecting the considered assessments by other experts as fake news.

I'll never forget being told in a heated and agitated outburst by one relative that I was just not seeing what was all too clear to Sally's real family. She was the source of evil and disharmony. By contrast, her parents (and other siblings) were loving and devoted Christians who were simply doing their best to cope with an impossible and oppositional daughter!

On another occasion, the door to my office was left off its hinges after being slammed by Susie's brothers. They had just stormed out after I had suggested that perhaps the very negative and harsh interactions between Susie and her mother may be contributing to her ongoing distress. They took the opportunity to swear loudly me and threaten their sister with expulsion from the family.

Given that this family were all members of a religious group that preached inclusion and kindness, I was somewhat taken aback. For those who believe there are no risks associated with convening family meetings, I'd like to note that things do not always go to plan. I did not count this as one of my greatest therapeutic moments.

Of these young women who were otherwise diagnosed as having 'adjustment disorders' or 'personality disorders', about half went on to develop much more severe mood disorders, including bipolar disorder. For most, formal diagnoses were not made until they had a very discrete episode of severe depression, psychotic depression or mania following childbirth. As that was often 10 to 15 years after my first meeting, it reinforced to me that we often do not know what will happen next in those who express their depressive vulnerability at any early age.

Sadly, for several their early-onset mood disorder was complicated later by alcohol or substance misuse. That itself often resulted in further medical complications. At this stage, a number of these 'young' women have reached menopause and are now experiencing a further deterioration in their mental health during this challenging life, and physical, transition.

I'm reminded of these stories today, as I've been going about one of my weekly tasks – the clinical supervision of a young psychiatrist. As usual, I was talking about how I don't really buy many of our favourite operating principles – things we use every day to make clinical decisions that may rest on shaky foundations and, with advancing science, will probably fall over soon (like labelling all young women like Susie, Sally, Sarah, Samantha, Sadie, Sofia and Stella as simply having personality disorders).

Part-way through this discourse, the younger psychiatrist explained to me how she has been strongly encouraged by our public hospital system to 'depolarise' as many young women as possible. The implication was that other psychiatrists (like me) who are keen to detect the early phases of serious mood disorders, such as emerging bipolar disorder, are now creating more illnesses that don't really exist. By relabelling these young people as personality disorders, we can then safely exit them from formal psychiatric care! A win for the system, but potentially a disaster for the young person.

So much of our current work is very narrow. We reconstruct the past to fit our preconceptions and rapidly close the door on the future.

Sarah does survive, and inspires

'Seriously, Ian, you must be the world's worst f***ing psychiatrist! After 30 years, I'm still seeing you and still struggling to stay alive each day!' Many would agree that Sarah's perspective about my lack of professional capability is entirely justified.

My only rather insipid reply is, 'Sarah, it's great to see that you are still alive.'

Given the extent of Sarah's psychiatric morbidity (adolescent-onset eating disorder, severe recurrent bipolar disorder, post-traumatic stress resulting from previous childhood abuse and later sexual assault as an adult), concurrent physical ill-health (chronic severe lung disease, recurrent severe infection and impaired immune function), complicating alcohol and drug addiction and social isolation (due to lost adult relationships and recurrent miscarriages), I have often wondered how Sarah has persevered in the face of overwhelming adversity. When she was much younger, and while still receiving treatment in hospital, she often left the ward to get herself a job in her chosen profession.

A simple trauma narrative just doesn't explain the complexity of Sarah's illness, life course, complications or capacity to survive. She has attracted almost every psychiatric diagnosis possible and there is no doubt that the extensive period of sexual abuse by a family member during her development, and subsequent episodes of sexual assault as an adult, have played critical parts in her journey. But what of the other physiological, medical and social factors? And, what explains her remarkable capacity to thrive, form relationships and function when psychologically well?

Family distress as a reaction to and not a cause of disorder

As I've got older, I have developed a greater empathy for the parents (and siblings) of many young people who come to care with serious behavioural disturbances. By contrast, in these more normative situations (basically where there is no evidence of prior abuse or neglect by family members), clinical teams comment extensively on what they believe to be the abnormal, anxious or distressed behaviour of the parents (see 'Bella's story' on page 133). In many of these situations, the family distress, an overt frustration with the health system, is largely a reaction to the confronting situation in which they find themselves. It's not the cause of the young person's psychological disturbance.

Transgenerational family trauma: cause or effect?

For many families, the whole narrative around transgenerational trauma is very hard to unravel. Fathers with bipolar disorder and alcoholism, who were abused by their fathers, sexually abusing their daughters, who in turn present with depression, eating disorders and repeated self-harm (things like self-cutting, burning, overdoses and attempted suicides). Mothers with depression, who were sexually or physically abused by their fathers (or grandfathers), tormenting or neglecting their own children. It would be easy enough to say that it's just trauma perpetuating trauma across the generations.

But that seems to miss the point. There are very complex interactions happening between abusive or violent experiences, neglect, various forms of mood disorder (notably clinical depression or bipolar disorder) that are themselves often complicated by alcohol or other substance misuse. In many cases, the actual mood disorder (particularly among fathers) has never been treated. The specific diagnoses are now varying by age, gender, and other cultural factors. Perhaps most clearly in Western societies, there is an increasing incidence and younger age of onset of depressive disorders, eating disorders and suicidal behaviour in young women.

The lack of access to any mental health assessment in previous generations, and its consequent association with disrupted interpersonal relationships, family breakdown, domestic and intrafamilial violence is worthy of consideration. Not all previous generations were simply bad parents or siblings – many were also unwell. The ongoing effects of untreated illness included alcohol and substance misuse, social isolation, poverty, discrimination (in the workplace and social organisation), and breakdown of interpersonal relationships.

This perspective does not seek to excuse any such violent, abusive or neglectful behaviour, or diminish its toxic effects across generations. Instead, it simply seeks to recognise that for many families the combination of untreated illness, vulnerability to major mental disorders like clinical depression and the repeated (and transgenerational) experiences of violence, abuse and neglect are often considerably more complex than any simple genetic versus environmental (nature versus nurture) model of causation can explain.

So, what about epigenetics?

The area of new biology that has most excited those with an interest in environmental factors has been the birth of the discipline of epigenetics. As defined by the US Centers for Disease Control, it is 'the study of how your behaviours and environment can cause changes that affect the way your genes work'. Generally speaking, this is a very broad conceptualisation. It basically says that in many important areas of biological function, the environment has the capacity to either down- or up-regulate those biological signals coming from your genetic makeup.

A more restrictive notion of epigenetics is that not only does the environment moderate the signals emanating from the genetic code in your own lifetime, but that this change in DNA signalling can be transmitted across generations – that's a much more radical and frankly anti-Darwinian notion.

A whole range of factors (smoking, diet, infections, physical activity) has been demonstrated to affect these epigenetic processes and, potentially, affect the risk of disease. From a behavioural perspective, there has been great interest in what types of environments, particularly in utero or in childhood, may affect the DNA in such ways as to affect emotional or cognitive development.

Two strands of work are important. One relates to normal development, while the other relates to specific examples of the impacts of adverse environments. The first suggests that early parenting practices, of physical warmth and care, become encoded in those systems that regulate stress responses in later life. The other line of work looks at how early adverse environments – most notably childhood adversity (sexual or physical abuse, emotional neglect) – might induce very negative changes in brain growth factors as well as those same stress-response systems.

It would be fair to say that there is much active research looking at the many ways environments change those genes that regulate nerve cell growth and function throughout life. Some will lead to new treatments and promote better function in this next generation, and possibly beyond.

TAKE-OUT TIPS

- It's the doing, not the talking, that fixes the problem.
- Despite what most people think, it is not usually an acute threat or sudden life event that really matters to the onset or course of depressive disorders. It's ongoing, unavoidable interpersonal stress.
- It's not simply one parent, or one mother–child interaction, that rules the (developmental) world. Humans, and other primates, develop best in small but wider social groups.
- Chronic, unresolved and not easily fixed stressors are what really matter (relationship, financial, work, social).
- Call for outside help sooner rather than later.

12

Gene–environment Interactions: The Holy Grail!

The 19 December 2003 'awards' issue of *Science* included a provocative headline: '*Science Breakthrough of the Year: #2 "Decoding Mental Illness"*.'

It's not often that mental health research is anywhere near the top of the leaderboard for breakthroughs in science. The accompanying editorial in one of the world's most prestigious scientific journals noted that researchers had identified 'particular genes' that could explain why illnesses like schizophrenia, bipolar disorder and depression run in families, and how they could so 'distort the brain's information processing and nudge someone into mental illness'.

Specifically, the research demonstrated that the variation in the gene for the serotonin receptor 'increases the risk of depression only when combined with stress'. That is, two things appeared to matter. One was serotonin availability in the brain (that critical happiness chemical and the one that the Prozac-like drugs regulate to treat anxiety and depression). The other was an active interaction with exposure to particular life stressors. So, it wasn't simply one (biology) versus another (environmental) events. It took two to tango!

The Dunedin Multidisciplinary Health and Development Study also suggested that the same genetically determined variation in the serotonin system made some people more prone to developing anxiety in the face of threat, and that this was linked with brain-imaging studies demonstrating 'heightened activity in a fear-focused brain region called the amygdala'. In other words, we can now see that part of the brain which recognises a life-threatening risk (lion leaping out of the long grass) light up ever more brightly in those with this particular genetic predisposition.

Game over? Not yet . . .

In 2003, we hoped (prematurely and, sadly, wrongly) that the mystery about which underlying genetic factors led to vulnerability to anxiety and depression had been solved.

Only trouble was that the results didn't really stack up. Early critics looked hard at the statistics, and compared the analyses with other studies. After much fierce debate the consensus now is that all of these studies that just look at one very specific or 'candidate gene' (that is, largely acting on one biological pathway), do not reveal what is really going on under the hood.

I did have some of my own favourite 'candidates' running in this race, like the gene that regulates how dietary folate influences the blood level of an amino acid (homocysteine) that, if too high, can damage blood vessels in the brain. Also, low folate and other B-group vitamins have previously been linked with anxiety and depression. So, we were keen to know whether folate supplementation might work as a treatment for depression (or at least in those carrying a genetic risk).

I was also keen about brain derived neurotrophic factor (BDNF), a chemical that stimulates the growth of new nerve cell connections in the brain, and whose production varies according to your own genetic code. Our brain imaging studies had shown reductions in the size of key brain structures (like the hippocampus, which controls short-term memory) in people with depression. Other work had suggested that long-term use of antidepressant medications tended to increase the size of those same brain regions. A more general theory suggests that all effective therapies (medical or psychological) share a common factor, namely the generation of new nerve cell connections. So, to this day, BDNF remains a protein of intense interest and is seen as a possible target for a whole range of antidepressant medicines.

At that time, in the early 2000s, many studies proposed a large number of these candidate genes as possible causes of depression. The real hope was that they would rapidly lead to more targeted or effective treatments. But very few findings have ever been replicated. So, none really changed how we do things, or delivered a new treatment.

This is an important aspect of science. There are many discoveries every year in medicine. Very few last – largely because they depend on chance or the rose-coloured glasses of the investigators (not fraud). Typically, once the rest of the scientific and medical research world quickly turns its attention to testing the robustness of the original claims, many new avenues turn out to be dead-ends.

The stress-vulnerability or stress–diathesis model of clinical depression

Most clinicians work with a very basic stress-vulnerability or stress-diathesis model of the causes of many physical and certainly most mental disorders. The 'stress' is the events in your life that appear to trigger the onset of the depression. The 'vulnerability' or 'diathesis' is what it is about you personally (be that genetic, biologically or prior experiences) that makes you descend into this state right now. In other words, the cause is not simply one or the other – the stress or the vulnerability. It's a unique interaction between the two. Why does this key (the event) unlock your lock (the vulnerability) at this specific point in your life?

In its simplest form, this is another way of presenting individual risk. Basically, if you have never smoked you won't get smoking-related lung cancer or if you have no access to alcohol, you won't ever be an alcoholic. No key, then the door is never unlocked. But, on the other side, not every key unlocks your door.

'Life is stressful and then you die'

For most mental disorders, like clinical depression, the common view as to what is the big environmental toxin, the real cause, is stress or, these days, trauma. That is, past or current stressors that are reported by a person with depression to be harmful.

As stress is an intrinsic part of life, we can't simply remove it from the environment, though occasionally people do promote removing all stressors from schools or workplaces as a mistaken way of preventing mental illness. In fact, some degree of stress generally leads us to perform our daily tasks better, and the mastery of challenging situations through childhood and adolescence is an essential developmental task.

We also recognise that stress comes in many different shapes and sizes and, often, has different individual and cultural meanings. While there are intrinsic factors (probably largely genetically determined) that put each of us at different degrees of risk, we don't expect that to lead to illnesses, like clinical depression, without some degree of exposure to emotional or interpersonal stressors that trigger its onset.

You may have a strong family history of depression but have never had an episode of depression in your life. There's a fair chance that you are genetically vulnerable but, to date, nothing extra has happened to tip that balance from vulnerability to illness. By contrast, your brother (who probably carries a similar genetic risk), became seriously depressed after losing his high-flying professional job and his wife leaving after the money ran out. On the surface, it looks like those particular events (major losses and interpersonal crisis) were enough to tip him from vulnerable to ill.

As outlined in the previous chapter, the stressors that are clearly associated with an increased risk to clinical depression include:

- a small number of childhood-related factors (childhood sexual or physical abuse, emotional neglect); or,
- situations in the adult environment – such as abusive interpersonal relationship, chronic unemployment, major physical illness, care of a newborn or disabled child, care of an elderly parent – that are often chronic, repeated and not easily prevented or changed by actions of the person affected.

How many versions of the stress-vulnerability explanation exist?

So, what the stress-vulnerability explanation model is really trying to say is you need both, intrinsic risk-vulnerability and environmental stress, to take you over the edge. But, this is often interpreted in two quite different ways.

First, is the simplest: just add up the risks. We all have a certain number of intrinsic risks (things you've inherited or are in your genes), but, on their own, you never get sick. However, when you then add some very specific environmental stress (birth of a newborn child, onset of a major physical illness, marital separation), these are the extra risks that all together take you over the edge. Finally, the straw that breaks the camel's back!

Here, it's the combination, but not either alone, that breaks your normal coping system, physiologically and psychologically, leading to the 'nervous breakdown' or, more technically, the onset of an episode of depression. For chronic, unrelenting stressors, the concept is less one of acute breakdown and more one of nervous exhaustion.

According to this simple 'add it all up' version, there is no interaction between the two types of risk, meaning as the dose of either genetic risk or environmental stress increases, the size of the risk does not multiply. Let's imagine you need five risks in total to go over the line. So, any three plus three is sufficient to bring on an episode of illness.

Much more interesting, and probably much more accurate is an explanation where there are true gene–environment interactions. Here the effects of each are compounded. Instead of 3+3=6, you start to see 3x3=9! Very rapidly, and often quite unexpectedly, someone who had little idea that they were at risk is way over the line!

This second explanation is the holy grail. Partly, because everybody wins. Those who argue the importance of genetic influences are satisfied, while those who say the environment is always critical (and that is the thing you can most easily change) are equally happy.

Just one small problem: is it really true?

In reality, the onset of clinical illness may not require either the genes or the environment each to have big effects. One or the other, and not necessarily both, may be most relevant to you (or your family's) situation.

That is, if the threshold for the onset of clinical depression is a theoretical score of 3 and you have a large enough genetic load that gives you a score of 5 on its own, then you could get depressed anywhere and at any time (no specific trigger required). As we now know that many different genes are involved, and they can all add up (see Chapter 10), this scenario is entirely possible. If you are one of those people with a very high genetic load, don't blame the trauma – work on how best to reduce your own risks. Remember, just because you have the genes does not mean that you won't respond to treatment or that the pathways those genes affect cannot be altered by smart interventions.

By contrast, if the environmental insult is big enough (prolonged child and adolescent sexual abuse by a parent) and the environmental stressors alone gives you a score of 5 or more, then your individual genetic risk may be largely irrelevant. You're in a high-risk category – but just like those in the high-risk gene group it does not mean that you won't respond to treatment or other interventions.

Turns out, there is good data to support the proposition that, for many individuals, strong genetic factors or strong environmental factors on their own do provide much of the explanation for risk of the onset of clinical depression. Individuals can say with some certainty 'nothing has really gone wrong for me recently, I just got really depressed' or, by contrast, 'I had always been fine, until I got trapped in this really bad and abusive relationship'.

For the scientists, and for many clinicians, these fairly simple statements about the causes of depression are very unsatisfying. We much prefer the interaction or more dynamic model. It's more intuitive and fits better with our preconceptions. We all tend to think of mental ill-health as one big train wreck between ourselves and our circumstances. It also fits best with the real-world data. Most people with a family history of anxiety or depression don't get clinically depressed. Most people exposed to trauma don't get depressed either.

While clinical depression is common (lifetime risk of about 15–25 per cent) nowhere near those numbers have any evidence of very highly stacked genetic (3+) or environmental (3+) risk. So, we have been very keen to find substantive evidence for our favourite theory (multiplicative) or our second-best (additive) 'genetic plus environment' explanation for why depression is so common.

Studying gene–environment interactions in the age of GWAS

Over the past decade the science of how best to decode our genes and provide much better explanations of genetic risk has rapidly advanced. Why focus on one or two genes, when you can screen the 25–30,000 possibilities and then start to add up how many combinations really matter? This new method (whole genome sequencing) is combined with very large international efforts to join up clinics and population-based registries of people with each of the major conditions. These massive investments (known as Genome Wide Association Studies – GWAS) lead to much more blue-sky thinking, and challenge many of our basic assumptions.

So, we are now well down the road to quantifying how your own genes add up to put you at some degree of risk of things like clinical depression. But other very interesting things emerge. It turns out that while we generally think that your genetic profile ('vulnerability') and then what happens to you ('life stressors') are independent of each other, for many conditions that's not quite true.

One aspect of this is fairly clear if you stop and think about it. Kids with severe ADHD often have a high genetic load. Consequently, they often go on to do risky things, like crashing off skateboards and falling out of trees. They can struggle at school. So, they experience more bad events, and then chronic stresses, not as a cause of the condition but as a consequence of their higher genetic risk. Those additional problems can then contribute to more behavioural and emotional problems, and worse social and educational outcomes, for those same kids.

For things like clinical depression, these patterns are not so clear. Those same genes that are putting you at risk of developing depression may also be influencing other aspects of your emotional life – like your temperament, tending to make you more anxious, more sensitive to criticism, more likely to overreact to fairly minor upheavals in your daily life and more likely to report that others have treated you harshly.

So, even before you develop the illness your genetic makeup may be playing a role, increasing the risk that those things that are most likely to upset you will actually occur! That is, some of this is not simply happening by chance. The situation can then be compounded by the fact that once you have had depression you are then more likely to have other things go wrong – lose your job, your intimate partner leaves, other important relationships with friends and family breakup. So, more adverse events pile on top of what occurred before you got depressed.

As we enter the third decade of the 21st century we can start to draw some new conclusions about the relationships between genetic risk and life-stressors. While some people do have a very large genetic risk and some have experienced very bad environments, for the majority of those affected both are playing rather more complex roles.

While most people can tell the story of what is happening in their life now, and what they believe mattered in their childhood, very few really factor in their own likely genetic – or epigenetic – risk. It's not something you can see or easily test. But this is all changing rather quickly. It is likely that genetic testing will enter the clinic in the very near future. When it does, it doesn't mean that there is nothing you can do about it. What it will mean is that rather than just saying life stress caused your depression, you will need to work on reducing your own underlying vulnerability.

TAKE-OUT TIPS

- Just because you have very high genetic or environmental risks for clinical depression doesn't mean that you won't respond to treatment.
- The true relationships between genetic risks and environmetal stressors are only just emerging.
- Most people with clinical depression don't have an overwhelming genetic or environmental risk – so let's avoid simple explanations that aren't true and don't lead to redcucing long-term vulnerability.

13

Genes and Environments in the Aftermath of COVID

Most of my previous discussion of the interplay between genetic vulnerabilities and various life stressors was focused on those things many people already know something about: what runs in their families (genes) and their own life circumstances, including events that they have experienced as traumatic. So, much of my description spelt out the types of brain pathways those genes might be influencing (brain-nerve cell connections, concentrations of brain chemicals like serotonin, the brain's hormonal responses to stress) and the types of environments that elicit the most emotional responses (childhood abuse, traumatic break-ups in personal relationships).

But all of that is a rather narrow view of the things that are in play – and it leaves out a lot of things that people don't really know anything about. Among these are the extent to which their genes underpin their immune responses to infection, the way their sleep–wake cycle reacts to light or changes in season, the way their brain reacts to the ups and downs of sex hormones like estrogen and testosterone, or the way some people react badly to cancer therapies or some antiviral treatments.

Most of us are unaware of how these factors affect our risk of developing clinical depression, or why mental ill-health can suddenly come on at different stages of our life. This is where the experience of the COVID-19 pandemic, and some of its ongoing ill-effects, such as 'long COVID' become really interesting. Many of those prolonged-illness experiences that are now being described are not new.

Very similar experiences were reported after the Spanish Flu pandemic of 1917–19, and after each major viral epidemic since then. Much of my own research has looked at these experiences after other common viral (e.g. glandular fever) and non-viral infections. The same set of body and brain symptoms (fever, aches and pain, tiredness, daytime sleepiness, poor night-time sleep, lack of pleasure in daily activities and 'brain fog' – poor concentration and memory) are reported consistently.

What turns out to be really important for many people is not which bug attacked them but their own (genetically determined) immune response. The bigger and nastier the initial immune (inflammatory) response, the worse the acute illness (all the way from days in bed to the ICU for some) and the longer the recovery. These responses are all designed to kill the bug quickly, but if they don't turn off again quickly – they really hurt you. In the worst situations during COVID it was a person's own immune response that killed them. That explains why the first effective treatments (corticosteroids) turned out to be those that suppressed the acute immune response.

The key issue here is that the immune response doesn't just affect the body – it has big effects on some important brain systems, most notably the 24-hour sleep–wake system (see Chapter 14) and its own links with tiredness, mood, memory and concentration. If you have genes that put you at risk for both a supercharged immune response to the bug *and* you also have genes that make your sleep–wake cycle fragile (clues include being easily upset by things like shift work, worry or jet lag), then you may be at very high risk of getting depressed post-COVID (or any other severe infection). The only thing is, you won't know that till it happens . . .

The same experience has been noted in a range of other 'medical' situations, like cancer therapies, other antiviral and hormonal treatments, or following life situations that really mess with your sleep–wake cycle (adolescence, post-childbirth, menopause, ageing). So it's not simply genetic risk to depression that matters, but additionally genetic risk to a disturbed circadian cycle. And then there might still be other genetic factors in the mix that break the camel's back – like the genes underpinning your immune response to a viral infection or your brain's response to changes in sex hormones.

These things are not simply the interactions between genes for depression and life stressors but rather interactions between quite different sets of genes that you may be carrying. And then suddenly they might all come together at the one time – like after a COVID infection. Lots of people will now say, 'I can't be depressed after COVID because I never got depressed before – even when really bad things happened in my life.' And besides, 'I'm not really sad – it's just that I can't enjoy anything, I've got no energy, I can't think straight, and I wake up just as tired as when I went to bed.'

As the scientific hunt gains momentum for which sets of genes correspond to different brain and body systems and how they put people at a greater risk of depression (and in what circumstances those genes actually matter), we are likely to learn a whole lot more about things we really had no idea about. It's vital not to get stuck believing that each of us already knows what has caused our depression. That belief may lead us up some seriously wrong finger-pointing or therapeutic dead-ends.

PART 3

THE BIOLOGY OF DEPRESSION

14

The Neurobiology of Depression

> Ian, would you and your mates just get on with it – I want to know what is really going on in my head, not just what some doctor or psychologist makes up on the day. They often seem to know less than me.
>
> – Jackie Crowe

It's important to stop and summarise where the neurobiology of clinical depression is at. It's probably the thing I get asked about the most in my clinical and public media roles. People want to know how their brain works and, when ill, what's gone wrong in their mind *and* their body. They want to know what the relevance is of the underlying biology to all phases of depressions – prevention, early intervention, treatment, recovery, and prevention of relapse.

Turning thinking about depression on its head

As we dive into the neurobiology – meaning simply the biology of the brain, the mechanics that sit under the hood of clinical depression – it's best to put my perspective upfront. Contrary to much discourse, it's really disturbed 'emotional' (or limbic) circuitry that is in the front seat and driving the experience. Dysfunctional thinking is in the back seat and just dragged along for the ride. We've had extensive (anatomical) brain maps of these emotional circuits in humans and other animals for decades. But, courtesy of modern brain imaging, we can now track their activity in life.

The emotional brain or 'limbic' circuit and its connections

From an evolutionary perspective, the emotional circuits are very old, sitting deep within the modern brain and well away from the new 'cortical' grey (thinking) areas that cover the surface. Consequently, we still share the emotional elements with many other species. They regulate essential survival functions like sex, eating, physical activity, fear, sleep–wake and emotional signalling between members of the same species. These are the more instinctive and reactive parts. The 'cortical' or thinking regions developed much later in the evolutionary journey and are more elaborate in mammals and primates.

The emotional or 'subcortical' regions are tightly linked with the two major output systems from the brain to the rest of the body – the brainstem, which is the main electrical system that then becomes the spinal cord (regulating not just motor activity but heart rate, breathing and other critical responses), and the hypothalamic-pituitary axis (HPA), which is the main chemical output and controls the release of the key stress (corticosteroid), sex and other regulatory hormones.

The most important element of the emotional circuitry is the limbic system. This includes, in the temporal lobes, the amygdala (the fear centre), the hippocampus (the memory centre) and, running from the frontal lobes back across the brain, the cingulate gyrus (see Figure 1). These key structures are then linked with other subcortical nuclei – the basal ganglia, which include the caudate, putamen and globus pallidus. All these structures are on both sides of the brain. While the subcortical regions play a key role in regulating motor activity, they are also strongly linked with the hypothalamus (the brain's air traffic control tower that connects to the pituitary gland) and other major brain connecting systems, such as the corpus callosum, the major white matter path for exchanging signals between the left and right hemispheres of the brain. In turn, these circuits are linked to the cerebellum at the back of the brain, which coordinates all our complex movements through the signals it sends down the spinal cord.

The most basic element of the emotional circuitry (or 'limbic system') is our 'fear circuit'. It is centred on the amygdala (fear

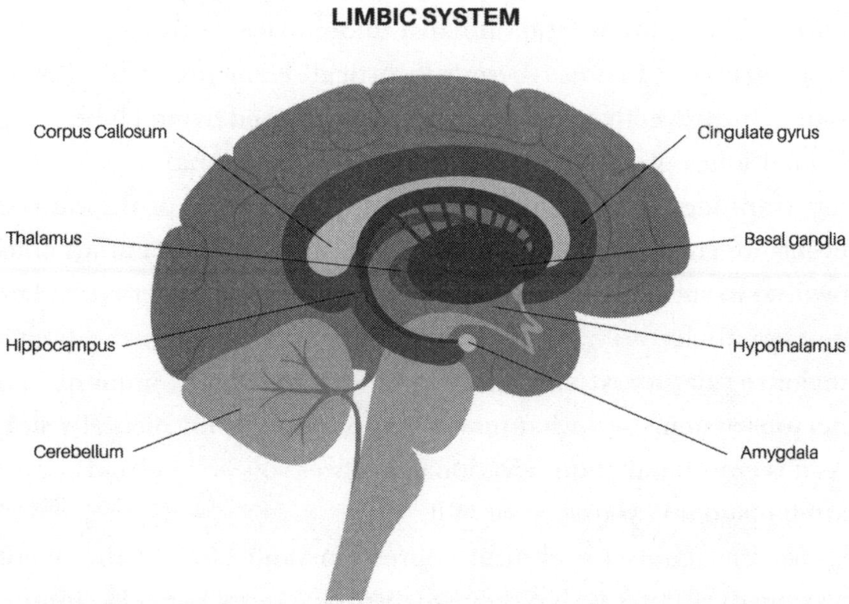

Figure 1

central), which sits on top of the hippocampus (memory central), located in the temporal lobes. It's fascinating that fear and memories are so intimately linked, presumably providing an evolutiuonary advantage. They allow us to immediately recall (and avoid) those things we've learnt previously are life-threatening! Humans are wired just like most other species so that we feel, react and respond to survive first and then think about the consequences later.

The fear circuit controls our immediate motor (reflex) responses, as well as connecting directly with the top of our spinal cord to increase heart and breathing rates, and blood pressure. As it also links to the brain's regulator of our hormonal responses to threat, the hypothalamus, it can signal the rest of the body to release appropriate stress hormones, like cortisol. So, this fear circuitry encodes our behavioural responses to threat from the outside world, equipping us to mount our immediate 'fight or flight' responses. From an anxiety and depressive perspective, they also give rise to the 'freeze or flop' responses that are often observed in animals (and humans) under extreme threat.

In primates like us, these 'subcortical' elements of the limbic system link directly to our much more developed frontal lobes. The frontal lobes play key roles in linking our emotional responses to our thinking patterns, and the ongoing evaluation of the various events we encounter. But this emotional circuitry has a mind of its own, so to speak. It drives the whole physiological experience. The emotional circuitry, via its connections back through the body's major regulatory systems – the hormonal, metabolic, immune and nervous systems – is what makes you physically and mentally sick. As it is emotional and not rational, it leaves you well beyond simple attempts to talk yourself out of it.

So, the reality for clinical depression (and most of the major anxiety disorders) is that they are disturbances of very old circuits, essential to survival, and come with very tight links to major physiological systems (neuronal, hormonal, metabolic, immune). They are systems that are not easily overridden by signals – that is, thoughts or intentions – from the new cortical or thinking parts of the brain. Emotion trumps thought every time – in both speed and intensity of response. It's often very hard for modern humans to come to terms with this biological reality.

Think about it. You can't just tell yourself to go to sleep. You can't just tell yourself to be hungry when you're not. You can't just tell yourself to be attracted to someone you are not attracted to. You can't just tell yourself not to be afraid when you're feeling threatened. You can't just tell your heart to go faster or slow down. You can't just tell yourself to feel physically well and energetic when you're sick.

One of the most confusing things for people when they are clinically depressed, and they can't give an easy explanation, or the original trigger has long passed, is trying to reconcile the lack of a rationale with the utterly terrible way they feel. The bottom line is that those emotional circuits that do regulate how you feel, not what you think, are off on their own non-cognitive, non-rational trip! Your consent has not been sought, and your objections are not heard.

Which circuits really drive clinical depression?

A dysfunction of the limbic circuit (amygdala, hippocampus, anterior cingulate gyrus and its frontal lobe connections), acting in concert with its brain–bodyvarious connections (HPA, SNS, circadian system) lies at the heart of clinical depression (see Figure 1 on page 217 and Figure 2 overleaf). If the limbic system is disrupted, it doesn't matter what you think – you will have trouble with sleep, eating, sex, fear, motor behaviours, hormonal function (notably increased and persistent release of the corticosteroid stress hormones), metabolic

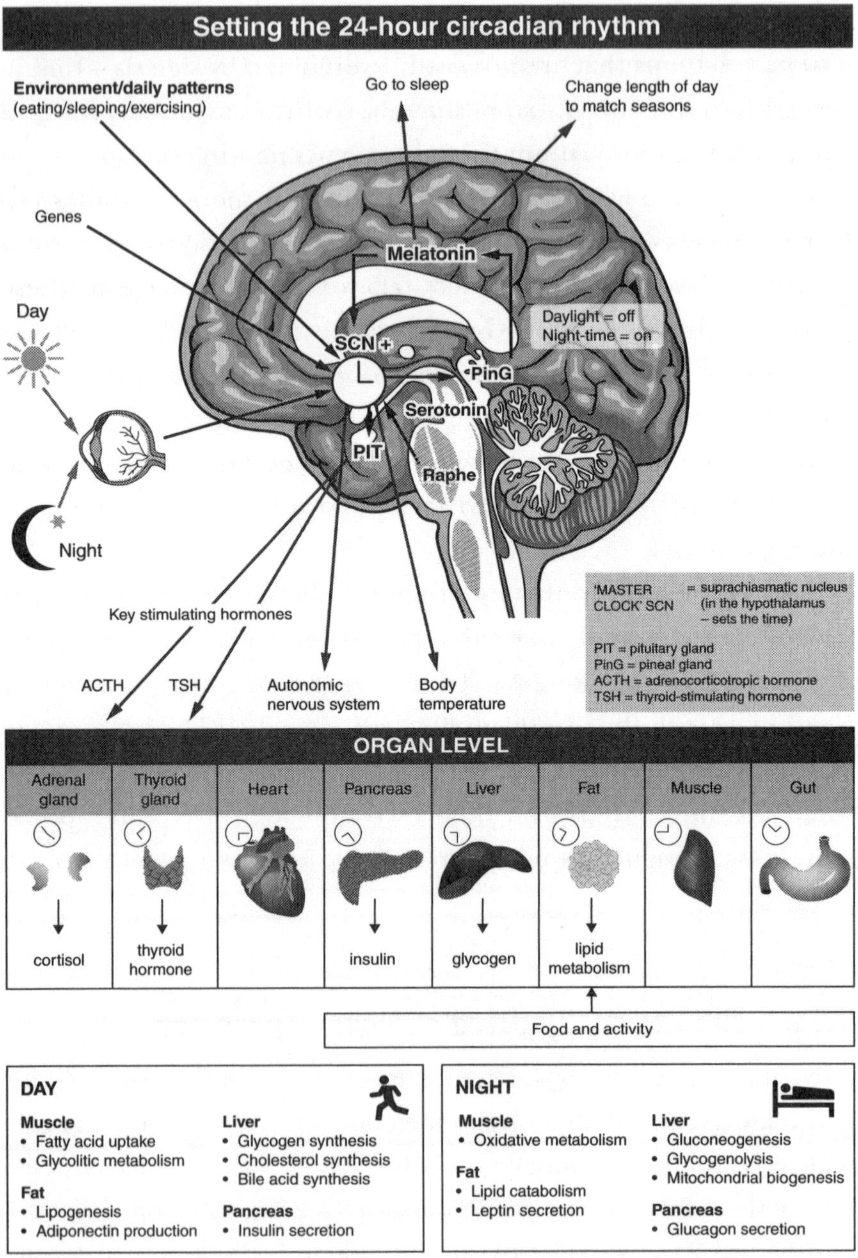
Setting the 24-hour circadian rhythm
Environment/daily patterns
(eating/sleeping/exercising)
Go to sleep
Change length of day
to match seasons
Genes
Melatonin
Day
Daylight = off
Night-time = on
SCN
PinG
Serotonin
PIT
Raphe
Night
'MASTER CLOCK' SCN = suprachiasmatic nucleus (in the hypothalamus – sets the time)
PIT = pituitary gland
PinG = pineal gland
ACTH = adrenocorticotropic hormone
TSH = thyroid-stimulating hormone
Key stimulating hormones
ACTH
TSH
Autonomic
nervous system
Body
temperature
ORGAN LEVEL
Adrenal gland
Thyroid gland
Heart
Pancreas
Liver
Fat
Muscle
Gut
cortisol
thyroid hormone
insulin
glycogen
lipid metabolism
Food and activity
DAY
Muscle
• Fatty acid uptake
• Glycolitic metabolism
Fat
• Lipogenesis
• Adiponectin production
Liver
• Glycogen synthesis
• Cholesterol synthesis
• Bile acid synthesis
Pancreas
• Insulin secretion
NIGHT
Muscle
• Oxidative metabolism
Fat
• Lipid catabolism
• Leptin secretion
Liver
• Gluconeogenesis
• Glycogenolysis
• Mitochondrial biogenesis
Pancreas
• Glucagon secretion

Figure 2

system (affecting blood glucose and insulin regulation), immune system (which protects you from infection and cancer) and regulation of the cardiovascular system (heart rate and blood pressure) and nervous arousal system (sweating, hyperventilating).

While some people have vulnerabilities in their emotional circuitry prior to ever being depressed, the recurrent or persistent experience of clinical depression does further damage to these cortical–subcortical paths. Getting treatment early and effectively, and preventing recurrence, all become high priorities once you appreciate that the underlying machinery is being damaged by the ongoing illness. Once seriously depressed, the brain takes a while to recover fully from the physiological as well as the psychological injury.

So, the more we know about the underlying brain mechanisms, and the more that you can find the model that best fits your own illness experience, the more likely we are to implement strategies that get you out of the hole and repair the damage, and help you to stay well long-term.

Watching the brain in life

In the early 1990s, we first had access to one of those most remarkable developments in brain-imaging techniques, magnetic resonance imaging (MRI). We were fortunate that a professor of radiology facilitated our early access to this new technology at Prince Henry Hospital in Sydney. He thought it was as likely to be relevant to our clinical work as it was for our neurological and neurosurgical colleagues.

At the time, this view distressed two sets of colleagues. The first were those who championed traditional psychological (or 'brainless') theories of causation and the second were those ('mindless') colleagues who believed that only neurologists and neurosurgeons should access such brain-focused techniques. They perpetuated the view that if a behavioural, emotional or cognitive problem was the direct result of structural brain change, then the patient no longer had a mental health problem!

Much more brain imaging research uses MR technology, not just to look at the structure of the emotional circuitry, but also its activity in life via 'functional MRI'. It makes use of the way that blood flows preferentially (to deliver glucose) to the most active brain cells. So, you can watch which parts of the brain are doing the work, and who they are doing it with (the circuit), at rest or in response to various external stimuli.

These approaches have underpinned a newer classification of brain circuits or 'networks'. The three that are most important from a mental health perspective have been described as:

1. *Default mode network (DMN):* This network, which closely maps on the limbic system described above, was first seen to be the most active when someone was *not* doing active tasks. It was thought to reflect what the brain was doing while not required to do anything else. But it is actually very active when thinking about the past or worrying about what might happen in the future – things lots of us do while not being forced to respond to the outside world! It's been associated with concepts like 'mental simulations' – thinking through future scenarios based on past experiences. It also appears to be overactive when we are lost in our own internal world, ruminating on past mistakes or future misdemeanours. It's now of great interest as it seems to be most affected by things like 'mindfulness' and 'meditaton', as well as the new wave of psychedelic compounds that are being actively promoted as novel interventions for treatment-resistant depression, post-traumatic stress disorder and addictions.
2. *Salience network (SN):* This is the network that connects part of the cingulate gyrus (which is part of the emotional circuitry) with other cortical parts of the brain (insular cortex) that have

been linked traditionally with emotional responses like empathy and compassion, as well as consciousness, self-awareness and interpersonal experiences. Its main role is to filter our attention to stimuli from the external world that most demand our attention. The goal is to respond verbally and non-verbally in the most appropriate ways to social context. So, from a depression perspective, it's a key part of the brain's functions that we need to be working optimally.

3. *Central executive network (CEN)*: This network does the hard work of actively manipulating information in real-time so that you can respond appropriately and rationally (by thinking about all the information available to you), given the constraints you face (or the agreed social rules for responding), and the need to focus on solving the problems or challenges immediately in front of you. Anatomically, it connects key frontal and more posterior cortical (grey-thinking) brain areas. It's most active (in contrast with the DMN) when you are trying really hard to solve problems – a major challenge for those with clinical depression. When we are functioning well (and we are not depressed or distracted by an overactive DMN), these parts of the brain should be really active.

These three networks are in a complex, interconnected dance with each other. When one goes up (the DMN), the other (the CEN) goes down – or, for the mathematically oriented, there is an inverse correlation between their patterns of activity. The SN is actively associated with both of these other networks and may be thought of as the mediating influence between the two – deciding whether or not we need to actively respond (a task for the CEN) or switch off from the external world and focus on our own personal concerns (the task of the DMN).

We have now reached a fascinating point in tracking these networks, not just by blood flow (using MRI) but also by new electrical techniques – applied to the skull or even deployed directly on the brain surface! We can start to see whether these anatomical networks behave in the ways we predict and, more importantly, if they were directly stimulated (electrically or magnetically), would those networks be engaged, leading to different behavioural outputs.

This could include (via individual and guided brain stimulation) things like:

- An end to ruminative thinking, and dwelling on past mistakes or future errors (through manipulation of the DMN);
- An enhanced focus on aspects of the interpersonal environment that are most relevant to our emotional and social world (through stimulation of the SN); and
- A return to a focus on goal-directed responses to real and immediate environmental challenges (through manipulation of the CEN).

A few caveats before we dive right in

First, whatever I say today will be, at least, partly wrong tomorrow. In five years' time, I hope that it will be significantly wrong, due to major advances in the field. That's the nature of real science. It's especially the case for brain and mind sciences. The situation today is very different to what was known as little as ten years ago.

We still have limited understanding of how the brain functions normally, let alone how it misfires in specific disease states. This is particularly so for the complex emotional, cognitive and behavioural tasks it facilitates. From an information technology perspective, there are major gaps in our conceptualisation of just how all those cells, and the very complex connections and networks between those cells, come together to provide us with the incredible thoughts, feelings, perceptions and social behaviours that we take for granted in everyday life.

Quite often when I'm asked to explain (preferably in plain English) some complex or challenging brain-linked behavioural change, I reply, 'Don't know . . . None of us really know at this stage. But here's our best guess . . .'

These concessions of how limited our knowledge is differentiates us from other sources of truth – like philosophy, personal insights, religious beliefs, sociopolitical ideology and many traditional psychological (notably 'psychoanalytic') perspectives. We don't have a theory of everything, or a theoretical perspective that can be adapted to explain every new observation.

My late father, a professor of cardiology, would frequently ask me whether there was anything really new in the brain-science world – or just more opinions?

He had formed the view that much academic work in psychiatry was based more on opinion than fact. My reply: 'Dad, the brain is complicated. Unlike the heart, it's not a dumb four-chambered pump with a simple electrical system. And, it varies a lot – not just from person to person, but continually over the course of your life!'

Of course, that's one of the reasons I love to work in this area. Real complexity. As President Obama noted when launching the US BRAIN Initiative, 'We can identify galaxies light years away, we can study particles smaller than an atom. But we still haven't unlocked the mystery of the three pounds of matter that sits between our ears.'

Animal models of depression: a cautionary tale

We have relied heavily on animal models of depressive behaviours to test our theories of the causes of depression, as well as evaluating new treatments. In reality, the animal models are very limited proxies for the real thing. We have typically used rodents with very limited genetic variation to develop these models, and then conducted experiments within very constrained social and physical environments.

From a causal perspective, these approaches clearly don't capture the complex nature of human social systems and their patterns of inter-relationships. The experiments have a tendency to reduce these very important contextual elements to exposure to fear or interruptions to simple dyadic relationships (say, mother–child). The intricate pattern of human learning, adaptation by experience over time and dependence on social context is artificially reduced to simplistic notions of reward-dependent learning.

From the perspective of evaluating new treatments, these experiments may well have led to an undue focus on what works well to overcome 'defeat' in rodents. Inadvertently, this may have directed attention away from other relevant biochemical, immune or nerve cell pathways. If it didn't work on the rat or the mouse, then it won't work on humans!

Of course, there are much more interesting species to consider. Domestic dogs have more human-like personal and social characteristics, and for other key considerations like the oxytocin-bonding systems, may even have co-evolved in partnership with us! It's not surprising that many people consider dogs to be better companions than other humans and that they're often proposed as very effective antidepressant treatments.

As we move to primates, and eventually to our close relatives among the great apes (orangutans, chimpanzees, bonobos and gorillas), we can recognise the similarities in behaviour, temperament and social systems. Our willingness to conduct mechanistic research on our nearest cousins has declined rapidly in recent times. These days, most experimentation that is relevant to mental health or brain health is largely observational or involves non-harmful measurement of key social and individual behaviours, preferably in real-world settings. We are still learning key insights from this work, like the ways in which patterns of physical activity or social behaviour are actually transmitted across generations.

The bottom line is that for most common mental disorders like clinical depression, which are played out behaviourally and physiologically within complex social and physical settings, our animal models are of limited utility.

When it comes to our brains, we humans are all very different

That's my second big caveat before I jump into more general statements about the neurobiology of depression. As you move from person to person, we vary much more inside our own heads, neurobiologically and, as a consequence, emotionally, behaviourally and cognitively, than we do in any other body organ.

And, within the one person, we are changing dramatically over the course of our lives, with constant changes in brain structure, such as nerve cell connections within the brain and brain circuit rearrangement. There are major changes happening constantly, and often very rapidly during critical periods of development – in utero, in the first few years of life, in late childhood, across the many phases of adolescence (from a brain perspective there are at least four major phases in that decade of life), the child-bearing and child-rearing years, mid-life (particularly related to menopause) and on into later life.

When illnesses strike at any age from childhood onwards, these normal changes in brain structure and function are potentially disrupted. The changes may be temporary or have long-term consequences. So the brain, and those downstream systems it regulates within your body – metabolic, hormonal, immune, nervous, gut – also change as a consequence. Your brain is affecting your whole body all the time. So if the brain becomes sick, it affects the body too.

Some important qualifying factors (it's never simple . . .)

When trying to understand the nature of the neurobiology of clinical depression(s), there are other important factors to consider, like:

- Age of onset of the illness – the younger the age, the bigger the impact on brain development. True clinical depression is rare before puberty but increasingly common after that.
- Treatment responsiveness – the earlier and the more effectively the illness is treated, the less harm done to the brain and the body, and the greater the chance the brain and the body have of getting back to normal.
- Chronicity or recurrence of illness – the longer the duration of episodes of illness and the more episodes of illness a person has, the more likely that enduring harm is done to the brain and the body. This includes putting you at increased risk of heart disease or diabetes in mid-life or dementia in late-life.
- Physical health problems that are associated with the onset or persistence of clinical depression. Some episodes of illness following medical events like major viral infections, stroke, head injury or treatment for cancer, are not simply a psychological reaction to the impacts of that other illness. Rather, it is more likely that those diseases have disrupted critical parts of the brain machinery that regulate normal emotions and cognition.
- Other concurrent problems like misuse of alcohol and other drugs. The more that people who are clinically depressed self-medicate with other neurotoxic substances, the more harm is done.

There is no one simple type of clinical depression(s)

Another problem we have with the public discussion of major depression, and the licensing of new medical treatments or diagnostic tests for clinical use, is the false assumption that we are talking about one homogeneous illness, and that one type operates across all people, of all ages and at all the different phases of illness.

While the public promotion of major depression has been a major public health success (see Chapter 3), for the purposes of delineating the complex neurobiology, and underlying disease mechanisms, it is problematic.

Sadly, this rather simplistic concept is repeated in much public information and clinical guidelines for health professionals. While these are designed to promote best therapeutic practice, often they can be quite misleading. That's because to generalise about major depression is about as useful as talking about cancer without specifying that we are talking about breast, lung or bowel cancer, and then without clarifying how old the person is and at what stage of illness are they presenting for care.

One illness, one causative pathway, at any age – doesn't really work for mental disorders

Key assumptions were made about the fundamental disturbances in brain function in association with the major psychiatric disorders – namely, that if a true disease process was active, it should have the same biological characteristics, independent of the age or individual characteristics of the affected individual.

This very simple assumption was based on the cancer, infection or heart disease comparisons. If, at any age, you have leukaemia or a solid tumour like bowel cancer, or a disrupted heart rhythm, or a bacterial meningitis, then the same pathological features are evident in all cases.

So the logic ran that if clinical depression, or bipolar disorder, or schizophrenia, or autism were present, then we should find the same defining neurobiological features and the same behavioural signs at any age. But brain development is going on from minus nine months to about 25 years in most people.

Throughout this very long developmental period, the brain is undergoing constant changes, affecting what cognitive, emotional or behavioural functions we can display. Clearly you can't have a speech disorder before you can talk! You can't have a problem with your gait until you learn to walk. Similarly, you may not have a particular emotional or cognitive disturbance before the underlying brain function has actually developed.

'Age-dependent phenotypes' – what we can see is age-dependent

Although certain brain systems may be disrupted right across the life span – like a person's emotional response to environmental stimuli – what we actually observe will depend on the age, and stage of brain and social development, of the individual.

For practical purposes, we refer to these issues as studying the onset and course of age-dependent phenotypes. The phenotypes are what we can observe behaviourally, but also measure empirically, on the body or inside your head. Some illness states just cannot be observed until the relevant brain circuitry is in place.

The brain is particularly sensitive to the onset of certain illnesses when it is passing through some of these key developmental periods – puberty and mid-adolescence for onset of first episodes of clinical depression and, for older females, childbirth and menopause.

Most importantly, the reality is that clinical depression from a neurobiological and mechanistic perspective is not a single entity. What is presented here is our clinical and research groups' best ideas as to what are some of the key processes. We combine the best available evidence from genetics, developmental paediatrics, lifetime trajectory mapping, brain imaging, circadian medicine, immunology and metabolic sciences.

One final caveat: the groupings described here will only ever fit partially with the experiences of any individual. While each person may have clinical features that largely map one subtype of depression, matching neurobiological changes in one major domain (like, say, the body clock), they are also likely to have features from the other domains. There are no mutually exclusive groups – and we are probably only half right with our current model. At the end of the day, it helps to know which grouping best describes your situation, as it may lead to better treatment choices.

Clinical staging

One of the most important clinical concepts that the Brain and Mind Centre has pursued with my great friend Professor Pat McGorry and his Melbourne colleagues is the transfer of the concept of clinical staging from general medicine to clinical psychiatry – particularly as it relates to major mood and psychotic disorders. (See the Recommended Reading for more details on this topic.)

In general medicine, clinical staging is standard practice – particularly for the management of each type of cancer. Early stages are associated with less intensive or less toxic treatments and offer better prospects for long-term survival. Fundamentally, it is a better way of matching specific treatment choices to the phase of illness a person is at when they present for care. It also strongly encourages an early intervention perspective. Basically, the earlier you get treatment, the lower the impact on your life.

Most depressive disorders have their onset after puberty, rising then across adolescence and early adulthood. This is at the same time as brain, body and social developments are themselves also changing rapidly – and in complex ways. So, the neurobiology of these early phases of illness is also complicated and changing continuously – that is, the adolescent's hormones, sleep–wake cycles, emotional and cognitive capacities are changing. Our models of neurobiology try to capture these various dimensions: clinical staging, depressive subtypes and normal adolescent development (see Figures 3 and 4 on pages 233–234).

Childhood precursors and adolescent onset

Although we focus on adolescence, many parents report that their kids had other emotional, behavioural or learning issues earlier in childhood. Lots of relevant positive (nutrition, education, warm parenting) and negative (infections, head injuries, drug exposures, alcohol, assault, abuse or neglect) environmental exposures also take place in the womb, or throughout those earlier childhood years. These affect brain and body development, and may be the basis for later vulnerability to the onset of depressive disorders, after puberty or in adult life. Any model of the neurobiology of depression needs to describe these earlier pathways of childhood risk and then, why the disorders themselves begin in adolescence (see Figure 4).

Other key biological change points

Fortunately, for most of us life is long and complicated. There are more transitions than just childhood and puberty. For women, the transition through childbirth is a critical risk period. For most of us, our lives are now much more complicated than the original evolutionary plan. Back then, we only needed adults to get to 25–30 years for the species to reproduce and survive. But, now that most adults live into their eighth and ninth decades, there are other important biological turning points that are relevant. These

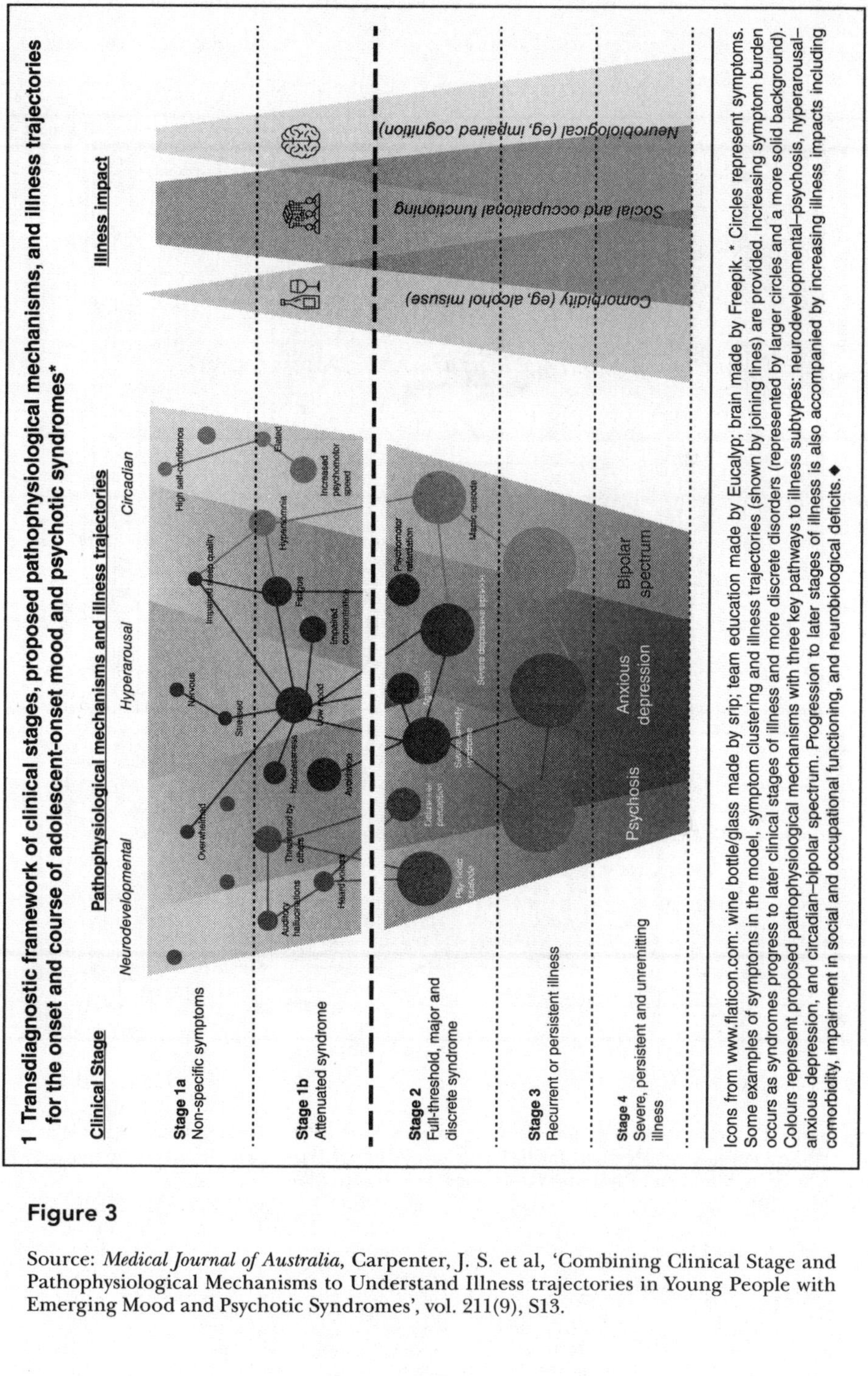

Figure 3

Source: *Medical Journal of Australia*, Carpenter, J. S. et al, 'Combining Clinical Stage and Pathophysiological Mechanisms to Understand Illness trajectories in Young People with Emerging Mood and Psychotic Syndromes', vol. 211(9), S13.

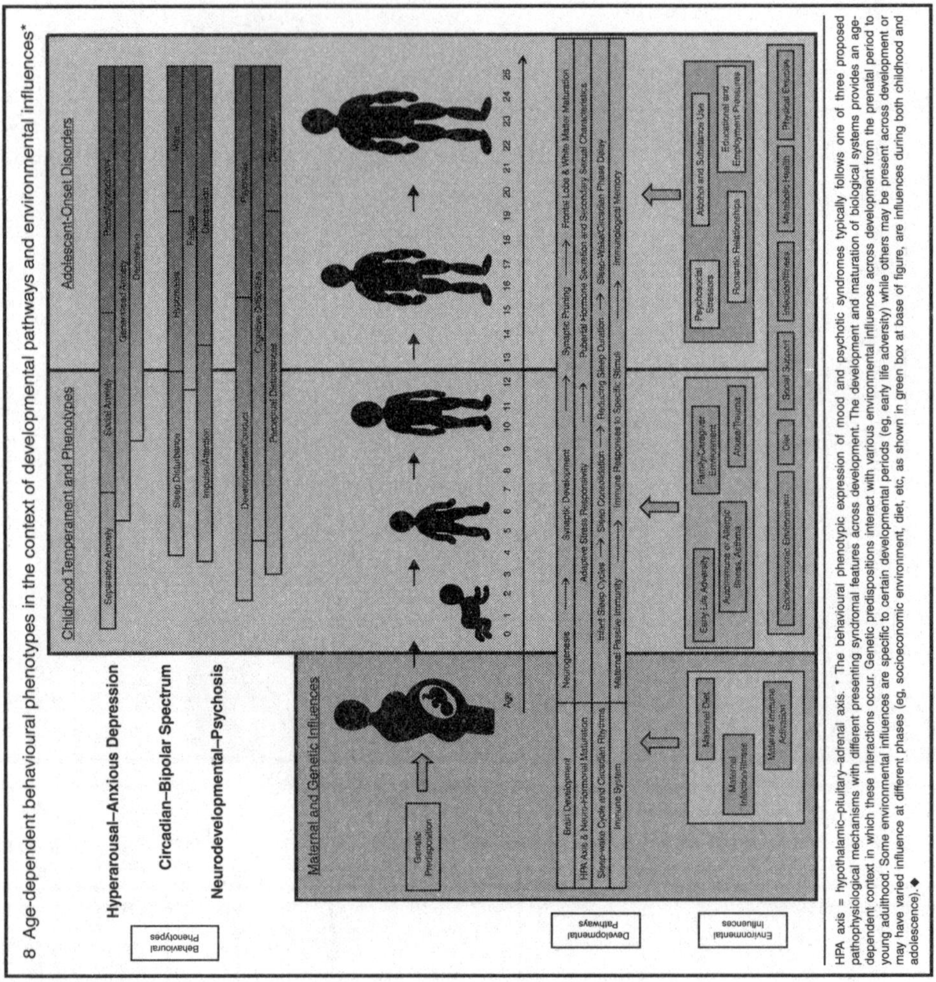

Figure 4

Source: *Medical Journal of Australia*, Carpenter, J. S. et al, 'Combining Clinical Stage and Pathophysiological Mechanisms to Understand Illness Trajectories in Young People with Emerging Mood and Psychotic Syndromes', vol. 211(9), S19.

include menopause for women and the illnesses that become more common with ageing – such as blood vessel disease and potential degeneration of brain cells in association with dementia.

KAY'S PERSPECTIVE

Kay is a middle-aged woman who has survived breast cancer, early-onset clinical depression, other physical disability (linked to profound fatigue) and a tough personal life. Her first episode of clinical depression was a severe post-natal event, suggesting a significant contribution by either hormonal or circadian factors. Antidepressant medications, cognitive behavioural therapy, increased physical activity and improved sleep cycles all helped.

Just when Kay had got most things that really mattered to her sorted (new intimate relationship, financial stability, improved physical health), she went into menopause and had a severe recurrence of her clinical depression. Her menopausal state had not only disrupted her mood and contributed to the return of fatigue, but also her poor night-time temperature regulation was ruining her sleep cycle. Sadly, due to her pre-menopausal breast cancer, hormone replacement therapy (that boosts estrogen levels) was not an option. Clinical depression is often more effectively treated in women like Kay when estrogen replacement is added to the treatment mix.

In my office one day, while simultaneously crying and laughing, she just yelled out, 'Which male god ever thought menopause was a f***ing good idea?'

My reply: 'You think this was planned? Kay, let's face it, from an evolutionary perspective, most women would have been dead many years before they ever got close to menopause. This is not a god-imposed or intentionally-designed problem.'

Co-occurring medical, psychiatric and substance misuse disorders

Clinical depression doesn't often occur entirely on its own. Many people will have other disorders of the mind (say, OCD) or the body (such as infection or cancer). These all have their own effects on brain and body health, and on the underlying neurobiology of the depression. All of this makes the formal neurobiological assessment of each individual considerably more complicated!

Clinical depression subtypes: different brain, body and system changes

So, after taking account of age of onset, childhood precursors, critical life transitions and concurrent other medical, psychiatric and substance misuse disorders, we have proposed that for adolescent-onset clinical depression there are three main subtypes or trajectories that demand attention, and are fundamentally linked to different underlying brain mechanisms (see Figure 3 on page 233).

1. *Anxious Arousal:* a lifetime pattern of exaggerated emotional responses to environmental stressors. In childhood this is associated with anxiety (separation anxiety, school refusal, anxious temperament) and, following puberty, becomes increasingly associated with anxious depression in the teenage and young adult years. The anxiety here is not normal and is easily tripped over into a more profound fear response. The typical prolonged hyperarousal state that follows an environmental stimulus drives downstream hormonal, metabolic, cardiovascular and immune changes. The overstimulation of excitatory pathways within the brain does further damage to the 'emotional' brain circuits, while the persistent overproduction of the body's stress response hormones (most notably cortisol), does damage to the

rest of the body. People with this subtype of clinical depression are most likely to have the onset following a major life disruption or when exposed to unresolved stressors (abusive intimate relationship, chronic illness, prolonged unemployment). This form is the most common, recurrent across the lifespan, and most easily confused with normal psychological responses to distressing circumstances.

2. *Circadian:* a lifetime pattern associated with difficulties maintaining regular body rhythms, most notably of the 24-hour sleep–wake cycle. Much more than low mood, it is linked with fundamental loss of pleasure (particularly in things like food, sex, physical activity), low energy, observable changes in speed of motor movement, weight changes (usually weight gain) and variations in response to factors like light exposure and season of the year. It is likely to come on in association with natural shifts in light–dark cycles (changing seasons), forced disruptions of sleep–wake cycles (like postnatal, shift work, intercontinental travel), or normal developmental stages where sleep–wake cycles are shifting (post-puberty and adolescence, menopause). While less common, it is the one that has most shared characteristics with other subtypes like 'atypical' (which is common in many young people), bipolar depression and melancholia. Many of these display similar observable signs, such as slowed movement and thinking, but also the sudden 'on–off' pattern. It is that characteristic and sudden 'on-off' switch that is not easily explained by other neurobiological or environmental factors.
3. *Neurodevelopmental:* a trajectory of impaired brain development, often linked with obvious childhood difficulties (delayed motor or speech development, specific learning difficulties, impaired emotional responsiveness), that post-puberty becomes increasingly associated with social disconnection, poor emotion regulation, misinterpretation of environmental and

interpersonal cues, psychotic-like experiences. Although the least common trajectory, it has also been the most neglected, even when very obviously associated with suicidal behaviour, social exclusion and active discrimination.

Other forms of clinical depressions that have their onset in specific circumstances include:

1. *Perinatal depression*: a good example of two different subgroups – prenatal slower onset anxious–arousal type, and postnatal sudden onset circadian-type depression, amid a cascade of external (sleep deprivation, disrupted circadian cycles, new interpersonal dependency, disrupted intimate relationship) and internal (a tsunami of hormonal changes, including oxytocin linked with breast feeding) factors.
2. *Late-onset depression*: a standout case of structural brain changes in older persons, typically due to underlying but undetected blood vessel disease.
3. *Depression in the context of another medical condition or treatment*: common severe illnesses like heart attack, stroke and cancer, along with a range of rarer hormonal diseases (say, Cushing's syndrome, where the adrenal glands overproduce corticosteroids; or polycystic ovaries), and other medical treatments (immune therapies for cancer or chronic infection), are all associated with markedly increased rates of depressive disorders. Typically, many people in these situations assume (wrongly) that the depression is an understandable psychological response to the consequences of physical illness.
4. *Post-infective depression*: a classic combination of an immune storm following a severe infection, linked with the disruption of key regulatory systems, most notably the circadian system. In the post-COVID and long-COVID era, we are likely to see a big upswing in the numbers of these cases.

5. *Autoimmune and other immune-mediated forms of depression*: where your own antibodies attack your own brain cells, or cells elsewhere in the body.

As an aside, we have always seen people with secondary depressive or other neuropsychiatric conditions who have clinical depression as a consequence of primary brain disorders, such as stroke, multiple sclerosis or epilepsy. Optimal management requires the expertise of a multidisciplinary team of specialists, who offer a much wider variety of medical, psychological and behavioural therapies.

The brain circuits that regulate mood and cognition

Brain circuits are the fashion of the day in neuroscience. For many major mental disorders (like clinical depression) and more complex neurodevelopmental conditions (such as autism), or neurological disorders (like multiple sclerosis), the disruption of the relevant circuits is our real focus. Before the late 20th century, most direct brain research relied on collecting brain tissue after death to study these circuits. Now we use modern brain imaging techniques to study them in life.

There are four major insights to clinical depression:

- First, the key emotional circuits are old, non-verbal and not rational. For some species, they may be thought of as the fear circuitry and are, therefore, most related to the anxious–arousal type of depression. Even in more developed species, they still do the basic survival functions – food, sex, fear, sleep, socialisation – and don't need words.
- Second, when perturbed, those circuits are uncontrollable.
- Third, it's often emotions that drive our thoughts and not the other way around. Humans try to explain whatever is happening

to them (see Chapter 11) and like to believe that their thoughts are in control.

- Last, the circuits are changed constantly in their strength and connections by experiences – rewards or punishments driving reward-based learning. This is a characteristic shared with most other species, and generally requires minimal conscious processing.

The brain-related causes of depression are often in the non-thinking parts of the brain

We humans have a certain inbuilt arrogance about our place in the evolutionary tree. Complex forms of language, speech, thought, communication and, of course, consciousness obviously set us apart. From a neurobiological perspective we attribute these capacities to the size and complexity of the cerebral cortex – the grey matter – that is so richly developed in humans.

This arrogance has often resulted in the assumption that all major disorders of cognition, emotion or behaviour arise from disturbances in these thinking parts of the brain and, worse, that we can simply use that part of our brains to detect the underlying causes of those conditions. So much psychological theory places conscious thought above all other attributes. At its worst (in the ongoing spirit of Descartes), it completely separates cognition and emotion from their underlying physiological structures.

How does the environment alter the development of the brain machine?

In most serious neuroscience, there has never been any doubt that the environment plays a critical part in shaping the growth and ongoing function of the brain.

The real questions relate to:

- How does this actually happen? How does the environment really get in and set off an episode? We need to know which regulatory systems (or circuits or networks) are most affected by changes in the environment.
- Which environmental factors have large impacts? Rather generic notions of stress, poverty, adversity, diet or lifestyle are not that helpful.
- How can the brain and its regulatory systems be manipulated in a positive way by various medical, psychological–behavioural or social interventions?
- At what points in normal development or during other at-risk periods (like childbirth or menopause) is it possible to deploy relevant prevention or early intervention strategies?

The circuitry is changing constantly in relation to the environment

At the microscopic level, one key perspective is that the major circuits are not simply analogous to an electrical circuit – that is, they are not 'fixed' or 'rigid'. The connections between the various elements are changing continuously. The basic cellular elements, the physical connections between nerve cells – the synapses – respond to ever-changing environmental stimuli.

So a key insight from modern neuroscience, and confirmed in living humans via brain imaging techniques, is that the basic cellular template for brain activity varies constantly in structure (the number of connections between nerve cells goes up and down) and function (meaning the activity of the chemical receptors on either end of these connections).

In addition, other supporting cells – most notably the glial (or 'glue') cells that provide the basic scaffolding for neurons and their synaptic connections – are also highly responsive to environmental stimuli. Previously thought to be rather passive observers, they are now recognised as active players too.

More modern views suggest that microglial cells, which are the most immune-responsive and mobile, are not activated in response to major traumatic or infective events, but rather function as everyday electricians. They are constantly reshaping these key physical elements of the basic brain circuitry in response to a vast range of internal and external signals.

Most importantly, the brain is not simply distanced from the environment, being protected physically by the skull and biochemically by the blood–brain barrier (a tight cellular wall to protect the brain from circulating toxins). This historic view of the protected brain included the notion that it was separate from the rest of the body's immune responses – one of the most active systems we have for protecting us from environmental threats. Turns out, the reverse is true. The brain is highly responsive, physiologically, to many stimuli, including light, immune and, biochemical signals. It is constantly changing its own structure to optimise its responses.

Another relatively recent but key insight is these active brain cells (neurons and glial cells) don't just respond to positive or physical challenges, but also to the withdrawal of key environmental information. If you lose sensory input, through loss of hearing, diminishing eyesight or loss of social interactions with others, you start to lose the rich connections between cells that maintain these functions.

For the brain, social information is as important as sensory signals

One of the most complex stimuli we respond to is the human face. One face is very complex; large groups of faces are many times more complex. Yet, humans need to be able to decode complex emotional and behavioural signals, within such groups, to survive.

So, during critical periods of early childhood and later adolescence key social experiences drive the development of the limbic circuitry, hardwiring us to read and respond in socially advantageous ways. This shapes behaviour that will later promote reproduction, tight emotional bonds within kinship groups and successful child rearing.

In early childhood, stimuli such as touch, smell, comfort, safety and facial expressions of key parenting figures drive the development of the emotional circuitry. Fascinating brain imaging studies that examine the amygdala's activity during adolescence indicate that it is no longer excited by its own kin, but by the social behaviours – notably facial expressions – of other adolescents!

When I was a medical student in the late 1970s, basic teaching about brain development and brain structure was very static. You were born with a certain brain capacity, and unless something major went wrong (a genetic variation that results in Downs syndrome, or severe birth trauma or head injury), the brain would develop along a rigid, genetically programmed timeline.

The result was that most of our brain's main motor and sensory functions are organised in early childhood, and then we rapidly acquired other cognitive and emotional skills pre-puberty. After that, not much to see (except for the impact of pubertal hormones) until it started to decline, degenerate or, at best, just slowed down in later life.

Now, the notion of the dynamic brain constantly rearranging itself, including its basic cellular elements, is a radical departure from that earlier thinking. This concept, now popularised as neuroplasticity, is a very attractive one – and clearly a major help when trying to change public perceptions about the inevitable decline that will follow any damage to the brain. In particular, it is critical to challenging the long-standing myth that brain-related conditions, including many mental illnesses, are intractable.

Which environmental stimuli are deeply encoded? Which ones can cause disease?

You might think that this radical new concept of neuroplasticity means it must be relatively easy to fix any major problem with the circuitry that has gone astray in disorders like clinical depression. Another level of this neuroplasticity relates not just to the cells and circuits, but also the underlying genetic code and, specifically, the way that its messages are turned on or off by the environment. To be even more radical, those environmental changes to the code may have happened to your parents or grandparents, and then they were transmitted across generations to you.

So, while the brain, and its underlying cellular structures and genetic code, may be constantly changing, it also has a large degree of permanence – just like many of our other basic physical characteristics. As with all other aspects of human development, if the environment has specific effects on the brain during critical developmental periods, then we may well expect that these are much harder to change.

When we start to think about the circuits that really matter to mental disorders like clinical depression, the ones that stand out are those that regulate brain development and repair (neuroplasticity – with very specific respect to immune responsiveness), stress-responsiveness (fronto-subcortical and their links to the HPA and SNS) and the circadian (24-hour sleep–wake) system.

It is very unlikely that environmental factors cause massive disruption to the functional capacity of any of these circuits (excepting in the most extreme circumstances, like massive head injury or severe brain infection). What's more likely is that earlier experiences set later levels of responses and stable patterns. It's like setting a temperature range for your home air-conditioning.

What are the upper and lower limits, and what do you do if you suddenly find yourself way outside those preset conditions? Any change here will affect how quickly you respond to a threatening event, how much anxiety you experience along with that threat, how capable you are of keeping your own fear under control while you take appropriate evasive or protective action.

So, the environmental changes that matters most are physical things that might seriously disrupt these well-established responses. The most obvious of these is the role of the 24-hour day–night light cycle and the way it regulates our sleep, activity and feeding patterns. When the external pattern is regular, most of our linked mental, behavioural, metabolic, hormonal and immune functions align with the external signal.

If the incoming signal is slowly changed (as in changing seasons), we slowly adapt without major disruption – unless we are vulnerable for other reasons. Being vulnerable here means being more fragile than others due to your own genetics, or because of your own behavioural patterns (working night shifts or other more chaotic forms of shift work) or because of other major disturbing events like childbirth (where the mother is typically forced into the infant's four-hour sleep and eating schedule).

If you are exposed to a one-off threatening situation, like an intruder in your house late at night, that elicits an immediate fear response – with its associated increased heart rate, breathing and sweating, signalled via the SNS, and increased cortisol release via the HPA – and if the situation is resolved quickly (it was your own son creeping in late in the dark), the initial set-point of the system will in all likelihood remain unaltered.

But there also may be a degree of sensitisation to any particular stimuli so that when approaching that threat again, the individual is already primed to respond. This is the case of learnt responses that become hardwired, if repeated often enough – just like Pavlov's dogs who learnt to salivate to the sound of a bell. So, if you re-enter a situation where you have previously been very afraid, you are likely to experience that fear response on exposure to any of the linked stimuli (the look, the sound, the smell), even if the actual threat never resurfaces. From an evolutionary perspective, it's good to be prepared.

Unfortunately, if the threat is repeated many times over, or is unending, or you are unable to escape, your hardwired stress response is soon overloaded. If this happens during childhood or early development, before all the set points have been put in place, you may never learn to respond appropriately. The brain becomes wired to respond in maladaptive ways – meaning over-responding, under-responding or not responding at all.

Reverberating circuits: the ones that just get stuck

Long before we had brain imaging to watch the brain in action, scientists and clinicians correctly hypothesised that a range of psychiatric disorders, like OCD, other chronic forms of anxiety, and some depressive disorders may be due to brain circuits getting stuck. These reverberating circuits – just going around and around, resulting in the same behaviour, thoughts and actions – are relatively impervious to outside signals to stop.

It's like the wheel of death on your laptop – once it's up, doing whatever it's actually doing in the background, you don't have any choice. It's time to reboot and hope you haven't lost whatever you were working on!

The concept was also applied to certain types of clinical depression, particularly those associated with severe ruminations, motor agitation (uncontrollable pacing), stereotyped motor behaviours (picking, scratching) or the sudden onset of obsessional thoughts (everything is infected) or compulsive behaviours (handwashing, checking doors or locks).

Ruminations – excessive and intrusive thoughts focused on very distressing or negative memories, beliefs or interpersonal experiences – are the most common. These are very distressing thoughts, often coloured by guilt, regret or remorse, that you just can't get out of your head.

The on–off problem – where's the switch?

For more than a century, psychiatrists have agreed that the best way to distinguish various major mood or psychotic disorders is to separate those that are largely unremitting versus those that are essentially cyclical (they come and go). The implication is that cyclical disorders, like clinical depression and bipolar disorder, must have some basic biological switch that can be triggered to turn the episode on or off.

These on–off switches can occur very rapidly, spontaneously, in response to treatment or in association with other environmental changes like the change of seasons – 'on' in autumn and then 'off' again in spring. A favourite practice in clinical psychiatry is to make sure you prescribe new treatments in spring when they are most likely to work!

So, as we think about circuits as being the underlying structural brain elements, we also need to explain how the activities of these circuits are turned on and then suddenly off again. For the three major paths that we track, only the one linked to the circadian system, which embraces seasonal changes, has a clear 'on–off' switch that is tied to the changes in the external environment.

There are other cyclical factors linked to these on–off phenomena. For post-pubertal and pre-menopausal females, the most obvious cycle is the normal monthly menstrual cycle. Conditions of that hormonal system (such as polycystic ovaries and endometriosis), commonly occur after puberty and are then also associated with the adolescent onset of clinical depression. Additionally, many women do experience changes in the severity of their clinical depression alongside the various phases of their menstrual cycle, with the premenstrual period often being most severe.

The circadian system: a model of on–off circuitry

Some circuits have more natural cycles, most notably the 24-hour sleep–wake or circadian (body-clock) system. We are all familiar with the fundamental switch between being awake and being asleep in a 24-hour cycle. So, normal sleep or normal activity turn on and off again each day. We are also well aware that the length of these periods varies across different seasons (shorter activity in winter, longer in the summer), with the greatest risks of onset of clinical depression being in the brief transitional (autumn) period between summer and winter.

For the circadian system, we do know that the major driver of the switch is light exposure, recognised through specialised light receptors in the retina at the back of the eye, which send a signal to the coordinating centre in the brain (the suprachiasmatic nucleus, SCN – see Figure 2 on page 220). The SCN is the conductor of a complex orchestra of hormones, chemicals and signals that, without tight central control, likes to wander off to play their own tune. Fascinatingly, none of those other complex body systems work to a 24-hour clock – so much for the 'intelligent design' of our basic physiology.

Not only does the SCN keep the time for all the other components, it drives the internal brain systems to release the natural sleep hormone melatonin after dark. There are other parts of this system, most notably the morning cortisol and afternoon orexin arousal systems to be kept in line with the signals being sent by the SCN. So for circadian systems, we do have a working model of where the neurobiological switch lies and some of the environmental factors that set its routines.

People who have very irregular day-to-day circadian cycles, or a preference for staying up late at night, or who oversleep (particularly during their teenage years) or frequently report that when they wake from sleep (independent of the duration of their sleep) they still feel very unrefreshed, are all at increased risk of having clinical depression. Regular strong patterns of sleep do help to protect against depression. For these people, it's likely that the SCN is doing a poor job of keeping the orchestra on the agreed tempo or even sometimes on the same melody.

For many people with clinical depression, it's likely that the circadian switch is faulty, being over-responsive to minor everyday changes in light or activity. Of more interest is the ways that some antidepressant medications may worsen the problem (like SSRIs), while others, such as melatonin-based agents, or mood stabilisers, like lithium carbonate, may help to keep this system under control (see Chapter 23).

As my Irish grandfather noted after migrating to Australia, and moving his family close to one of Sydney's most beautiful beaches, his mood was so good he was never going back to the cold and dark west coast of Ireland! He did attribute his strong sense of wellbeing to a daily coastal walk, sunlight, an invigorating morning swim in the surf, and then home to lunch and work.

The more we investigate what drives an optimal circadian system, and its linked metabolic, hormonal and immune cycles, the more we find that in humans it's the timing (and intensity) of light exposure that is really important. It's interesting that so much artistic representation of the experience of depression uses metaphors or images related to fading light, darkness or clouds descending.

So, what makes sensitivity to light exposure vary from one person to the next? Part of the answer is genetic. Given the very different conditions under which humans live and work, and that clinical depression occurs everywhere in the world despite the big differences in light exposure, it's not just a matter of how much daylight is out there.

It may be the case that being either too sensitive to light changes is a problem for some (consistent with theories that suggest that those experiencing depression actively avoid direct sunlight exposure), while for others it's their relative insensitivity to light that leads to low mood, low energy, overeating and low physical activity.

As with many aspects of the neurobiology of mood disorders, there may be individuals who are at either end of this spectrum, or it may be the case that light sensitivity actually changes – that is, it's different during the times when someone is depressed.

It's always amused me greatly that rodents have been used as the workhorse for animal models of depression, given they have the exact opposite response to the light–dark cycle as humans. When it gets dark they wake up, just as we are thinking about going to sleep! We conduct most animal experiments during the day, which would be the normal sleep period for rodents. It would be like waking us up at 3am and asking us to perform a whole set of new cognitive and motor tasks.

What role does the (neo)cortex, the thinking brain, play?

Humans are very different from most other species largely as a consequence of the size and sophistication of the cortical – the newer thinking – parts of our brain. These are the convoluted grey matter layers that cover the surface of the brain and are connected by various white matter cabling fibres to the older sub-cortical grey matter nuclei and the other elements of the limbic system.

Within the cortex, it's really the frontal lobes that underpin the marvellous cognitive and creative capacities we cherish – and make us feel so special or separated from all those other creatures on god's earth. Technically, neuropsychologists classify most of those features as executive functions – the higher-order and decision-making part of the whole organisation. When we are thinking, these are the areas where the lights are on.

For those who come from the business and corporate worlds this is the C-suite, the 'chief executive'. This is all about strategy. Complex planning. Predicting consequences. Integrating past experiences with new challenges. Holding back information, perceptions, opinions from those who may be hostile or not trusted. Shifting responses and changing preset ideas in response to new environmental contingencies. Making the right calls, at the right times and in the right settings. It's a heavy load.

For those who prefer more artistic comparisons, the frontal lobes are like the conductor of a very disorganised orchestra. Many sections, when left on their own, choose their own score, start to improvise and generally behave in chaotic and divergent ways. When persuaded to come together, operate in the same time sequences (echoing the circadian system) and focus on the greater good that can only be achieved by tightly coordinated and centrally controlled activity, fabulous experiences follow! The conductor doesn't actually make any sound – the output is entirely dependent on the actions of others. So it is with the prefrontal cortex.

Hierarchically in the brain, it seems appropriate that this section sits at the front (believing it is in the driver's seat) and on top of those cognitive, emotive, motor and physiological functions that the subcortical and more posterior parts of the cortex need to then operate and implement. It creates the illusion that conscious thought actually drives behaviour – that our behaviour, including our emotional responses, are premediated, well thought through, rational and commensurate with the environmental circumstances.

The brain actually matures, not so much by developing new pathways, but by strengthening its inhibitory connections. So, the real task of frontal lobe development is the maximisation of the stop button. That might be a pleasurable, funny, risky, thing to do – but now is the wrong place and wrong time, and others may be hurt or offended. The cortex is telling the sub-cortex, 'Yes, there is a time and place for pleasure – but not now!'

Certainly, when you knock out the frontal lobes, permanently through head injuries (it's the first part to hit the windscreen) or temporarily through substances like alcohol, you can see some of the ugly consequences. Disinhibition, loss of social awareness, impulsiveness, and loss of control over emotions like anger and sadness. Floods of tears interspersed with violent outbursts. Risk-taking and poor judgement become the order of the day. Pleasurable, and some would say more primitive drives – notably sex and food – become all-consuming.

When the frontal lobes are injured, the altered behavioural states that follow are not limited to unrestrained beer and skittles. Another common form is one of profound apathy, loss of motivation, and lack of engagement or responsiveness to the outside world.

The frontal lobes are, however, a very complex brain region with different functions being variously linked with different internal zones. From a behavioural perspective, it's those regions right at the front (prefrontal cortex) and two particular regions, the dorsolateral (off to the sides) and orbito-frontal zones that really matter. Both have extensive connections to other key brain regions, including the cerebellum, at the back of the brain.

An aside: make use of your cerebellum

The cerebellum is critical to the coordination of our very complex motor movements – like playing the piano or violin, touch-typing or maintaining our balance while running and simultaneously executing other motor tasks, like hitting a tennis ball. However, it also plays other roles in our broader cognitive and learning capacities and has complex feedback loops with the frontal lobes. It allows you to perform complicated motor tasks without having to concentrate. In fact, if you try to focus on the task ('Where is that "A" key on the keyboard?'), you'll mess it up!

If you want to distract yourself from the kinds of ruminative thoughts associated with anxiety or depression, head to the piano, pick up the violin, start typing, play tennis with friends. You'll find it helps to turn those other negative (including the DMN) circuits off!

The frontal lobes are the last part of the brain to reach maturity in humans. That process doesn't really get underway until after puberty, and continues on into early adult life. As males enter puberty later than females, for young men that process can continue well into their 20s. As I say to the parents of 16- to 18-year-old men in trouble, 'Don't worry, he still may grow a brain.'

From a purely evolutionary perspective, it is intriguing that humans reach physical and sexual maturity (usually by age 14 or 15) many years before our brains develop a real capacity for judgement, foresight or complex planning. It's not hard to understand why many cultures developed practices of arranged marriages and systems whereby complex relationship planning was left in the hands of much older adults. Very interestingly, many cultures delayed the transfer of full legal rights until the age of 21 years – much closer to the biological realities of brain development.

A good deal of the body's energy consumption is taken up by the brain, and when awake and concentrating, the frontal lobes take up more than their reasonable share of the available resources. Many neurobiological studies (brain pathology, brain imaging, neuropsychology) have focused on frontal lobe function in people with clinical depression.

One of the most curious early blood flow research experiments I worked on back in the 1990s involved having people lie in the dark – apparently not responding to external environmental cues – while we scanned their frontal lobes. People without depression typically had a great deal of activity in these areas, even though nothing was going on in the external world. Their minds were hard at work, even in the dark. Many of those with more severe depression had very little activity at all. The lights were on but nobody was home.

More elaborate studies of the brain, and the frontal lobes, have been conducted over the past 25 years, using elaborate new technologies. In those with more classical and severe depressions, where spontaneous thoughts and actions appear to be diminished and the person appears lost in their own world, the frontal lobe structures appear to be altered, their main functions are diminished, and the complexity of their connections are reduced. The C-suite has lost its usual capacity for smart or measured responses to environmental or cognitive challenges. It has become entirely internally focused.

In other types of depression, especially those in younger people with more significant anxiety and less severe depression, it has been suggested that overactivity in various prefrontal areas may be the more common finding. Clearly, the structure–function relationships are complicated, but we are on the way to unravelling these various paths.

Fronto-subcortical loops: chicken or the egg?

So, given there are critical loops between the thinking prefrontal cortex and the rest of the 'doing' brain, who sets off the dysfunctional activity between these key circuits?

Those who believe that the frontal cortex is driving the car really like the idea that dysfunctional thoughts are driving disturbed emotions. Those who assert that clinical depression is a rational response to environmental stressors also like to point the finger at the frontal cortex.

But some of us prefer the view that the subcortical parts, the doing brain, drive the car over the edge, and that the frontal cortex is actually a backseat driver, providing constant criticism.

While for some people dysfunctional thinking patterns do seem the likely culprit, for many others they do not persist once the episode of clinical depression has ended. That is, the dysfunctional thought patterns, being driven by the frontal cortex, are a consequence and not the cause of the depressive episode.

Late-onset depression: the exemplar of the subcortex in the driving seat

> I was having a drink with my old teacher – he's 102 now – he
> was about 97 at the time, and I poured him a drink.
> He clicked my glass and said, 'Excuse me for not dying!'
> – I kind of feel the same way . . .
>
> Leonard Cohen: introduction to 'Tower of Song',
> London 2008 concert

The importance of these new brain technologies in revolutionising our thinking about the neurobiological basis of many clinical mood disorders was highlighted for me almost 30 years ago by the case of a most elegant Spanish-speaking man, Gerardo. He was in his early 80s. He was brought to hospital by his wife and children who were at a complete loss to explain his sudden change in mood and behaviour.

Two weeks before, Gerardo had awoken and confessed to his wife that he believed he'd done terrible things to her and his children, and that he deserved to be punished. He wanted to die. Given his conservative background, and life-long Catholicism, he believed that he deserved punishment in this life and, very shortly, in the next. He was agitated, constantly pacing the floor, wringing his hands compulsively.

Gerardo's impending sense of doom was overwhelming. No amount of reassurance from his family had any impact. He was inconsolable and had stopped eating. Although he spoke softly and deliberately, Gerardo communicated his anguish mostly in non-verbal facial expressions and through his constant rocking motion when seated in a chair. He stopped responding to the warm embrace of his family. Their loving and caring husband and father appeared to have vacated his earthly form.

Gerardo closely resembled the figure in Van Gogh's 1890 painting 'Sorrowing Old Man (At Eternity's Gate)'. That painting is frequently used in clinical teaching and public discussion of mental illness to give visual life to the concept of 'total despair'. Van Gogh himself wrote, 'This is far from all theology – simply the fact that the poorest woodcutter, heath farmer or miner can have moments of emotion and mood that give him a sense of an eternal home that he is close to.'

There were no objective signs of a major change in Gerardo's brain function that might otherwise accompany a stroke or some other brain event. He could speak, walk, eat and respond in his usual manner, though, according to his family, at a much slower pace than usual. That slowing in the speed of thought, cognitive responses, speech and motor activity, interspersed with periods of intense psychic and motor agitation, has long been held to be characteristic of true melancholia or severe clinical depression, at any age.

So from a classical psychiatry perspective, Gerardo had a severe depressive illness, which had historically been referred to as 'involutional' melancholia (used to describe depression associated with ageing). As is typical of the field, the theories of its onset in older persons covered the usual spectrum from distinctly psychological (a failing of personality traits in older age), to being a simple variant of typical manic-depressive illness (now called bipolar disorder) in older persons, right across to more distinctly medical explanations, related to degenerative brain changes (i.e. dementia) in the elderly.

Before the advent of new brain imaging techniques, Gerardo would have been screened for a variety of possible primary medical disorders, which can accompany these types of unexpected disorders in older persons. But, with the arrival first of computerised tomography (CT) scanning of the brain in the 1970s and then MRI in the 1980s our capacity to look at the brain while a person is alive was a key development.

For clinical psychiatry, MRI has particular advantages. You can see the state of structures deep within the subcortical brain and the white matter cables that run between the various grey matter thinking regions.

In Gerardo's case, the MRI scan demonstrated a single discrete lesion in the sub-cortical region – an 'infarct', basically a water-filled hole. The most likely cause was a sudden loss of blood flow to this critical region – in other words a very small stroke.

Due to his very rapid deterioration, Gerardo and his family agreed to a course of electroconvulsive therapy. Fortunately, he responded quickly and soon made a full recovery. Gerardo walked out of the hospital, upright, with a spring in his step and in locked arms with his wife. His smile was warm and his handshake strong. Some 30 years later, Gerardo's daughter came up to me at a public event, to tell me that her father then went on to live a fulfilling life.

When retelling Gerardo's story, I often show Van Gogh's painting alongside a drawing from a children's book I acquired in the US. It, too, depicts an older man, sitting alone beside a window, with a rundown, damp and grey cityscape visible in the background. The story outlines how the old man's son and grandchildren have moved away to the country, leaving him tired and despondent. The son decides to come back and take his father with the rest of the family, resulting immediately in a return of his normal smiling face, sunshine outside, and the scene is filled with bright colours. So many of our stereotypic myths about depression, ageing, social stressors and approaches to care are captured in that one children's story.

By contrast, Gerardo's real life story is rarely told. It challenges pre-existing and enduring myths about the relationships between ageing and depression, and the role of physical health factors that we often can't see.

Default mode network: new ways of watching very old brain circuits

As outlined earlier, new brain imaging techniques now allow us to watch what various brain circuits are really up to as they go about their daily tasks. Much attention in depression research has been focused on the behaviour of the 'default mode network (DMN)'. It appears to be a network that is most active when you are doing nothing at all. So, engaging in very active and goal-directed behaviours turns the central executive network up, while turning the DMN down. Consequently, it may be one of the most effective ways (along with mindfulness and meditation) of breaking out of the inner cycles of anxiety, depression and ruminative thinking. I'm reminded again of the saying, 'We don't get well to go to work, we go to work to get well!'

Hypothalamic-pituitary-adrenal axis: the stress-response system

In previous decades, the best method for studying disturbances in brain function in clinical depression was to backtrack through one of its natural windows, namely the hypothalamic-pituitary-adrenal axis (HPA). The hypothalamus is part of the brain, a rich collection of nerve cells clustered into highly specialised sub-nuclei, receiving signals from many other brain regions.

Most importantly, the hypothalamus links directly to the pituitary gland. It has two parts, with the anterior pituitary being the master regulator of the body's major hormone-producing glands (the thyroid, adrenals, ovaries, testes), while the posterior pituitary regulates two major hormones: oxytocin (for breastfeeding, but also a key regulator of social behaviour within the brain) and anti-diuretic hormone (which regulates water levels within the body).

It's been known for decades that clinical depression is associated with an abnormal release of the stress-response hormones (corticosteroids and adrenaline) and that the source of this dysregulation wasn't the adrenal glands themselves, but rather the brain's regulation of the HPA.

In people with severe depression, the daily pattern of cortisol release (which is normally high early in the morning and then falls towards midday) is perturbed. It remains abnormally high throughout the late morning period, not responding to the normal 24-hour cycle, as if continuing to prime the body to sustain its stress response. This puts the body on continued high alert even when there is no obvious reason.

High cortisol states, usually in response to infection or injury, are normally shut down soon after they are turned on. The anxious-arousal form of depression makes the assumption that whatever the environmental trigger, the body has tripped into some form of ongoing but inappropriate stress-response. This prolonged response does damage to the body, and potentially the brain, over time.

Much debate has followed as to the various levels at which this feedback-driven system was failing, but the basic problem remained. The system was overactive and causing further damage. The extent to which this overactivity only occurs during the episode of illness, is a pre-existing vulnerability, or is a long-term consequence of ongoing illness, remains largely unresolved.

One new take on all this is that the HPA-axis abnormalities do not relate to any particular adult diagnosis, but rather represent a specific example of a gene-environment interaction – namely, the long-term impact of childhood trauma. From this perspective, the adverse environment caused damages to this most fundamental regulatory system, and its consequences include things like suicidal behaviour, earlier age of onset of depression and resistance to treatments.

The debate about inappropriate function of the HPA axis (too much or too little cortisol), in response to either environmental impacts in childhood (childhood abuse) or later in adolescence (sexual assault or physical violence) or adult life (war veterans, domestic violence in marital relationships), lies at the heart of the pathway by which too much stress makes us physically sick.

But two other questions arise. First, what has gone amiss upstream – meaning at or above the hypothalamus (in the brain) – to precipitate this ongoing dysfunction? And, second, how does this system turn itself on and off to match the cyclical nature of the clinical illness?

On the first question, it's likely that upstream dysfunction, specifically in the fronto-subcortical circuits, results in downstream effects on the hypothalamus. So, the HPA is not responding normally because the upstream brain signals are off.

For the on–off question, it's more complicated. This stress-response system normally comes on in the face of specific environmental events. Most importantly, from the perspective of clinical depression these are not often one-off major life events but more prolonged stressful and unresolved life circumstances – dysfunctional marital relationship, chronic unemployment, prolonged and disabling physical illness. The cumulative effect of this prolonged stress overwhelms the otherwise short-term arousal and stress response. This would then constitute the 'on' mechanism – the dam wall breaks, and the flood of downstream physiological disruptions follows, mediated by the HPA.

But how does it turn off again? Before the advent of modern treatments, more severe episodes lasted months to years. For less severe episodes, spontaneous recovery certainly occurs, and the time frame of episodes is quite variable. One suggestion is that when younger, the episodes are shorter but with progression over time they become more prolonged and less prone to recovery. In other words, there is a loss of resilience over time – meaning the inability to spring back to normal after a negative event.

Another suggestion is that chronic illness leads to a resetting of the threshold (up or down) for normal functioning. Humans learn to adapt to the most amazing environmental stressors. Even when faced with major acute or chronic stressors, the *majority* of us do not develop an anxiety, depressive or post-traumatic disorder.

To pick up the theme from earlier, the fact that we get distressed (or overwhelmingly stressed) is not so interesting compared with how quickly most people recover. So for these stress-response disorders, where spontaneous recovery occurs, we assume that the internal threshold has been down-regulated to cope better with the new external realities.

New attempts to turn the prolonged stress-response and the dysregulated HPA-axis mechanisms off

The assumption that the relationship between the prolonged stress response and clinical depression is driven by HPA-axis dysfunction has driven decades of research that targets this pathway. Most of this research was focused on the assumption that the hypothalamus produced too much Corticotrophin Releasing Hormone (CRH), which is a hormone that helps stimulate the release of other stress hormones.

The most famous – and now failed – example of this approach was the development of new medicines to block the hypothalamic signal to the pituitary gland – namely, CRH-1 receptor antagonists. If the hypothalamus is driving the pituitary to produce too much cortisol and, as a consequence of prolonged production the feedback loops are dysfunctional, turning down the whole system would have major therapeutic effects – at least in theory.

After a series of basic science and clinical studies, the bottom line is that CRH-1 receptor antagonists just don't work. As has happened many times before, great in theory but below average in practice.

Non-specific ways to reduce inappropriate and prolonged HPA activity

Importantly, non-specific medical therapies (anxiolytics like benzodiazepines), other antidepressants (notably SSRIs, but also older tricyclic antidepressants), most psychological therapies and other effective self-care interventions like yoga, meditation and mindfulness all target reduction of these stress-arousal systems – but at those circuit levels, especially fronto-subcortical, that sit above the HPA axis.

Other new approaches to reducing unwanted arousal: does oxytocin have a place?

Humans rely heavily on social group cues to moderate their own stress-arousal responses. If everyone around you panics, you're also more likely to panic. If the social group pulls together and mounts an effective, or at least purposeful, response to adversity, then individual arousal is much reduced. We are just not that good on our own.

So, how can we make use of that social effect? One way is by promoting group rather than individual behaviours to reduce stress-responses. Interestingly, one can also think about that in biochemical ways. The hormone oxytocin not only facilitates the release of breastmilk but plays an essential role in reinforcing the importance of close social relationships – not just between mother and infant – but also very much between intimate adults. It has been investigated for its anti-anxiety effects and has been proposed as an adjunctive treatment for depression.

Is brain neurogenesis the answer? (Although, what is the question?)

It is commonly suggested that impaired brain repair mechanisms (neurogenesis or neuroplasticity) are at the heart of prolonged or treatment-resistant depression. That is, after being destabilised by the environment, and the brain circuits having been disrupted by the onset of the depression, if these systems are not operative then the brain can't turn the process off. This line of thinking is driven by brain imaging studies that demonstrate progressive loss of brain cell connections in association with the duration and severity of illness, and the positive effects of treatments on restoring those connections.

Perhaps the immune-inflammatory response is driving the car?

I was attending a medical science meeting in the US three years ago when a bright young scientist (the people who do the hard lab work) came up to me. She was working in the captivating new field of 'psychoimmunology' and was very excited about it. She asked if I had heard much about it and whether it was influencing our work.

I remarked that many of my colleagues had made major contributions to the field in the late 1970s and early 1980s.

So, the candidate in much discussion of what is driving disruption of brain circuits in clinical depression may well be an old candidate with a new face! It's the activated immune system. When your immune system is turned on elsewhere in the body (in response to infection) you see inflammation – which is an acute immune storm, designed to kill the bug (though it may kill you in the process).

The local immune response is not only accompanied by pain, swelling and redness at the site of infection, but also by acute illness behaviour: fever, loss of appetite, sleepiness, low energy, widespread aches and pains, and general malaise. Observe a young child with a viral illness or watch your pet dog when they get sick – they do the same thing: lie down, be quiet, stop eating and go to sleep. Interestingly, their cognitive functions also slow down, along with their motor behaviours. Parents of young children will also be aware of the irritability that may accompany the state.

Most adults who have had a severe viral infection are well aware of these whole-body and brain effects. This behavioural pattern, which had been described for centuries, was much more actively documented in the late 20th century. These included situations where the immune system was activated (in response to chemotherapy or radiotherapy for cancer) or where new immune therapies were being used to treat chronic infections like hepatitis or other inflammatory conditions (like arthritis). They also included situations very close to my own research interests, namely post-infection, and particularly post-viral fatigue and other depression-like states.

Those with an active interest in clinical depression also recognised the very close similarities between the behavioural characteristics presented in these specific situations and clinical depression. These overlaps were of great interest because of the long-noted associations between autoimmune diseases and clinical depression.

The stereotyped responses that occurred across species (fever, reduced motor activity, slowed movement, increased sleep, reduced feeding) are actually triggered by chemicals (the pro-inflammatory cytokines, with great names like 'tumour necrosis factor') released by activated immune cells (which also have great names like 'natural killer cells') that then circle back to the brain. When active in the brain, they induce these complex behavioural and whole-body changes. In this situation the brain itself is not inflamed. It's simply responding to feedback signals from elsewhere in the body.

Only recently did we find out that the brain does receive active immune signals from the periphery, and immune chemicals are a normal part of the biochemical repertoire that brain cells (and glial cells) use to communicate. Of particular importance is the extent to which immune cells are highly responsive to the external environment. In other words, they constitute a major pathway by which external signals become incorporated into brain chemistry, and then the way that leads to secondary changes in brain structures – including those circuits that regulate mood and cognition. As a result, new immune therapies are being explored as potential antidepressant medicines.

So whatever happened to the monoamine theories, like serotonin imbalance or deficiency?

When discussing the neurobiology of depression, from a circuit or trajectory perspective, you may have noticed a distinct lack of emphasis on basic biochemical theories. Chemical elements are the common signalling mechanism between nerve cells and include classical elements like the monoamines (serotonin, noradrenaline and dopamine) but also other novel factors like a range of chemicals produced by activated immune cells.

Pharmaceuticals have been the hallmark of major advances in clinical medicine (as distinct from surgery) – think antibiotics, anti-inflammatories, immune therapies, analgesics and pain relief, chemotherapies, medicines that treat heart failure or correct abnormal heartbeats, blood-thinning agents for life-threatening blockages of blood vessels. In most instances, the treatments have only an indirect relationship with the cause of the problem. Rarely does the body have a shortage of these things, and they certainly do not go back in time and fix the precipitant to the illness. Only very rarely are they truly curative.

Essentially, they are pragmatic. They relieve symptoms. They shorten the length of illness. They save lives. They reduce disability. They allow people to get on with their lives – even if the illness (and its daily impacts) is not entirely contained. Most real treatments have side-effects, short- and long-term. They target key regulatory pathways – just like the brain circuits that underpin clinical depression.

However, the monoamines (serotonin, noradrenaline and dopamine) have occupied a very special place for the last 50 years in the theories of the causes of clinical depression. The bedrock of this prolonged preoccupation has been their therapeutic benefit. Medicines that increase the concentration of one or more of these signalling factors between nerve cells – the literal chemical space between one nerve cell and the next – relieve depression. Those serotonin-based compounds appear particularly good for anxiety, obsessions, ruminations, and mood; the noradrenergic compounds for anxiety and energy; and the dopaminergic compounds for motor activation, energy and pleasure.

Additionally, a variety of monoamine depletion experiments, in humans and animals, had suggested that if the brain was drained of the relevant chemicals – of serotonin for mood-related functions and dopamine for movement-related functions such as Parkinson's disease – one could induce the symptoms that were characteristic of clinical depression.

This preoccupation with the role of the monoamines, especially serotonin, reached its peak in the early 2000s with the publication of research that genetic variations in the serotonin transporter gene interacted specifically with life-stressors to *cause* major depressive disorders (see Chapter 12). Only problem was the gene-environment interaction didn't stand up to further detailed scrutiny.

Since then, many brain imaging, pharmacological, and brain tissues studies have continued to try to understand the ways in which these key chemicals interact with the key circuits (limbic, circadian, fronto-subcortical) to regulate their basic functions – and how they turn clinical depression off.

A cautionary note relates to the price paid for regulating these pathways. While serotonin-based strategies turn down an overreactive system, they appear to have the opposite effect on sensitivity to light signals in the equally important circadian system. This leads to more disturbed 24-hour sleep–wake cycles and greater destabilisation of all of its linked systems (eating, metabolic, immune, hormonal). Therefore, while serotonin-based strategies are a good option for those with anxious-arousal type disorders, for those with more circadian-type clinical depression, they are generally problematic.

Do all drugs have a common target or at least a small number of relevant targets?

The neurobiological question that is often asked is whether the many therapeutic options (medicines, physical treatments, psychological therapies) all target the same brain regions – despite the fact that they were often designed for quite different purposes.

A good example of this relates to neurogenesis – the rebirth of new nerve cell connections (or even new nerve cells in key regions like the hippocampus). It appears that all effective treatments do induce new nerve cell connections. From this perspective, the true therapeutic effect of any antidepressant strategy may rely on its capacity to promote long-term structural changes in the brain (and its emotional circuitry) and not rapid changes in chemical concentrations of things like serotonin.

An evolutionary perspective on depression

A new area of interest in psychological and neurobiological theorising about the experience of depression is an attempt to view it through an evolutionary perspective. What advantage could it have to human survival to retain this distressing emotional and behavioural response, given that it so often leads to premature loss of life and disability?

The simplest explanation is that it's an in-built, brain-controlled, emotional and behavioural response, just like pain. As with acute pain, depression is evoked in response to harmful environmental challenges (probably in relationships) and signals the need to withdraw from a toxic or chronically distressing interpersonal situation.

But just like pain (or its close cousin, grief), that doesn't mean we think it's a great thing to experience – or that we might not make use of modern methods to prevent it. Just imagine dental procedures, accidents and injuries – or major surgery – in the pre-anaesthetic era! And the relief when treatments became available to address chronic or disabling pain. It's very hard to function if you have chronic pain. Similarly, it's very hard to engage with the world if you are chronically depressed.

Another more 'normative' view is that depression is just one of many emotional responses that are hardwired in our brains – like fear, anger, sadness, grief, joy and elation. This emotional range is critical to maintaining our relationships with other humans in our social group, and particularly important to the protection of our vulnerable offspring. They signal to others in our group how we really are on the inside, before and beyond the development of any verbal capacity. They inform those close to us what we need them to do in response. Humans without such emotional forms of social communication just couldn't maintain the social groups that have ensured our survival.

Depressed mood, sadness and tears may also inform us about how we really are, typically overriding our more rational explanations or our active denial of our own distress. Sometimes it's really important to stop, withdraw, take stock and reflect. We can't run on adrenaline and overactivity all the time. Our normal stress responses need to take time out and recoup – that's as much to promote our physiological and brain recovery as it is to take time out psychologically.

Another particular form of depression, the atypical type characterised by loss of pleasure, low energy, more sleep and weight gain (particularly likely to come on in autumn and end in spring) is clearly close to the hibernation states in other mammals. Lots of other highly evolved species also have other strong seasonal patterns of complex behaviours like migration (e.g. birds, whales) or reproduction. So, it's likely that some of these episodic behavioural changes that make us more or less active, more or less socially engaged, more or less engaged with food or sex, had survival advantages for many of our close animal relatives, and that propensity has been preserved in us as in many other species.

As discussed earlier, one of the most basic survival tools for every species on this planet is effective adaptation to the 24-hour light–dark cycle imposed by the daily rotation of the earth. Humans, having evolved to be diurnal mammals, are active during daylight and relatively inactive or asleep at night. Much of my own research is now directed to unravelling whether it's a genetically inherited or environmentally determined breakdown in that normal adaptive cycle that gives rise to a broader range of mood and other health disorders, including atypical depression, bipolar disorder and prolonged fatigue disorders.

This general line of discourse, about the evolutionary history of depression and other emotional states, however, is often used to argue that there is no legitimate role for treatments in moderating its depth or consequences. This goes as far as suggesting that many children, and most notably teenagers at the peak ages of onset, should be left to experience whatever distress or harm may result. ('Just let the children cry.') This is what is required to foster normal personal and social development. It's a view that also fundamentally rejects that depression may exist as an 'illness state', well beyond being at the end of a spectrum of negative emotional states.

In truth, many illness states are the result of some normal body system that is critical to survival or reproduction breaking down or no longer responding to the usual control mechanisms. If your immune system mounts a tsunami-level response to COVID-19, it's much more likely to kill you and not the virus. In such a circumstance, we are fairly comfortable making the key distinction between a normal healthy response and a life-threatening illness. Many effective treatments for infection, or other immune disorders where the immune cells attack your own body, use medications that turn down that essential response quickly.

All body cells have a normal turnover process, which uses in-built mechanisms to program their own timely death. If this normal process goes astray (or if other aspects of this normal cell replacement program go astray) cancer may result. Again, there is no real argument that at some point the 'normal' process is an illness with life-threatening potential. So, while depressive emotions and behaviour may be hardwired into humans, that doesn't mean the process can't deviate so far physiologically and psychologically from normal as to constitute a legitimate illness – and one that benefits from active clinical interventions.

For those of us who work with people confronted by life-threatening or chronically disabling depression, this view would be rather academic if it didn't potentially do more harm than good. If someone says to you that your depression is just a normal, adaptive response, in-built by evolution to promote your survival, feel free to challenge their assumptions. In fact, if evolution were left to take its course, and was combined with a lack of modern medical interventions, most of us would be dead long before our 30th birthday.

TAKE-OUT TIPS

- Emotions, not thoughts, are in the driver's seat. They react to threat first. Thinking is slow and comes later.
- While challenging dysfunctional thought patterns is, for some, a productive treatment strategy, it's not thoughts that are driving the problem.
- Engaging in specific, focused tasks turns various parts of the brain associated with anxiety and depression down!
- In the end, restoration of normal brain cell connections may lie at the heart of effective treatments for depression.
- New strategies, including those that target the immune system, are under development.

15

The Health (And Death) Consequences of Depression

The two most important reasons to treat clinical depression are to relieve distress and anguish, and prevent loss of life due to suicide or other accidents and injuries. Another much under-appreciated aspect of providing earlier and more effective treatment is to improve physical health.

A landmark study from a huge population-based study of 1,487,964 people who were born in Sweden between 1982 and 1996 reported the massive impact of youth depression not only on premature death but also on the onset of many other medical conditions. The study compared those who were diagnosed with depression between ages 5 and 19 years with those who were not depressed, and then followed up the participants between ages 17 and 31 years.

The bottom line was an increased risk of many other illnesses, including autoimmune, neurological, hormonal, metabolic and sleep disorders, infection, and heart and lung problems. The risk of premature death from all causes was increased by six times, the risk of suicide by 14.6 times.

So, next time someone – in the general public, media or health professions – suggests that young people (particularly those with more severe depression) don't really require assertive medical and psychological care, you may wish to bring these confronting statistics to their attention.

Previously, I went to some length to emphasise that people with clinical depression are very sick physically and that they're at much greater risk of developing other major medical conditions in mid- and later-life, most notably heart disease, metabolic diseases and, eventually, dementia.

So, what is going on that drives such bigger risks of other medical conditions?

If your most important regulatory systems (hypothalamic-pituitary adrenal axis, sympathetic nervous system, metabolic, hormonal, immune and circadian) are poorly synchronised with each other and either persistently over-responding or under-responding to everyday environmental stimuli, you may not be surprised to know you're predisposed to a wide range of other life-threatening conditions. For those who say that the problem is all in your mind, and not in your body, you may wish to bring these basic body facts to their attention.

The awareness of this intimate and direct impact of mental ill health on physical health has been recognised since the earliest days of medical science. What is more intriguing, and very hard to explain is why this obvious link ever got lost. Possibly, two major factors are at work. One is the continued drift of clinical psychiatry away from its original base in clinical medicine into general psychology. Psychiatrists used to work closely in big hospitals with people who had epilepsy, brain infections, failed adrenal glands, cancers and heart or lung failure, which were all associated with major behavioural and cognitive changes – most commonly, clinical depression.

The other is the increased super-specialisation in clinical medicine. As each area has become more preoccupied with the most reductionist elements of each body organ, cavity or system, the interconnections between those systems – and the fact that they are all part of the one larger organism, which then inhabits a complex social and physical world – is not widely appreciated. Perhaps because practical advances in brain science have not kept pace with advances in other areas such as cancer, infection and immunology, the central organising and coordinating role of the brain has also fallen away from view.

In my time in medicine, it has been a pleasure to work with other great physicians, notably in immunology and infectious diseases, as they've never constrained their interests to one body organ or one cavity. It's the nature of infection, and immune activation, that when affected, the whole body is sick – the illness is systemic and only rarely local. The fact that the brain is intimately engaged is no surprise to them.

Sitting with a young psychiatrist recently, I asked, 'So what do you say to physicians you consult about the medical problems experienced by your patients with severe mood disorders?'

He replied, 'I ask their opinion whether the other medical condition is the cause of the psychiatric condition.'

I enquired, 'Do you think that there is often a simple answer to that question? And is it really the right question to be asking?'

By this I mean that by the time a person with clinical depression has one or more major medical problems, the real issue is not necessarily whether one is causing the other but rather: how are we best going to manage the total combination of life-threatening or disabling conditions?

Premature cardiovascular disease is the big killer

People with clinical depression are very likely to be at high risk of premature cardiovascular disease via a large variety of internal and external (lifestyle) factors. For internal, think things happening inside the body systems, like excessive overstimulation of the SNS. In a study led some years ago by my colleagues in Melbourne, they recorded noradrenaline surges in the blood of people with clinical depression (via tubes that reached right to the source in the heart). These surges were so extreme that even the cardiologists were shocked. When people say you can't die from a heart attack while having a panic attack, or during a clinical depressive episode, I'm here to tell you that you can (due to the spasm in those arteries to the heart).

For external (lifestyle) factors, think high rates of smoking, obesity, reduced physical activity, complications of medical treatments and lack of access to timely medical care. Our goal should be to reduce all of the relevant contributing factors and manage *both* the clinical depression and the increased risk to heart disease.

While attending a meeting with cardiology colleagues a while back, I was being very defensive about the possible metabolic side-effects of the medications we prescribe – things like increasing weight or early onset of diabetes. One of my colleagues, who had seen the direct results of mental illness in his own family and the benefits of expert mental health care, just laughed.

He said, 'Come on, Ian! First, you should focus on keeping people alive and helping them to recover – then we can all contribute to keeping them well after that. Compared with other areas of medicine, your interventions aren't even close to causing the serious harm (diabetes, liver toxicity, heart failure) we see in other fields.' Reassuring and direct advice. Though my colleague does spend far less of every day responding to the negative media about the real value of the heart treatments he prescribes!

My colleague is not unusual. I've had the great pleasure of working with the National Heart Foundation of Australia over the last two decades. They've always reaffirmed that clinical depression, along with social isolation, are major risk factors to coronary heart disease and premature death. The hardcore sceptics are in psychological and social medicine, not cardiology.

Many other metabolic and immune-related diseases co-occur with depression

Along with cardiovascular diseases, many other conditions but most prominently metabolic diseases (insulin resistance and diabetes) and immune-related diseases (of the skin, thyroid, veins, brain, kidney and musculoskeletal system) can co-occur with depression. There is a chicken-and-egg question here. Is one causing the other or are they both due to the same (but hidden) underlying factor?

Importantly, all these associations were noted long before the arrival of our new medicines or their widespread prescription. But often that medical fact is presented to little avail. If we can simply blame the new antidepressant drugs, then you can be sure that the negative emphasis will be the focus of much public commentary.

In response, I'm tempted to get really direct: 'Just which condition do you want to die of first? It's going to be depression, long before diabetes or heart disease. Please tell me so I can ignore treating your depression now and just focus on preventing a heart attack in thirty years' time, assuming you'll still be here.'

The reality of course is that if we neglect the depression now, we're ignoring what is really life-threatening. But if we also ignore the other long-term risks then we're not doing the best we can do for the person with depression. So, I treat the urgent one (depression) now, and do my best to minimise the chance that that treatment does significant long-term harm.

Circadian system: is this the real underlying cause?

In recent times the question of which brain-based system might really constitute the main hidden reason a person is at much increased risk of clinical depression, *and* also obesity, diabetes and premature cardiovascular disease, has focused on circadian dysfunction – your 24-hour sleep–wake cycle (or 'body clock').

Circadian medicine has become a very fashionable area of medical research and multifaceted whole-body medicine. The awarding of a Nobel Prize in 2017 to the scientists who described the basic molecular mechanisms of the brain clock certainly helped bring it to very public attention.

There are good reasons to believe that it is the central regulator of most of your basic body and behavioural activities over each 24-hour period. It's the thing that gets you up in daylight, provides energy during the day, tells you when you are hungry or tired and ensures you go to sleep in darkness. When it's disturbed over long periods, it might help explain a large increase in risk of depression *and* premature mortality from other physical health problems.

Fortunately, the optimal preventive measures are readily available. They include daily physical activity, light exposure, reduced weight, regular sleep–wake cycles and ceasing smoking. To those we can add other medical or behavioural treatments specific to your own circumstances.

In those with markedly increased risk, treatments that target the circadian system directly (like melatonin-based antidepressants) may be preferable to those which inadvertently disrupt that system (like SSRIs).

Smoking

The one big factor that really matters in reducing the long-term health consequences of depression, particularly the increased risk of premature death, is quitting smoking. Those with depression smoke daily at much higher rates, at all ages, than their non-depressed compatriots. The young people we see presenting for care already have much higher rates of smoking than their age-matched peers. The recent surge in vaping in Australia is pushing up smoking rates in those same young people. Older people with depression who smoke daily have often tried unsuccessfully on many previous occasions to quit smoking.

The evidence that smoking causes depression, along with many other physical health problems, continues to rise and be supported by very sophisticated statistical techniques like Mendelian randomisation (see Chapter 10). There's a range of theories as to how smoking increases the risk of depression, particularly as you age.

One obvious pathway is the damaging effect of smoking on both the large and small blood vessels that deliver oxygen to your brain. With modern brain imaging techniques, we can see more clearly how much damage is being done, especially to those who have smoked daily from a young age. Where chronic smoking has damaged the lungs so that less oxygen is getting into the blood and being delivered around the body, the brain is especially at risk. Nerve cells, and specific parts of the emotional circuitry, like the hippocampus (see Chapter 14) are sensitive to low oxygen ('hypoxia'). Smoking is also associated with increased evidence of inflammation throughout the body, and it's now recognised that such immune-mediated changes impact on the brain to increase your chances of developing depression.

On the other side of the coin, does being depressed drive people to smoke or to find it very hard to quit? Again, new statistical approaches support the theory that depression causes people to smoke. For quitting, the story is somewhat different. Many people with depression do quit, especially when strongly encouraged to do so by their families or health care professionals. However, many also report that they have tried on multiple occasions but have found it very difficult to cope with the heightened anxiety and agitation during the initial withdrawal period. Common anti-depressants (such as bupropion, which increases dopamine) have been used to help reduce craving.

While the relationship between clinical depression and smoking is complex, and varies by age and other factors, it must remain our highest collective priority to stop young people taking up smoking and assist those who are depressed and continue to smoke, to quit. That is, if we really want to reduce premature mortality from physical health causes among those with clinical depression.

So, the sequence is fairly clear. Provide accurate information about the medical risks and keep treating the depression. Encourage every active attempt to quit – with or without additional nicotine replacement. If relevant, consider using medical therapies (i.e. bupropion, or varenicline, which blocks nicotine in the brain) that may help to reduce craving during the hardest early phases of quitting.

Of greatest importance, however, is the agreed partnership between the clinicians involved and the person with depression and their family to manage these significant physical and mental health risks, together.

Sometimes, we just forget what's really important to the people we assist. One of our most vocal advocates for youth mental health caused me considerable embarrassment in a national mental health meeting when she exclaimed loudly, 'Ian, I've been going to one or another of your youth clinics for seven years now, and no one has ever offered to help me stop smoking!'

As the son of a professor of cardiology, and sometimes fierce anti-smoking advocate, it was a major red face for me.

But she was right. We were always so focused on managing her major mental health problems that this other major threat to her life had largely been ignored – or maybe we just assumed it was someone else's problem.

16

Vaccines and the Future of Clinical Depression

Is there any medical issue more discussed in the COVID-19 era than the rapid development of an effective and safe vaccine? Vaccines are such powerful tools. They stand as live monuments to the success of modern science. They prevent disease onset, prolong life and reduce unnecessary disability and suffering.

To the great majority of people, and certainly those who have ever lived with the ravages of unrestrained epidemics, there is no argument that we wish to be rid of smallpox, polio, measles and tuberculosis for good. Though incredibly difficult, the challenge of developing new vaccines for illnesses like malaria and HIV/AIDS remained a global priority. The pursuit is not controversial. These are the conditions in which prevention is obviously a far superior option to treatment.

Some years ago, I was involved in an academic debate about whether we should be striving for a vaccine for major mental and developmental disorders. The range of conditions that were raised as examples included autism, schizophrenia, drug addiction and major depression.

The proponents of such a medically focused approach were principally in the US and strongly linked with major advances in basic and developmental sciences. In such settings, these scientists were less focused on other possible public health or non-medical alternatives.

It might seem fanciful, but the possibility of one or more biomedical and highly targeted vaccines is a science-possible not science-fiction concept. For each of the major pathways to autism, schizophrenia, clinical depression or drug addiction, putting a block in the right brain circuit, especially in those known to be at high genetic risk, could prevent onset or recurrence of the condition. We do know blocking dopamine release in subcortical structures of the brain does stop the symptoms of psychotic disorders like schizophrenia. So, we could target that chemical pathway before the illness ever happens.

We also know a great deal about the reward-based circuitry that underpins drug addiction, and so we could disrupt or permanently block those paths. We know the stress-arousal circuits that underpin anxiety and depression. We could focus on reducing or blocking activation of that system in response to threatening environmental cues.

The issue of disrupting brain circuits has progressed considerably in other areas of neurology and neurosurgery – most notably in the treatment of Parkinson's disease. While this is not being done as a preventive measure, it is certainly now a common therapeutic option.

Even though a Nobel Prize was awarded in 1949 to Portuguese neurologist António Egas Moniz for developing brain surgery for major psychiatric disorders (Moniz is also credited with inventing methods to visualise blood vessels in the brain), the history of psychosurgery in clinical psychiatry is typically a bad one (remember *One Flew Over the Cuckoo's Nest*?). This was largely due to its widespread, poorly regulated and often inappropriate use from the 1940s right through to the late 1960s.

In recent years, with the advent of more targeted neurosurgical techniques (basically the same as those being used to treat Parkinson's disease), and because the surgery does not involve destruction of brain tissue, there is much interest in using new brain stimulation technologies to treat severe and refractory clinical depression.

Is illness eradication where we are headed?

The vaccine debate forced all involved to think more deeply about illness eradication and its broader social and personal implications. When narrowly defined, and limited to the most severe examples that were associated with shortened lives and persistent disability, most clinicians tended to agree that eradication should be the goal – although whether vaccination was the best method was then hotly debated.

For the prevention of drug addiction and major depression, where exposure to major environmental risk factors (such as substance availability, childhood sexual and physical abuse) could be managed in other ways, many people are attracted to less intrusive – and non-medical, public-health type options.

But the debate also raised more complex issues for mental disorders. If we had strategies to eradicate these conditions, would we be destroying or diminishing some core element of our own humanity – diverse, valuable and alternative ways of thinking and feeling? This includes phenomena that are not just linked with psychotic experiences or melancholic states but may also be linked with altered states of consciousness, personal sensitivity, creativity or emotionality.

Some very romantic notions of mental illness, as simply being welcome extensions of the human condition have a long tradition, not only in clinical psychiatry but across the humanities, creative arts, literature and normative psychology.

Within these perspectives, there is also the opportunity now for an emphasis on greater inclusiveness and confrontation of discrimination. Rather than seeking to eradicate those who are 'deviant' or 'eccentric', we should be constantly expanding our notions of 'normality' to include those who think, feel and behave in ways that are different from the majority.

Linked to these cultural and social traditions is the idea that evolution has selectively preserved these disorders, assuming they impart some particular advantage to our species. Another commonly expressed view is that suffering of this type enriches personal experiences, creating unexpected opportunities for personal growth and deeper insights into the true nature of being human.

At the extreme end of these views are those who favour the notion of eternal redemption through suffering. Maximum suffering in this life as the necessary rite of passage to a better afterlife.

There is no doubt we are all very uncomfortable with the concept of meaningless suffering. As with other areas of 'effort after meaning' (see Chapter 11), we are drawn to attach personal and collective significance to these confronting aspects of our lives. Whether that significance justifies the suffering, or hinders legitimate attempts to reduce the impacts of such suffering is, in my view, quite a different question.

In reality, most clinicians are not very attracted to any of these evolutionary, romantic, sadomasochistic, religious, existential or philosophical propositions. They are not in favour of simply preserving these conditions. In my experience, neither are those people who have actually lived through these life-threatening and very distressing disorders. That's not to say, as with the lived experiences of others with life-threatening, disabling or chronic diseases, that people have not learned from, made productive use of or changed their views of life purpose as a consequence of their own illness journey. For those who have survived the turbulent journey of a major mental illness, when asked whether they would have preferred to have avoided it altogether, the answer is almost universally a resounding 'YES'!

Towards the development of a social vaccine

In recent times, a sustained emphasis on the pursuit of more effective strategies to prevent the onset or recurrence of severe disorders, like clinical depression, has emerged. But the concept has shifted from a very medical concept – a literal biomedical or 'injectable' vaccine to that of a 'social' vaccine.

It's an attractive alternative to other related concepts such as the social determinants of health (see Chapter 11). That is, while we have always recognised that there are complex upstream factors that affect the rate of disorders like clinical depression (i.e. social cohesion, economic status, employment, education, access to maternal health care, racism, discrimination, exposure to physical and sexual violence), this general approach has not led to many specific actions.

Much of this social perspective, however, is just too linear. It looks too far back and lacks the complexity, reverberating loops, and the fascinating interactive features of truly dynamic models of illness onset and course. By contrast, a more targeted focus puts emphasis squarely on factors that are close to the onset of illness. Relatively small but highly effective strategies that are used by lots of people could have massive benefits.

A social vaccine is not really a single shot, delivered on one occasion to impart lifelong protection against clinical depression. But it could be a set of specific interventions (like enhanced daily exercise, reductions in night-time light exposure, reduced binge-drinking among teenagers, reduced illicit drug use), preferably available to the whole population, delivered in a timely fashion, at the right developmental stages, to prevent the onset or reduce the severity of the illness.

In my view, humanity and our wider cultural traditions would not be diminished by the massive reduction in the prevalence of these disorders, but instead the richness of our collective lives (our shared mental wealth) would be greatly enhanced.

TAKE-OUT TIPS

- Specific strategies, if taken up by many of us, may help to reduce the number of people who get depressed.
- The main strategies that work are increased sound connection and activities to regulate our 24-hour sleep–wake (circadian) cycle.

17

No Simple Causes

Question: Are there no simple causes of depression?
Answer: Our aim is to uncover personal vulnerabilities: why are you, personally, really at risk?
Method: We will be neither 'mindless' nor 'brainless' in that pursuit!

In the very early days of my psychiatry training, Chris, a general physician-psychotherapist aged in his early 90s, came to spend a few weeks in our hospital. He'd come to refresh his diagnostic and therapeutic skills. His voice was quiet, his speech considered, and he was the master of the thoughtful pause. He was bright, alert, curious. His advanced age and healthy white beard, along with his warm and empathetic style, gave just a hint of Santa Claus.

Such a commitment to the pursuit of new knowledge was remarkable. My view was that we had much more to learn from his experiences than he was ever likely to learn from us.

In longer conversations with Chris, his more enduring concern was not that he lacked the skills to deliver expert care. Rather realistically, he worried if he took on new cases, now that the people he was treating would outlive him! As his commitment was to take each journey as a trusted companion, he wanted to keep his side of the bargain. He wondered whether we'd developed any ways (courtesy of new brain imaging or biochemical techniques) to shorten the course of that journey.

Chris's experience was that many of the most important aspects were not revealed early in the illness. Any truly successful model, most relevant to the specific needs of an individual and which could form the basis for a more enduring management plan, required an enduring partnership of expert knowledge and deep personal insights.

During this brief period, a woman in her late teens – let's call her Jane – was admitted to our hospital. She was very distressed, frightened, agitated and extremely unpredictable. She had already taken a series of chaotic actions (walking down a freeway, jumping off a high wall, swimming out to sea) that had put her life in danger.

Sadly, Jane was unable to give any coherent explanation of her internal world. Her mind was dislocated. Her family were overwhelmed by the sudden disruption of her mental and emotional capacities. Her mother's anguish was profound and she cried out, 'What has caused my daughter to be this way? Will she ever recover? Can she ever lead a normal life again?'

My first thought was a wish that anyone who considers the practice of clinical psychiatry as putting pseudo-medical labels on normal emotional states could witness this acute dislocation of a young mind, and its devastating impacts on Jane's family. To me, this is the clear mission of our specialist branch of medicine. To understand, and as quickly as possible fix, this debilitating and life-threatening illness.

What was evident, at that time in the mid-80s, was that we didn't have a straightforward explanation for such an acute 'mind-dislocation'. Our therapeutic options were rather generic. Basically, protecting an individual from self-harm, providing professional and compassionate care in a hospital and prescribing a limited range of sedative and other more therapeutic medicines.

These days, we have a whole new series of tests, explanations and therapeutic options. In retrospect, I suspect that Jane had a rare form of autoimmune disease that attacks the brain (often in females, in late adolescence). Today, we might consider a range of immune therapies. However, despite these diagnostic and therapeutic advances, for the person affected by a very severe illness, and the family and the clinician, the challenge to our everyday assumptions about normal mental health and behaviour remains as daunting as ever.

Chris, however, saw this same young woman through two complementary perspectives. The first was the realisation that we did not have a clear brain-based explanation for the patient's sudden behavioural and cognitive distress. Our area of specialist medicine lacked the diagnostic tools to deliver highly personalised or most-effective treatment options.

Chris's second perspective was more profound. His concern was focused more on how, after Jane recovered from this episode, she would incorporate this whole traumatic episode into her own life narrative. How could we help her to explain what she'd been through, and in a way that would not simply retell the story but rather inform her future choices?

Unlike that of so many younger colleagues, or those who have never really worked at the hard end of mental illness, Chris's approach was neither 'brainless' (i.e. without reference to the underlying changes in brain structure, chemistry or function that drove the episode) nor 'mindless' (i.e. without reference to the social context, past experiences or personal perception of the experience of being so dislocated from reality).

I often have the memory of Chris pop in my mind when a new person, accompanied by close relatives or confidantes, enters my consulting office. The unspoken anxiety among those waiting outside my office door is based on whether this encounter will prove any more enlightening than the many other professional consultations that have preceded it. The search for coherent explanations, and better treatment options that are both technically sound and personally relevant, is always challenging.

It's a marathon, not a sprint

As each new person enters my office, I'm guessing that some of their previous health care encounters may not have ended well. A reality of clinical medicine is that your own successes are well-known to you, while your mistakes and misadventures are dealt with elsewhere. From very early in my career, I was encouraged to take the view that the successful treatment of mental illness is a marathon, not a sprint. Declaring victory too early can end in tears.

Like many young clinicians, it's perhaps best to learn these lessons early. Unlike other areas of medicine, clinical psychiatry never offers heroic saves (those you might see in TV dramas that feature emergency rooms, operating theatres, brain surgeons and other legends of media medicine). The big differentiating factor for clinical psychiatry is that the journey of discovery (and recovery) is best taken in partnership with those directly affected.

As I've grown older, the clients I meet have got progressively younger – and are also presenting for care much earlier in their illness. That change in focus reflects three things. First, when I was starting my career, the main focus of adult psychiatry was on specialist assessment and management of middle-aged and older adults with severe, persistent or recurrent mood or psychotic disorders. Second, at the time I took an interest in the potential brain-related causes of these disorders, and their assessment through novel brain-imaging techniques, the most robust studies were conducted in older adults with treatment-resistant depression.

The profound effect of early intervention

The third reason is that these days there is a much greater emphasis placed on early intervention. This has led many of us now to focus our clinical and research efforts on adolescents and young adults who are traversing the peak ages of onset of the major mood and psychotic disorders (12–25 years). One big problem for this work is that the earlier in the illness course, the less certain we can be about causal factors, longitudinal course or the choice of best treatments.

For many of my professional colleagues, and some of the families they encounter, this retreat from the illusion of diagnostic or therapeutic certainty is challenging. If we cannot provide diagnostic precision (based on an objective laboratory test or brain scan), and clear evidence of the risk-benefit scenarios for options in treatment, then surely we should vacate the field (see 'Ruth's story' later in the chapter).

To me, this uncertainty can miss the point. As explained by Samuel Shem in *The House of God*, the true role of physicians has always been to 'be with' the person who is ill, throughout this very personal experience – no matter the outcome of the journey. Let's face it, medicine cures very few diseases. It does, however, quite often prolong life, reduce suffering and extend genuine and compassionate care.

'Being with' as the central responsibility of the physician

So, what is the essence of 'being with' that a physician might provide? Surely, if it's a companion the individual requires, then partners, families, peers or chosen others are the best choices. What is it that the physician can provide that adds real value? It includes technical knowledge about some of the intricacies of the condition that now afflicts that person. Of course, much of that general information is available 24/7 from the internet. Similarly, information about treatment options is out there – from professional studies, regulatory bodies, mass media and firsthand accounts.

These days, much is self-diagnosed and, where feasible, self-managed. Where such approaches are efficient, safe and effective, what's not to like about this wider democratisation of health care? Extreme versions do develop, particularly in mental health. It's not uncommon to hear that only the person with the illness, acting alone, can truly understand, choose and manage their own condition. Of course, this assumes that the cause(s) is knowable, the best course of action is obvious and that all effective treatments can be self-administered.

By contrast, the clinical encounter and the subsequent shared journey has always been about so much more than trading information or detailing treatment choices. It's a shared journey of discovery. Over time, I hope we converge on a path that genuinely leads to the best possible outcomes. The clinician is not a guide who has travelled this exact road previously – it is unique to each individual.

But it's likely that they've accompanied others and are more aware of the known pitfalls along the way. To quote that great philosopher Donald Rumsfeld, we are all constrained by the unknown unknowns. Most clinicians would contend that they at least have some useful knowledge of the 'known knowns' and the 'known unknowns', which may be very relevant to your personal journey.

Most importantly, it is not a journey that we are reluctant to take simply because we have limited tools and constrained knowledge.

The simple truth of early intervention is that the young person is on that journey and the sooner we provide more useful tools, the lower the likelihood that preventable harm will result. At this point, one cannot simply wish the journey away or abandon the young person (or their families and carers) to take it alone.

With middle-aged and older adults, we might assume that many have already travelled these paths. Fascinating to me, however, is that each new encounter is a new journey. Where things have not gone well, we need to reconsider prior assumptions and seek new options. But frequently, I'm most struck by the lack of a common understanding between a clinician's explanation and a person's own beliefs. To travel together we need to be using the same map, or at least agree on the desired destination.

Why is there sometimes a lack of agreement between clinicians and their clients?

Can this lack of agreement be simply explained by the lack of a common language – with the technical and professional explanatory stuff just not connecting with the personal and subjective experience? More likely, it's a lack of agreement to take that journey together. Even more important is the tension that comes from realising that the information is incomplete. For both the clinician, and the person and their family, there will never be a simple explanation of how they have come to be in this particular hole at this specific point in their life.

While the exploratory journey may throw up more pieces of information, it's just as likely new pieces will contradict previous assumptions. Over time each new phase may contribute to a richer picture, but it is likely that key information will remain incomplete and, sometimes, contradictory. For those in search of certainty, and the desire to have tight control over their future mental life, this can be disturbing. Sadly, many abort the journey early and adopt an overly simplistic social, psychological or neurobiological explanation. Rarely do these beliefs translate to successful long-term outcomes.

At critical points along the journey, the clinician and their client will still be far apart

Andrew came to see me a few days after his initial consultation with a life-threatening agitated depression. Fortunately, the prescribed medicine had had some benefits (and side-effects). But, much more coherently and somewhat more forcefully, Andrew was able to tell me why my 'mindless' conceptualisation of his illness was just all wrong, and now that he was a bit better (after two nights' sleep) he was 'strong enough' to fix it himself. He was convinced of the cause and so now knew the right path out.

From my perspective (and that of his family), his belief was at its most 'brainless' point. His understanding was entirely psychological, and entirely unique to his circumstances. For him, the way he was behaving (agitated, pacing, ruminating, not sleeping, losing weight, unresponsive to other's views, child-like stubbornness but also suicidal thoughts) bore no resemblance to anyone else – and certainly not any diagnostic or clinical category. It was simply a personal, and existential, crisis. There was no brain or mechanical element driving his actions. If not for his family's insistence, he would not have been in my office. He had no need for this kind of expertise. He could sort it.

When I raised the issue, that the next step involved blood tests and brain scans (given his age and risk factors), he scoffed, 'So, you do think there are things going on in my head. What a waste of time!' As usual, I departed into a short explanation of why at his age, and at this time in the journey, these were necessary steps – not so much for Andrew, because he wasn't really hearing any of this, but rather for his family – as they were overseeing his safety and calling the shots.

The real task

In our field, there is perhaps the maximum confusion between the search for the cause and the more important task – the search for the safest, fastest and enduring way out of this hole. Like Lot's wife in the biblical story, looking back is very risky. Focusing on finding the best ladder out is the immediate and life-saving challenge. Cries of 'you can't treat the illness without knowing the cause' are simplistic and, as in most of medicine, just plain wrong. Removing the inflamed appendix, restoring the blood flow to a blocked artery to the brain, recharging the disturbed electrical system to the heart, delivering the endangered foetus (and saving the mother's life) are not delayed by the debate as to why this person, at this point in their life, has encountered this life-threatening illness.

Sadly, in mental health, this preoccupation with looking backwards still dominates much public discourse. While some of the genuine risk factors to the onset of major mood and psychotic disorders are known (see Part B), they may be irrelevant to the immediate course of action. Our goal is to construct an accurate picture of the lifetime journey of each individual that includes key historical information, but much more of what will really be useful will be learnt as the journey goes forward. If we are right about the true underlying mechanisms, (disturbed body clock, overreactive stress-response system, misfiring brain circuits) and those mechanisms are amenable to intervention, then we can change the course of the illness.

We never treat the average – it always misses the mark

The most common goal of medicine these days is to develop highly personalised therapies. It may come as a surprise to you that this has not always been the goal. In truth, the last century of medicine was focused on the standardisation of methods for assessment and treatment, so that the 'average' good could be delivered to as many people as possible. It's at the heart of most universal and collective health systems. Equitable care for everybody – a strong emphasis on access and activity – but relatively little emphasis on counting how good the individual outcome was.

The principal failing of these highly standardised approaches is that no person's individual journey through serious illness is ever average. Treatments that are simply delivered in a person-blind, 'on average', way rarely deliver the best outcomes. The truly skilled clinician doesn't operate in a cookbook-driven way. The clinician's task is to present the best possible match between the various treatments available and the very specific challenge of this individual journey. Each ladder, out of each hole, has its own unique characteristics (see Figure 5 overleaf). The challenge is to facilitate the design, construction and deployment of that ladder as quickly as possible.

Most young people, and their parents, plead with me to provide the correct diagnosis, the best treatment and the most accurate prediction of the likely outcome. An expert view may help to allay their fears and offer real hope. So, my rather imprecise offerings may, at times, seem meagre and off-putting. The quest for genuine discovery is not assisted by false offerings or overconfidence in one's own abilities.

What the best of my colleagues really offer is a willingness to traverse together the territory of mental ill health and its social and personal consequences. They do this with compassion, empathy and prior knowledge of the common challenges. Along that journey,

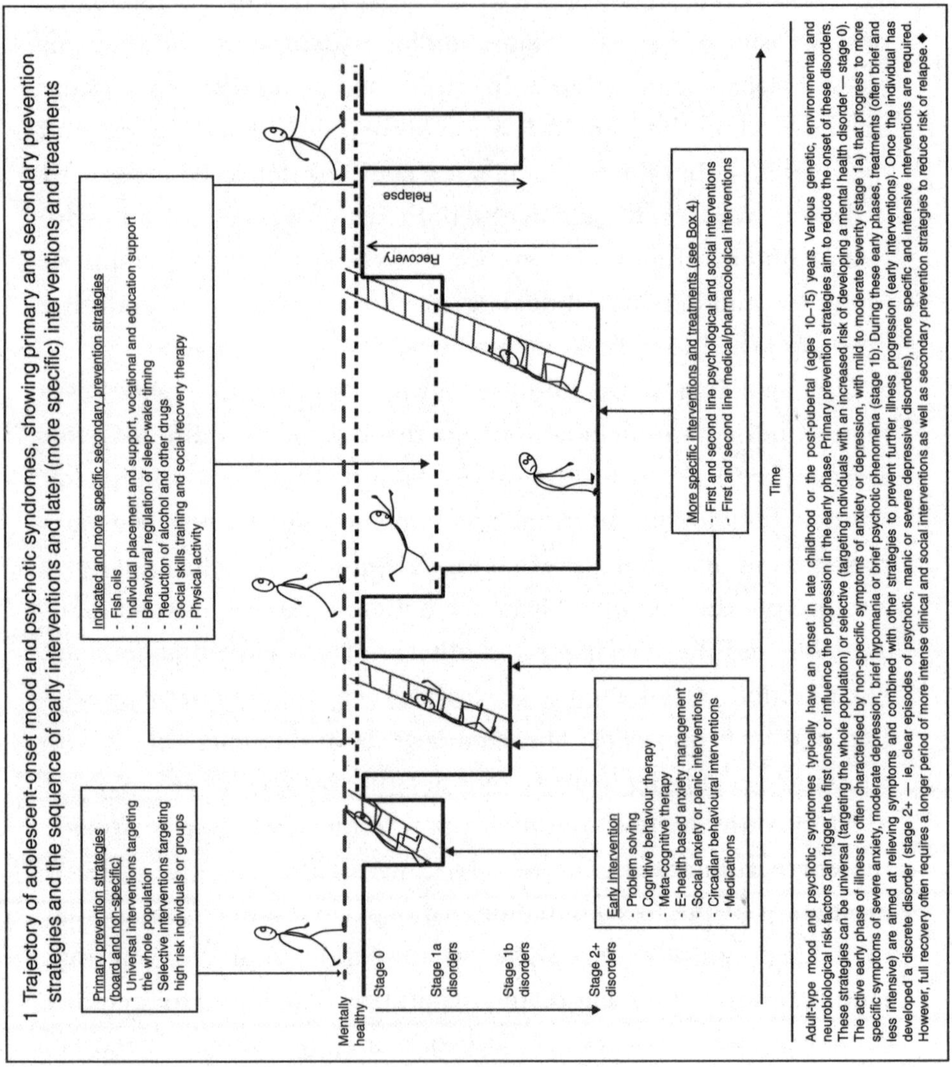

Figure 5

Source: *Medical Journal of Australia*, Rohleder, C. et al, 'Personalising Care Options in Youth Mental Health', vol 211(9), S33.

it's not uncommon that together we achieve a genuine consensus, bringing together the expertise of the clinician, the collective knowledge of medical, social and psychological research, and the experience of the individual and their families and carers.

Charting a common course

For those who know the geography of Western Australia, the journey we are on may be considered the equivalent of sailing west, against the fierce sea breeze, from the coastal city of Fremantle to Rottnest Island, about 20 kilometres off the mainland. What's really important to know is that Rottnest is the actual destination (in this analogy, the state of being out of the hole and planning to prevent recurrence of the illness). If you don't know that, and don't keep tacking back towards that destination, you'll soon be blown to shore or lost in the Great Southern Ocean.

The result of the collection of new information as we move along the journey is the detailing of the personal landscape that truly reveals each individual's underlying vulnerability. It's that which you can't really know about the ocean, or the wind, or the tides or about the seaworthiness of your own vessel before you step off the shore and into the sailing boat.

Your vulnerability (here, your boat) is not the illness experience itself (here, the sailing trip), but rather a stronger grasp of those opaque mechanisms that have put you at risk. In my view, such genuine understanding of the nature of that very personal vulnerability (not a long list of general risk factors) provides a solid basis for future action. Your boat needs to be much more seaworthy and able to withstand unexpected changes in the weather conditions.

For many people, the cause of their illness is never really known. Put bluntly, if we assist you to achieve a genuine insight into the true nature of your personal vulnerability then you may well be on the path to acquiring the tools necessary for a more productive life – to leave the devil behind. To set sail again, with much greater confidence of arriving safely at distant shores.

RUTH'S STORY

I'm in the habit of answering my phone to colleagues. So, when one of my close friends rang and asked me to see the daughter of a close associate (let's call her Ruth) who had just returned urgently from overseas, I was unlikely to say no. Such encounters are always challenging. Another young person's life has just gone seriously off course, and the family are sure to be distressed.

When families present to my office, no matter the age of the ill person, my practice, first up, is to get everyone in. On this occasion, three different perspectives emerged. The father was direct and wanted fast, concise answers. His highest priority was a correct and clear diagnosis, followed by effective actions. The best medical care would result in the minimum disruption to his daughter's life.

The mother also wanted the best possible explanation, but immediately took a broader view of the possible options. She accepted that the future course may not be so clear at this point. Ruth, the young adult whose life overseas had just come crashing down, was bewildered. Nothing really made any sense, though she was appreciative of her family's swift actions to bring her home and wrap her back within their close-knit support network. She could offer no clear explanation for her predicament. Nothing obvious had gone wrong. Her parents had provided her with access to a world of opportunity.

The clinical story was not simple. At the change of seasons, Ruth had experienced a series of uncharacteristic episodes of overactivity, poor judgement, disturbed sleep and reckless spending. These had been interspersed with other periods of low energy, loss of motivation, tearfulness and thoughts of death. Being on her own in a foreign country, she had increasingly withdrawn from her formal education.

While it was entirely possible that Ruth (who had had some earlier emotional difficulties that waxed and waned throughout her adolescence) was now headed towards the early stages of bipolar mood disorder, such a definitive conclusion could not be reached. Although there was a strong family history of the illness, the probability of a false positive diagnosis was still high. However, the chance that Ruth was at more risk of progression to a major mood disorder than many other young people could not be easily discounted.

After some considerable discussion of these complexities, Ruth's dad demanded a straight answer: 'Well, does she have bipolar disorder or not?'

I'm rarely short for words, and gave yet another highly informed, technically correct, but ultimately vague response. I even provided my collection of informative illness-course and circadian disruption print-out figures and charts to support the explanation. Finally, on the question of bipolar disorder, yes or no, I concluded, 'In truth, it's too early to say.'

The father was furious. I'd just confirmed what he'd always thought about the uselessness of clinical psychiatry. No straight answers. No clear solutions. Lots of half-truths and possibly credible theories, but no certainty. His fear that his precious daughter was in danger of heading down a path of lost life opportunities was palpable.

My recommendation was that while we provide an appropriate set of medical and psychological treatments, the real task would be to journey together over a longer time to see what might emerge. Given Ruth's age, 19 years, I suggested that we would need to be vigilant over at least the next two years, and that she and her family would need to monitor her mental health over the next decade. Although we didn't discuss it at that stage, I was also thinking that if she ever proceeded to have children, information about these episodes should be incorporated into any perinatal management plan. (There is a spike in onset of bipolar disorder in young women in their late 20s, often in association with childbirth.)

Ruth's dad was quick to suggest that what was required was another expert opinion – though perhaps from an actual expert! I agreed that such a course of action was entirely reasonable, as others in my profession may well interpret the same clinical information differently and, consequently, propose a different plan of action. Ruth's mum was quiet, considerate and appreciative of the complexities.

At times like these, I'm often reminded of the sage advice of my daughter (who is a very sensible public health physician): 'Dad, you've just got to get a (diagnostic) test.' The backstory here is that even if the test is weak, non-specific and unlikely to override your clinical judgement, it will certainly convince the sceptical patient, the estranged or overwhelmed family and at least some of the wider public that clinical psychiatry is as reality-based (reflecting the body's actual physiology) as other medical specialities.

As an aside the search for diagnostic tests in clinical psychiatry (the brain scan, the blood test, the microchip that can read brain electrical waves) remains our holy grail.

While some useful tests are already here, and more are on the way, it's more likely that the quest to find a very simple or specific diagnostic test will be beyond our reach.

When I next saw Ruth, she had indeed consulted one of my expert colleagues. 'So', I gently enquired, 'what was the outcome?' The father, in a somewhat annoyed tone, reported that my colleague had offered the family one of two choices. Ruth could have a formal diagnosis of bipolar disorder and immediately start on a relevant cocktail of antidepressant, mood-stabilising and sleep-restoring medications. Or, she could have no diagnosis, resulting in no specific treatment and ongoing observation. No middle ground. So the choice was left with Ruth and her family.

I'm sure my colleague presented these stark contrasts to help persuade the family back towards the middle terrain. That uncertainty is best summarised as: likely genetic risk; no clear precipitating cause; clinical phenomena consistent with recurrent depression and possible bipolar-like features; murky illness course with uncertain outcomes; and possible risk of progression to more serious or recurring illness. This summary is not the concise, all-explaining diagnosis, objectively verified by smart brain scans or blood tests, expertly managed answer that most of us would strongly prefer.

The end result: we all agreed to pursue the slow, steady and watchful approach that I had originally recommended. It will be some years before we really know whether this was the best road to take.

TAKE-OUT TIPS

- The 'average' treatment is never the best treatment for you.
- Finding specifically what works best for you may take some time and some genuine exploration of what makes you vulnerable to depression.
- Managing your own vulnerability is the equivalent of ensuring that your own boat (your mind and body) is seaworthy before you set sail across stormy waters.

PART 4

THE TREATMENT OF DEPRESSION

18

The Free Will Problem

Now that we know why clinical depression can't be explained away as either, 'It's in your genes' or 'It's how you were raised as a child', there's a danger we might appear to be endorsing the other extreme in this discourse, namely that of 'free will'. As if you can simply choose your own destiny, independent of any other constraints. And certainly not constrained by the physicality of your own brain functions, and its in-built emotional circuitry, or your own history.

Free will has a long and rich tradition in philosophy and religion and, perhaps even more importantly these days, the criminal justice system. To be guilty of a crime and deserving of punishment, the person needs not only to have engaged in an antisocial behaviour but also to have had a guilty mind ('*mens rea*' in Latin). That is, the person needs to have had the mental capacity to know that the act was wrong and to have chosen (or planned) to go ahead with it anyway. So, you committed the crime of your own free will!

I've sat with many senior people in politics, government and the law who frequently express the view that in some way people with depression choose to be that way or, more importantly, they don't choose not to be. A related concept is that a person with a very strong mind can *choose* to overcome adversity and not be destabilised by situations that cause distress to those other less strong, less resilient or more vulnerable minds.

Successful people who have not experienced (directly or indirectly through family members) mental ill health often assume that this is not a result of good fortune, but rather a consequence of their mental strength or other intrinsic talents. While sympathetic to the plight of others, they often lack any real empathy or genuine insight into the true nature of these problems.

While it is easy to criticise those from other professions, or the wider community, who take these views, it's not uncommon to hear health professionals express the same set of beliefs.

A lot of commercial resilience programs state that we are all able to easily 'rewrite our own stories', 'choose not to react', 'decide not to be depressed', 'rewire our emotions' or just 'think differently'. Beneath each of these self-affirmations is the assumption of free will. Implied in these hard sells is that a failure to succeed – to put things right by your own hand or by exercising your own power of mind – represents a failure of will, strength or motivation.

While this type of thinking has been bad enough in mental health, it is interesting that in the modern world of striving for self-actualisation, this triumph of free will over circumstances extends to fighting your own cancer or beating some terrible infection simply by recruiting your own mental power and strength – that is, choosing to be healthy! By implication, people who are sick (especially those who are mentally unwell) are those who have failed to take personal responsibility for their physical and mental health.

So, for these, positive-thinking advocates, no matter what set of biological or environmental circumstances has landed you in this dark place, and no matter what state of mind you are in at the time, you can *choose* to behave, feel and think differently – and intrinsically, positively, hopefully and without any obvious assistance from anyone else, let alone psychologists or other doctors.

For those who have had clinical depression, and during the episode of illness have experienced deeply the reality that they are simply not able to choose to be well, there is often the driving desire to get back to that normal state where we believe that we are in control of our own thoughts, feelings and actions. And that being normal and acceptable again has to be achieved without the assistance of medications, physical treatments or ongoing psychological supports.

This preoccupation with free will has even more insidious impacts than might not initially be apparent. For example, if one person believes that another person is not able to exercise their free will, then they're unlikely to want to engage with them personally, professionally or socially. The end result is that that person is likely to be excluded from relationships, social networks, education or employment.

As a result, it's very common to hear people (and often very successful people) say, 'I am well again, and I demonstrate this by my capacity to be in control of my own actions and decisions *without* the supports of medication or other therapies' – thus demonstrating, once again, their very active exercise of their own free will.

By contrast, issues related to depression and impaired mental capacity are sometimes dragged inappropriately into a variety of other legal and criminal settings. Typically, the presence of a diagnosis is used to seek to excuse the behaviour of someone who has committed a crime or some other antisocial act. That is, the presence of a disorder means that the person could not be held accountable (morally or legally) for their actions. All shades of grey are quickly lost.

My view is that the free will concept creates as many problems as its counterparts of genetic or environmental determinism. The notion that we exist, and feel, think and behave independently of the multitude of factors that have led us to this point in our lives, or the complexity of the current situation in which we operate, isn't tenable. So, the notion that we can simply choose freely is not tenable.

But the essential element missing from both the free will and deterministic extremes is that we do (individually or collectively) have the capacity to intervene to change the future course of events. How we achieve that change, and over what time period, are the core philosophies of this book devoted to evaluating the most effective treatment options for anyone who finds themselves in this space.

19

Everybody Needs Someone to Listen (Actively!)

Everybody needs someone to listen. Many are fortunate to have intimate partners, family or close friends who fulfill that need, particularly in times of crisis or prolonged adversity. That empathetic, non-judgemental response – delivered at just the right moment – can be life-saving.

Everybody who comes to professional care expects to be listened to. The stereotypical New York Psychiatrist (preferably with a strong Eastern European heritage and sensibility), and now the universal therapist, can often sit quietly for hours as their clientele unload their personal accounts. In my experience, professional therapists are mostly warm, intelligent, considerate and deeply committed to assisting those in psychological need.

But, is empathetic listening enough? Recently, I enquired of a middle-aged man who I'd been asked to reassess for his treatment-resistant depression, and who'd been in psychotherapy for over a decade: what model of illness were he and his therapist working with?

He looked stunned, and replied, 'She just listens.'

Rather stupidly, I went on to ask, 'But what does she say about your *condition*. What do you agree is the goal of the therapy?'

He looked even more confused, replying, 'She asks me for my conclusions.'

This journey of professionally endorsed self-discovery may seem entirely reasonable. There is no doubt that most people love it! Whenever client satisfaction surveys are done for this type of intervention, they always yield very high ratings. Who wouldn't enjoy the opportunity to be heard, affirmed and comforted? Or even have the space and time to think out loud, put options on the table and consider the choices before taking action?

Brief periods of psychological therapy can be highly effective for common forms of anxiety, depression and other life crises (like grief, relationship breakdowns and work disruptions). The chance to just get your head together by talking through these situations, and crying where necessary, in the presence of someone who is warm, skilled and non-judgemental, is not to be dismissed lightly.

While this may seem strange for a person in my line of work to say, I strongly prefer that both clients and therapists talk less and act more! When talking about yourself (or listening endlessly to someone unload) becomes a long-term alternative to substantive actions, I become quite critical.

I often remark to those in greatest need that we will both have succeeded when we are no longer talking and, instead, they're out in the real world – working, studying and actively engaged in substantive interpersonal relationships.

Some time ago, I was treating an angry and irritable middle-aged man, Josh, who headed a very successful IT firm. He had come to see me after storming out of marital therapy. His wife insisted that if he didn't get help himself, the marriage was over and he would not be seeing his daughter again. His business was in trouble due to a series of recent erratic decisions. Given the ferocity of his outbursts, his daughter was afraid for her own safety. She'd asked her mother whether she could move away with relatives. Fairly quickly, the couple's experienced therapist had suggested Josh's mental state was a much greater problem than the dysfunctional communication patterns between these life partners.

Like many men I see, he didn't want to see me. However, as he felt that his wife was 'holding a gun to my head', he reluctantly came in.

Within about ten minutes of being on his own in my office, Josh dropped the hostility and irritability and departed into a much more fascinating tale about his harsh childhood and the divergent paths he and his twin brother, Jake, had taken since that time. They'd grown up as privileged white people in a former British colony. Their father had encouraged the notion that to succeed they should never back down or concede any past wrong. He was strict, quick to punish, extremely moody and physically abusive. Collectively, the family believed that they'd worked hard and were entitled to their financial success.

As local events in that colony shifted, both boys were forced to emigrate. They left their family of origin behind and Josh moved to Australia, while Jake ended up in the US. Both then succeeded at university, married and had children. While Josh set up his own IT firm, Jake became a very successful medical specialist in New York. By their early thirties both were financially and socially well off – but miserable. Meanwhile, their father had descended into alcoholism and died, reportedly of a 'gun-related' accident.

Josh's brother Jake immediately went into long-term psychoanalytically orientated (Freudian) psychotherapy. He continued to see his warm, empathetic and non-judgemental therapist several times a week for the next ten years. He refused to take any antidepressant medication, despite the recommendations of his treating physician. Over that period, his first marriage ended, he was estranged from his two daughters, he remarried and was now separated from his second wife. There were unresolved financial disputes running from both the first and second marriages.

As Josh outlined the details of his brother's disastrous personal circumstances, he started to sob. The tears were mixed with anguish, frustration and grief. Josh saw himself as an entirely rational individual and could not reconcile the fact that his brother was a medical professional who remained engaged with a form of treatment that was clearly not working. But, at the same time his brother was also refusing any other medical therapy that might assist.

In long telephone conversations, whenever Josh challenged his brother to consider other therapeutic approaches, Jake would become extremely hostile and yell, 'I've just got to sort this out for myself. No drug is ever going to help me get to the bottom of all this!' It didn't seem to Josh that ten years of guided self-digging had ever really helped his brother.

So, now that Josh was faced with a similar dilemma the discourse was no longer theoretical but very personal. The stakes were high. There was no doubt that while both men did share very adverse childhood experiences, and had really struggled with anxiety and irritability in their adolescence, they had also gone on to lead very productive lives and form substantive family and personal relationships.

Having seen the outcomes of unsuccessful long-term psychotherapy for his twin, Josh wanted to know what other alternatives were available. We discussed the range of medical, psychological and interpersonal options that may be relevant.

What was also apparent, however, was how depressed Josh was at that first meeting. Naturally, he'd not disclosed to his wife or the marital therapist that he'd been having elaborate and violent suicidal thoughts. He couldn't sleep, was losing weight and had lost all interest in any physical intimacy with his wife. It was this very noticeable behavioural change, rather than his declining emotional state, that had precipitated the move to marital therapy.

After some considerable dialogue, we agreed that a trial of an antidepressant was worthwhile. Within weeks, Josh was feeling more optimistic about his future and about his capacity to behave quite differently in his critical interpersonal relationships.

It was that interpersonal aspect of his recovery that I found most interesting. Josh related that he'd always had an extremely short temper. Whenever he felt provoked, by even the most minor reason, he overreacted. Despite the dire consequences, he'd never been able to stop the harshness of his immediate verbal or physical response.

After taking the medicine (a selective serotonin reuptake inhibitor – SSRI) for some time, Josh related that while he still felt the emotional response, he had time to think before he reacted. His wife, daughter and work colleagues all remarked on this transformation. They noted that his 'personality' seemed to have shifted, matured and changed in a very positive way.

Josh's interpersonal sensitivity was no longer characterised by its previous 'hair-trigger', but by a new consideration for the perspective of the other. After some months, he went to see one of my favourite very practical cognitive-behavioural therapists. He kept seeing her regularly over the next six months. Later, a return to marital therapy was successfully negotiated and his business was soon back on its successful trajectory. He apologised to his daughter for his previous outbursts and was now spending time just being with her.

When I reviewed Josh's progress about a year after he had fully recovered, I was intrigued as to whether he'd shared his experiences with his brother, and whether he was keen to cease antidepressant medication. Indeed, he'd continued to speak with his brother regularly. Josh had shared his experiences with SSRIs and CBT and the unusual transformation of his personality. But, they no longer argued, as Josh no longer felt the overwhelming need to convince his brother to change therapeutic directions. Sadly, Jake's own circumstances continued to deteriorate despite the ongoing long-term psychotherapy.

So, we soon turned our attention back to Josh's own situation. Wrongly, I assumed that he would be keen to quit antidepressants, like most men who like to feel back in control of their lives. Additionally, he was having ongoing sexual difficulties associated with the medication, and physical intimacy had been such a key aspect of his marital relationship.

Josh's brief but direct response to my suggestion that we start reducing the medication, with the intention of stopping it, was a firm 'No way!'

He continued: 'Clearly, you've never been in a situation when you almost lost everything you really cared about. If you think I'm ever going back to the old me, living my life like Jake, and risking losing my family and my business, then you're very mistaken. I like the new me. People now think I'm a sensitive and considerate guy. I'm not, but it's definitely a much better me than before.'

I suggested to Josh that it must be a very unusual thing to have someone else (and a twin!) acting as your very own personal comparison. It's hard to know how much the parallel life experiences of Jake influenced Josh's own perspective, and his decision-making at the time of his own personal crisis. But it did provide a real-life, stark contrast.

While Josh drew some important lessons from his brother's experiences – without effective intervention you could lose most of what you cared about – Jake drew no comfort from his brother's positive experiences with SSRIs, cognitive therapy and brief but effective marital therapy. Jake remained committed to his unending journey of finding the 'real' cause of his distress and his ongoing interpersonal dysfunction.

All too often I hear many sensible people say, 'The hard work needs to be done by the person with the illness', 'They need to want to change', 'They need to make the effort' or 'You can't help those who don't want to be helped.'

It's an interesting, if harsh, perspective. Some aspects seem self-evident and entirely reasonable. Trying to convince the behaviourally disturbed, but completely recalcitrant, that they should engage with mental health professionals is certainly not an easy road to success.

In my view, we really need to shift from this reductionistic notion of 'real causes' to the more central questions: What's to be done, and what are the best tools for seeing real changes in people's lives?

TAKE-OUT TIPS

- While being listened to is essential in a crisis, it may not provide the answers you need.
- Real change is possible, and sometimes that results from having the experience of feeling and behaving differently.
- For some, taking medications that work provides that experience.

20

Facts, Alternative Facts and 'Truthiness' Around Clinical Depression

Brain and social sciences, and their relationships with mental illness, are constantly evolving. Some aspects are clear and, like climate change, there is real scientific consensus. These include the effectiveness and safety profile of modern antidepressant medicines, that the brain behaves differently in people with clinical depression and that major mood disorders do run in families. Other aspects, like the extent to which any specific genetic factors increase the risk to illness, what forms of prevention are really effective, and how much social or environmental factors such as previous trauma or serious viral infection matter, are more contestable. Which types of evidence should inform the specific choice of treatment for any particular person are serious ethical and practical issues?

In our era, where much information can be accessed on the internet, it can be very difficult to convey the true state of scientific knowledge. While the extent of scientific knowledge has always been constrained by its own culture and philosophical traditions, modern societies have generally recognised the extraordinary benefits from its widespread application. This is most obvious in many other areas of physical health care.

For those of us old enough to have experienced childhood diseases like polio, whooping cough, chicken pox or measles, the benefit of widespread use of simple and safe vaccines is evident. Some of us may still choose not to vaccinate our children or wish to dispute the authority of the state to require children to be vaccinated before attending school.

All these dissenting views are not the same as the active dissemination of false information, 'alternative facts' or what the comedian Stephen Colbert identified as the epidemic of 'truthiness' (untruths presented as facts), in Trump's America. Such things as 'Vaccines cause autism', 'Vaccines are full of toxins' or 'You can get natural immunity from just eating well.'

The misuse of information does not simply consist of the active dissemination of falsehoods. It can be more complicated than that. Risks may be deliberately exaggerated, or downplayed, for broader sociopolitical purposes.

To attempt to discredit the available science by proposing non-scientific alternative explanations is now commonplace. Strategies for advancing these perverse agendas are now well described. For example, see Naomi Oreskes's book *Merchants of Doubt.* According to her, the process is to 'keep the controversy alive' by constantly questioning the notion that any scientific consensus has actually been reached. Where there is real doubt, no substantive political or social action will follow.

Notable examples include various 'faith-based' campaigns against medical treatments for psychiatric disorders, with a particular focus on the 'abuse' or 'brain damage' supposedly being caused to children and young people. Given the profile and reach of this campaign in the US, its global impact is significant.

In the realm of clinical depression, there has been no shortage of high-profile clinicians (in child psychiatry and psychology), academics or researchers (in clinical pharmacology or statistics) who have been willing participants in this process. Particularly influential are those who are 'converts' to the cause – they say they were once committed prescribers of these treatments but are now determined to bring the real 'truth' to public attention.

So, what's all this got to do with clinical depression and other mental health issues?

Actually, lots. Most days in my work as a clinician, researcher, science communicator or public advocate, I'm confronted by the harm done by active misinformation about the nature of scientific consensus.

Recently, I was sitting with a senior politician, arguing for key investments in new systems of mental health care for young people. Those things would promote earlier intervention and more complex, multidisciplinary interventions for those with more severe problems.

He looked somewhat doubtful and said he was really having trouble reconciling my view with the anecdotal stories of a dysfunctional system and individual stories of harm. The reconciling of the systematic or science level of 'knowledge' with that of personal experiences is always very challenging.

Remember President Trump and his experience of COVID-19? His own illness course was clearly not the same as the more than 1 million Americans who died. But it had a major impact on his own view of the condition.

Living with any major condition, for the person primarily affected and their family and carers, leads to deep reflection on the experience. Increasingly, these personal experiences directly influence public policy and health service development. In my own research work, we give priority to answering questions that are directly raised by those with personal experience. We are committed to working in partnership with those most affected by answering those questions.

Despite these movements, many people who have endured experiences of poor mental health care, or have suffered harms from treatments, may well disagree. My summaries of the science, and my clinical experience with hundreds of people with major mood disorders, just don't match their own lived reality. In this book, I've tried to include many of those lived experiences that provide more personal descriptions consistent with my own and the wider science view.

A senior female journalist who often writes critically about the use of antidepressant medications, particularly in children and young people, frequently relates stories of young people who have had adverse experiences. Clearly, these personal experiences influence her reporting of other medical studies in this area and her preference for selecting stories of likely harms rather than achieved benefits.

Another journalist, in 2020, in the context of the ever-recurring debate about prescribing antidepressant medicines to children and young people, invokes the 2004 USA Food and Drug Administration decision to place a 'black box' on packages of antidepressants, as evidence of the clear problem with continuing to recommend such treatments.

Those more familiar with the details of this whole 'black box' controversy are likely to be aware of the major limitations of the initial analyses on which the recommendation was made. They would also be aware of the arguments that the warning has done more harm than good, resulting in an increased number of youth suicides. But for this particular journalist, all of this is just detail – the top line inference of demonstrable harm is enough.

As an aside, I really liked a 2012 ethics-based discussion of that controversial action by the FDA in the *American Medical Association Journal of Ethics*, which concluded:

'By making a public recommendation, the FDA undermined the evidential-neutrality in the advisability of treating pediatric MDD with antidepressants. The warning now becomes, in itself, "evidence" even though the FDA's decision was not evidence-based. A morally preferable route might have been to present the lack of evidence plainly and to reiterate the rationality of either choice. Allowing individuals to make their own decisions demonstrates a respect for multiple rational options in a context of evidential scarcity.'

In other words, let the evidence (as it currently is) speak first – then allow those most affected to make the relevant judgements.

By contrast, I am grateful to the many journalists and other media who on the basis of their own personal or family experiences, the negative impacts of a deficient health system or an uncaring society, or their own deep desire to improve the care options for those affected, have provided me with the opportunity to put forward the scientific consensus in the public domain.

Many are notable but I wish to draw attention to some particularly moving personal accounts that have laid the basis for both an ongoing and serious commitment to accurate reporting. (Thanks to Lanai Scarr and Ben Pike.) We have been fortunate in Australia that over a long period, positive support for more accurate reporting has been the dominant trend.

Peddling misinformation

Beyond those who simply hold dissenting views, there are those who actively peddle misinformation. Sadly, there is now another universe of 'alternative facts'. Commonly these reports allege that medical treatments are causing many suicides, or brain damage, and that this is mostly happening to children and young people.

Other more subtle actors play at misleading the public, and then accentuating these deceptions through media headlines. For example, a very common (US-based) tactic is to describe everyone under the age of 18 years as 'children' and then run sensationalist headlines alleging massive overtreatment of children with antidepressant drugs. The fact that the clear evidence from the US is to the contrary is of little significance.

Another tactic is to allege massive use of antidepressants in children under five years, as if those kids are receiving medicines for clinical depression. The reality is that these medicines are prescribed by paediatricians, developmental neurologists and other medical specialists to treat a whole variety of other neurodevelopmental issues, like autism and severe intellectual disability.

It has been common to confuse early intervention strategies for those aged 12–25 years with unrelated public health proposals to screen for neurodevelopmental problems in children under five. Headlines rapidly follow suggesting that proponents of early intervention for anxiety and depression want to medicate three-year-olds with antidepressants or antipsychotics.

In my own world, some of those 'academics' or 'health professionals' with strong views continue to try to prevent or disrupt ongoing and ethically approved research. It's hardly a defensible position for those seriously interested in scientifically validated truths. At other times, the attacks are simply personal, seeking to discredit the research findings by attacking those who actually conduct, or the agencies that support scientific work.

Presenting a spectrum of views, and a range of options, based on deep knowledge

A really interesting aspect of the COVID-19 era, and perhaps a reaction against the preceding period of 'alternative facts' and 'fake news', is a rebirth of interest in science-based expertise and deep knowledge.

I recently heard a quantum physicist say that what was required in her discipline was many more people who genuinely understood the complexity of the concepts and the depth of the challenges in bridging the gap between theory and useful technology. That deep knowledge was not acquired by a quick bridging course. It required long and serious immersion in the topic. My own view is that brain and mind sciences, and their effective application in preventing or treating mental illness, has a lot in common with quantum physics.

In my often engaging discussion with senior politicians, or individuals and their families, when I'm challenged about what is to be done, I often start by saying that these are our best options on the basis of current evidence – since both politicians, and those whose lives are affected, have to make decisions now, and do this on the basis of incomplete knowledge. While doing nothing is preferred by the armchair critics, it's not an option for those directly affected.

In addition to detailing what the options are, I do also try to counter the active misinformation that is so readily distributed across this field. So, in the spirit of where best to start, I find that it's helpful to dispel some of the most common and destructive myths about engaging in treatment, and particularly about the artificial notions of 'medicines = all bad', 'psychological therapies = all good'.

TAKE-OUT TIPS

- There is much science-based consensus about the effective treatments for clinical depression.
- Taking actions, preferably early in the illness course, on the basis of best available evidence is the smart and responsible thing to do.

21

Ten Myths About Antidepressant Treatments

JOHN'S STORY

John was a 52-year-old man who recently attempted suicide. He'd been clinically depressed for the past three years, had just lost his job due to poor work performance. His wife was on the verge of leaving him. He agreed after careful consideration to start a trial of antidepressant medication. After the consultation, he went home and told his 75-year-old mother of his intentions to now get medical care.

Her response: 'Is that really necessary? Aren't they the drugs that make you suicidal? Won't they make your depression worse? Won't you just be bombed out all the time? Don't you think you could just get through by going back to work or exercising some more?'

At one level, I get it. John's mum wanted him to get better, but she had seen enough of the 'bad press' to be worried about making a really tough situation worse. It's very hard to imagine that she would have the same response if John had come home and said that he'd agreed to urgent medical treatment for cancer.

Bad news sells

In this chapter, you'll see I'm a bit reactive to the constant retelling of half-truths, and the perpetuation of negative experiences, that are sometimes associated with the medical management of clinical depression.

Such grossly exaggerated negativism has the continued effect of preventing many of those who would really benefit from coming forward to receive effective care. It continuously reinforces the stigma – commonly referred to as 'pill-shaming' – imposed on those who take, and frequently benefit from, well-evaluated treatments. The negative stories sell books and, along with other anti-science and anti-medical campaigns, have a rich social media following.

The stereotype is that antidepressants 'just relieve the symptoms', 'act only as placebos', 'don't address the real psychological or social causes', 'drug you out', 'cause lots of damage', 'make you never want to have sex again' or 'make you more suicidal'. Overwhelmingly, the conclusion becomes that you are only really better when you don't need them anymore – and if that's the case, you probably didn't need them in the first place.

So, below, I've tried to limit myself to considered and slightly more 'academic' responses.

For those with an axe to grind (through personal experience or for other sociopolitical or ideological reasons), my opinions can be easily cancelled or ignored. I am a clinical psychiatrist who prescribes medicines, psychological therapies and other physical treatments. I am also someone who has worked actively with the pharmaceutical industry, testing new drugs, trying to work out how they cause either benefits or side-effects. With many others I'm attempting to find ways to predict who is most likely to respond to any particular intervention, either from clinical assessment or independent genetic, brain, blood, sleep or neuropsychological tests.

1. Antidepressant medications result in lasting emotional blunting.

Justin, aged in his early 20s, had previously been treated successfully for anxiety and depression. He was reluctant to go back on treatment when he experienced a recurrence, because of what he'd read online about the 'emotional blunting' in people who take antidepressant medications.

This exchange took place at the end of one clinical consultation. He'd been pursuing this issue very politely with his family doctor, and had received very reasonable responses: 'It's reported by a significant proportion of people' and 'It's one of the things we monitor closely in ongoing treatment.' All joined with an ongoing commitment to monitor for any untoward emotional or other physical (notably sexual) side-effects.

Just before he left, he threw me a curveball: 'So, Professor Hickie, what do you really think about the "blunting thing"?'

My reply: 'It's largely nonsense and fails completely to acknowledge how most people who are successfully treated welcome the return of normal emotionality! Let's not forget that the experience of depression is all about losing emotionality and being more restricted in the first place. In fact, when they are taking SSRIs, many people who don't fly off the handle so quickly, who don't now overreact to every stressful event, who are keeping their relationships intact or holding onto their jobs, are quite happy to be "different" now.'

2. Antidepressant medications cause loss of cognitive function (memory, attention, concentration, planning).

It's really hard to know who started this one or why it is still perpetuated. Many people with clinical depression have all sorts of objectively measured memory, concentration and planning problems at the height of their illness. The science is clear. To various degrees, modern antidepressant medications are associated with improvements in each of these functions. Much older anti-psychotic medications that are rarely prescribed now, or other sedative medications (commonly co-prescribed for sleep problems or anxiety), may cause sleepiness or a slowing down in some of these mental functions. It's likely that this is where this myth had its origins.

3. Antidepressant medications cause a loss of creativity.

As my great friend and playwright Neil Cole often remarks, 'Just try being creative, when you can't get out of bed or can't write any of your best ideas.' There is a lot of interest in the extent to which creative people, like artists, novelists, playwrights and musicians experience depression (or drown their sorrows in alcohol and other drugs) and whether there is a direct (brain) link between their experience of a profound mood disturbance and their creative output. What's important is that as a consequence of modern treatments many more creative people are now alive and well-functioning. These creative people have just as many ideas but are now much more likely to be seen or heard by the rest of us, by virtue of still being alive.

4. Antidepressant medications cause suicide.

Premature deaths due to suicide, self-harm or other accidents or injuries remain the major complication of untreated clinical depression. By contrast, large studies of people receiving antidepressant medications indicate the extent to which thinking about suicide or self-harm goes down in those receiving treatment. Most importantly, active suicide attempts and deaths also go down.

What can happen in a relatively small number of people receiving antidepressant medications, particularly in the early phases of treatment, is an increased sense of anxiety, motor restlessness or agitation. As that might exacerbate thoughts of self-harm or suicide in those who already have those feelings (whether they've told the doctor about them or not), it's important to have this discussion before commencing treatment and to monitor the early phases of care very closely.

5. Psychological treatments have no adverse effects.

One of my favourite studies when I was more focused on the impact of intimate relationships on the course of clinical depression, was of the short- and long-term impacts of marital therapy. Contrary to most people's expectations, the person with depression often got worse in the short-term! However, if the couple persisted, the person with depression then had a better long-term outcome.

It was very consistent with research from the 1970s on the impact of expressed emotion in the family home on the course of most mental disorders, including clinical depression. The basic concept was that if the person who was unwell was exposed to too much expressed emotion (including very critical comments), then relapse would shortly follow.

In my own practice, I sought to meet with couples, with the clear intention of co-opting the intimate partner as a 'co-therapist' – a very fashionable idea back then. Working together, one could hopefully reduce the degree of conflict that had often arisen in response to the loss of physical and emotional intimacy, sense of rejection and abandonment, guilt and shame.

The partner's frustration with being unable to change those distressing behaviours that were now so evident (floods of tears, irritability, unprovoked emotional outbursts, non-response to reassurance, non-response to positive changes, self-harm, social withdrawal, and rejection of intimacy) could be acknowledged. A vicious cycle of blame and guilt could be broken.

This all sounded fine in theory. In practice, it was much harder. Often one party (typically the non-depressed person) was on their way out of the relationship – as a result of years of frustration or because they'd found intimacy elsewhere. Often the depressed person had great difficulty participating in the joint sessions. Making the problems more overt made them feel worse about the negative impact they were having on those they cared for.

As an acute treatment, the timing was just all wrong. As I've got older, I've become more pragmatic and typically postpone this hard work until the person with depression is best able to participate. Later on you can make the best possible decisions for yourself, and those you care about – best done when you have recaptured your own capacity to express emotional warmth and physical intimacy.

Too many times with young people with depression, or middle-aged people with chronic illnesses, when the initial treatment hasn't worked and everyone is very distressed, I hear colleagues rush to 'send them to family therapy', 'send them to marital therapy', 'send them to long-term psychotherapy' – followed by 'even if it doesn't really help – well, what harm can it do?'

My answer: 'Lots – assuming that you do believe it is actually an active treatment and not just a glorified placebo!'

For starters, this rush to any psychological port in a storm can precipitate relationship breakdowns, exacerbate distorted beliefs, accentuate guilt and self-harm or postpone the provision of more effective treatments. If it really alienates those intimate partners or family who are closest and most able to provide 24/7 safe and sustainable support, then it is downright dangerous.

At the Cundill Centre for Child and Youth Depression in Toronto, Canada, my colleague Professor Peter Szatmari has led a fascinating study on identifying the adverse effects of psychological therapies for young people – particularly important as psychological therapies are usually recommended first-up for youth with clinical depression. It was the first time I'd ever heard a child psychiatrist come clean about the fact that such approaches don't always go well for the individual, or their family, and that those affected are often not provided with sufficient information to make the best choices possible.

In a public debate some years ago with another child-psychiatry colleague on the use of antidepressant medications in young people, I asked the simple question, 'So, just how do you treat a fifteen-year-old with severe depression who is actively suicidal?'

His reply: 'I admit them to hospital and hand the problem over to the other doctors.'

Astounding response, as the additional traumatisation that frequently results from admitting young people to acute psychiatry wards is now well recognised. And being in a hospital is not on its own an active treatment.

For someone who is known to use a lot of words – I was speechless at my colleague's response. We both knew too well that he'd just avoided taking any responsibility for the decision to prescribe a real treatment.

A similar theme has been expressed by those who track the course of illness from its adolescent onset through to adulthood. For half of those who have major difficulties as young people, such as depression, suicidal behaviour and self-harm, the problems don't persist into adulthood – so these colleagues recommend we sit, watch and wait.

Of course, this assumes that the young people will actually make it into adulthood, alive and not significantly scarred, mentally or physically, by their adolescent experiences. It also completely discounts the potential for altering the course of illness earlier and, potentially, preventing that progression for the other half who *do* drag their difficulties on into adult life.

Interestingly, when the same debate breaks out in other areas of paediatric medicine – think childhood seizures (epilepsy), diabetes or asthma – the community, parent and professional response is markedly different. Doctors don't just sit and wait, putting at risk the lives of those young people, short or long term.

As an aside, there have been important medico-legal cases that have established the principle that people with clinical depression have rights to receive information about and access to the full range of possible medical or psychological 'treatments'. Sometimes the law can be a very useful way of resolving ideological divides that do not operate in a patient's best interests.

The research-informed view now is that psychological interventions have about the same success rate as other medical therapies for mild to moderately severe forms of clinical depression (about 50 per cent clearly benefit, while 5 to 20 per cent deteriorate). Everywhere in the world, psychological therapies also cost time, money and opportunity. If you are not getting better, or actually getting worse, just providing more of the same may be the worst option.

6. Psychological treatments are equally effective as medications for all forms of clinical depression.

As outlined in Chapter 14, there isn't just one form of clinical depression. But the common portrayal of the treatment options often suggests just one illness – and that psychological treatments and medical treatments have about the same first-up cure rate, about 40 to 50 per cent.

One of the problems is that actual head-to-head comparisons aren't that common. For the less severe forms, typically meaning those associated with anxiety, the short-term response rate for medicines and reputable psychological therapies (like CBT) are comparable.

But, as depression becomes more severe, and things like agitation, suicidal behaviour, neglect of self-care, motor and cognitive slowing and social withdrawal intensify, or very specific features like psychotic experiences of delusions of guilt or hallucinatory voices emerge, the clear advantages of various medications, and combinations of medications, or physical treatments like ECT, increases.

Essentially, medical treatments do their best work when you are very unwell. The most suitable time for other psychological, interpersonal, behavioural and social interventions tends to be after recovery, to stay well into the future.

With regards to optimal care, the priorities should be what's the best *sequence* of care, the cost or availability of treatments (since all validated treatment options are better than none), personal preference, likelihood of unintended harm *and* that over the long term, what's the right combination of psychological, behavioural, social and medical therapies for you.

7. You've only really recovered from depression when you stop your medications.

Have you really recovered from diabetes when you can just throw the insulin away? Have you really recovered from epilepsy when you can just ditch the anticonvulsant medication? It's still a widely expressed belief that people have only really recovered from depression when the medicine has gone out with the trash. While clinical depression can run an episodic course, and there are many psychological and behavioural strategies that can help to prevent it coming back, the reality for many people with persistent or recurrent illnesses is that continuing medication is the best way to stay well, live longer and lead a productive life. It would be great if that medical reality was more widely acknowledged and socially accepted.

8. Antidepressant medications lead to worse physical health and then premature death.

Clinical medicine has two important goals – living longer and living better. Clinical depression, particularly when it starts in adolescence or the young adult years, shortens your life. All causes including self-harm, suicide, alcohol and drug use, accidents and injuries, and then other physical health problems, such as premature heart disease.

But what about the treatments? Don't they just make you fatter and sicker? Don't they hurt your brain more than the illness itself? The basic answers are no and no! Long-term studies of people have been successfully treated with antidepressants indicate that they live longer, probably have fewer changes in underlying brain structures and have better physical health outcomes.

That's not to say that careful, long-term, medical monitoring of the physical health of people being treated for clinical depression isn't necessary. Some of the medicines do result in weight gain and may then lead to diabetes or other metabolic complications. Finding the best treatment option for you is critical.

9. You can't treat your depression until you stop drinking (or using any other substances that you may be using to self-medicate).

If you have an alcohol or substance-misuse problem, even though we may well accept that you've been largely self-medicating for a long time, sadly, some doctors may not be in a rush to help – even though you're at higher risk of premature death, physical ill-health, other accidents and injuries, family and relationship breakdowns and loss of education or employment.

There's no doubt that people with clinical depression and concurrent alcohol or other substance misuse are harder to treat – more unstable mood, worse sleep–wake cycles, more side-effects from treatments, more risk of drug interactions, higher risk of self-harm and suicidal behaviour. So this requires greater expertise, more multidisciplinary care and careful use of the right sequence of treatments to move from your preferred self-medication to our other safer and more effective methods.

10. You're not really depressed – you've simply got a personality disorder and antidepressant treatments won't help you.

We all have temperaments (those emotional-setting things that make us ourselves), experiences and consequently 'personalities'. We all get sick and eventually die – from infections, heart or lung disease or cancer or from other mental conditions like clinical depression. Our personality does travel with us through the illness experience and will influence how we respond, positively or negatively, to the many challenges we face.

In psychiatry, the concept of a personality disorder wasn't ever meant to exclude other diagnoses, like clinical depression. In fact, many personality characteristics are themselves expressed differently at different stages of life and in different contextual and relationship settings.

Have you ever heard the ex-spouse/partner exclaim, 'They never behaved like that when we lived together?' The reality is that those things that seemed very fixed can change – and often do – in different interpersonal environments.

In clinical practice, one of the most important reasons to see you when you've recovered is to observe your normal personality, your regular interpersonal and emotional style, free of the distorting effects of illness.

Any time a colleague opines, 'They simply have a personality disorder (for women: borderline, obsessional or dependent; for men: narcissistic, paranoid or antisocial)', I simply enquire, 'Have you seen them when they're well?'

For many of my more junior colleagues, often the answer is, 'No – I've just seen them for twenty minutes in an emergency department, after an overdose . . . and by the way, they were probably still intoxicated . . .'

A good deal of my life is spent saying things like, 'I've seen him when he's well. You know, he is really warm, has a great partner and a solid work record. When he's unwell, things are quite different.'

Sadly, the diagnostic concept of 'personality disorder' is now one that is frequently misused in health services to exclude people from care or direct people away from medical interventions that may actually help.

ANNA'S STORY

I first met Anna almost thirty years ago. I was deeply engaged with people being assessed medically and psychologically for chronic fatigue. She walked determinedly into my office and said, 'Let's be clear – I'm not depressed, but maybe you can help.'

I dived into my usual lines, 'Although I'm a psychiatrist – and psychiatrists are medical doctors – I don't subscribe to a simple psychological explanation for these syndromes. I'm really interested in how critical brain systems, like the body clock, are disrupted by "medical" things like infection, or "mental" things like depression. But my main concern is working out which treatments may actually help people recover.'

Anna's response: 'Fair enough.'

After some lively banter, much negotiation and information updates on how the body clock works, I suggested a trial of 'antidepressants' – not for 'depression', but to treat the fatigue, aches and pains and brain fog.

Anna agreed to give it a trial.

When we reviewed the outcome of this trial three months later, Anna reported feeling much better – but the sexual side effects were a real negative. Anyway, she was headed back to work, and into a new relationship.

I next saw Anna ten years later after she was diagnosed and treated for early-stage breast cancer. The radiotherapy and estrogen-blocking medication had made her feel totally miserable. Her oncologist had said, 'You're depressed by the life-threatening diagnosis – go see that psychiatrist again and get back on antidepressants.'

Anna realised it just wasn't as simple as that. Her fatigue and brain fog were back, and her mood was low – not *sad*, but she just couldn't enjoy anything. No amount of rest made any difference – actually, more rest tended to make it worse.

So we soon agreed that reintroducing the antidepressant that worked last time was the way to go.

Again, Anna had a good response, but she was also annoyed at now being in a low-estrogen state. Was that making things much worse? And was that why she was much more obviously depressed this time around?

For many women, experiencing fatigue, sleep disruption and low mood during menopause (natural or medically induced), this is an important question.

What was clear for Anna was that she was more at risk of developing fatigue and depressive states than many other women who may have gone through the same life stages or medical treatments. But she was also prepared to accept that and try treatments like antidepressants. End result: she found interventions that worked for her.

22

The Real-world Experience of Taking Antidepressant Medication

The birth of effective antidepressant medicines, and a whole range of other antipsychotic and mood-stabilising agents from the 1960s onwards, was one of the most important developments in modern medicine. Prior to that people whose lives had been ruined by major mood or psychotic disorders were frequently hospitalised, and were also at very high risk of premature death. From then on, they have had the opportunity to receive treatments in their own homes and resume their personal, family, professional and societal roles.

Many decades later, it's very easy to take such advances as a given and be selectively blind to the benefits they have delivered. Like so much in modern medicine – vaccines, cancer therapies, keyhole surgeries, opening up of blocked blood vessels to the heart – we now take these significant leaps forward for granted.

A critical aspect of education in mental health is providing students with exposure to people who are living with severe mood or psychotic disorders, but do not respond to available treatments. To see what life is really like when these illnesses are left to run their 'natural course'. Unfortunately, this experience is often limited to medical and nursing students, with very little exposure for many psychology students and other health disciplines who operate outside more specialised centres.

Direct contact with those severely affected, and being witness to the impacts on their families and carers, quickly dispels naive notions that these disorders are simply normal social or behavioural responses to adversity. Or that they are easily fixed by 'placebo' therapies, able to be 'talked through' with a comforting friend or readily fixed by a simple change in diet or taking a holiday.

The fundamental disturbance in brain function, historically referred to as a 'nervous breakdown' or what I would prefer to call a 'broken mind', that accompanies severe forms of clinical depression manifests in:

- grossly distorted behaviour – cessation of eating and drinking, unconstrained pacing, self-hitting, rubbing, picking at skin and clothes and other forms of agitation, endless repetitive and pointless mundane activities, like dressing and undressing
- changes in normal physical movements and expressions – slowed walking and other motor movements, loss of facial movements, fixed and anguished facial expressions
- distorted and greatly distressed emotional expression
- impaired cognitive performance – inability to concentrate, remember, plan or shift from one cognitive task to another
- serious acts of self-harm or active suicidal behaviour that are often unpredictable and precipitous.

These things are apparent to even the most sceptical observer – assuming, of course, they have any empathy for the plight of those affected.

Measuring depression severity – neurobiologically

These severe forms are not 'depression estimates' simply derived from ticking enough boxes on self-report scales of anxiety, sadness, sleep disturbance, loss of libido, tiredness or appetite or weight changes. At the start of the modern clinical trial era, which was devoted to determining which treatments – medical, psychological, behavioural or social – worked most effectively, and for which types of depressive disorders – various rating scales, typically completed by trained clinicians, were developed to try to assess common symptoms of depression.

The most famous of these scales, the Hamilton Depression Rating Scale, was developed by a psychiatrist, Max Hamilton, and first published in 1960. It was the most frequently used in the early trials of antidepressant medicines. It placed great weight on the more classic physical (or somatic or neurobiological) features of severe depression and observable changes in motor movements, agitation, weight loss and sleep disturbance.

The people who participated in these early studies, and basically dominated clinical research until the early 1980s, were likely to be hospitalised, attending specialist clinics, having had many episodes, experienced suicidal behaviours, and were resistant to psychological or behavioural interventions. They were diagnosed as having more severe or neurobiological clinical subtypes – often referred to as melancholic, endogenous or psychotic.

It was the clinical image of these people that underpinned the concept of major depression, and its later standardisation for research purposes. At the time research centres were trying to investigate these clinical concepts with new genetic and other medical technologies. They were hunting for the neurobiological signals of the underlying brain mechanisms that caused these diseases. Additionally, they were evaluating the efficacy of new medications. This approach to research was taken up with gusto by the American Psychiatric Association and in 1980 gave birth to their diagnostic bible, the *Diagnostic and Statistical Manual for Mental Disorder, Third Edition (DSM-III)*.

Without a well-standardised diagnostic system, such fundamental research in humans couldn't proceed. As later conceded by the Director of the US National Institute of Mental Health (NIMH), Steve Hyman, this all went too far, becoming Stalinist in its implementation.

In the US, the DSM system moved away from promoting better research and licensing new treatments to being the basis of personal medical insurance. So, you couldn't get medical care without assigning one of these diagnostic labels. In Australia, and most other countries, we don't use such systems for reimbursing medical care costs.

Measuring anxiety and depression severity – psychologically

At the same time, there were other scale developments. These placed an emphasis on psychological distress and cognitive characteristics – that is, focusing much more on what you thought and how you felt (and not what others could observe). They were very important to researchers focused on the development of more effective psychological interventions, mainly intended for people with less severe forms of anxiety and depression.

The most important, the Beck Depression Inventory, dates back to 1961, and was developed by Aaron Beck, a psychiatrist who pioneered the concept that negative cognitions – longstanding self-beliefs, attitudes and distorted interpretations of the external world – were central to the onset of common forms of anxiety and depression. His work forms the basis of most modern cognitive-behaviour therapies (CBT). The 21-item scale is completed by the person themselves – that is, it's a self-report and not an independent-observer based rating scale.

So, two quite different traditions, focusing on quite different types of people, developed from the 1960s onwards. Both were seeking to bring more modern methods of measurement and standardisation to the field. But they had distinct intentions – for one, the determination of the most effective medical treatments for those with severe forms of clinical depression. For the other, it was to assist those whose lives were disrupted by more enduring cognitive and psychological characteristics.

The 1980s onwards – a collision of independent traditions

From the 1980s onwards the two fields began to collide in ways that have distorted much of the subsequent discourse. As described previously, the successful social and public health marketing of major depression led to a blurring of this fundamental distinction.

Psychiatric epidemiology, in the US and elsewhere in the world, went out into the broader community to find out how common major depression was, and who was accessing care. These studies were a genuine effort to understand the unmet need for care and how nations could best respond.

At the same time, the realisation that the new antidepressant compounds – most notably the selective serotonin reuptake inhibitors (SSRIs) – were far less toxic than their predecessors (the tricyclics and the MAOIs), eventually caused pharmaceutical companies to rethink their target audience.

This pivot in thinking in specialist psychiatry, public health and in the pharmaceutical industry, away from a focus on the most severe forms of clinical depression to the wider public significance, was a critical turning point. It led to an emphasis on providing medical or psychological care in everyday primary care and family-practice-based settings. It also precipitated open competition as to which type of treatment (medical versus psychological) was preferable for the many millions of people with less severe conditions.

So, since the 1980s the majority of people entering clinical trials that test the efficacy and safety of new antidepressant compounds, or new psychological therapies, are likely to have less severe forms of depression. It is also likely that the form of depression most studied is of the anxious-depressive subtype (see Chapter 14).

So what do most people experience when they take the common antidepressant medications?

When it comes to reporting the common experiences of people taking antidepressant medications we've tended to fall back on different types of information. This includes data from the clinical testing of a new compound (efficacy and safety trials), followed by more extensive trials in broader groups of people with major depression or other mood disorders, and then eventually the ongoing experiences of those who are prescribed these treatments by their physicians.

So, first, there is the systematic data collected from the 'registration' trials of each compound. These are the short-term studies that pharmaceutical companies must conduct. They detail both the positive benefits and the possible dangers. Here, we are mainly talking about studies of otherwise physically healthy adults who have been diagnosed as having major depression, but are likely to not express significant suicidal behaviours or have concurrent alcohol or other drug misuse.

The results are submitted to the various national regulators who give permission to distribute these compounds in each country.

The regulators also have an important ongoing role in monitoring the safety profile of these compounds and, if concerned, they may move to restrict their use. The most famous example of this was the 2004 FDA 'black box' warning about increased 'suicidality' among young people taking the new generation SSRIs. (See Chapter 20.)

If the regulators are really concerned, they may deregister specific compounds. More typically, they may issue a 'safety advisory' – as the Australian regulator, the Therapeutic Goods Administration (TGA), did in February 2021 for pregabalin and gabapentin – traditionally anti-epileptic drugs but now also used in complex mood disorders, like bipolar disorder. (The alert related to the potential for those compounds to be associated with abuse or dependence.)

The active role of national regulators: a case example for antidepressant use and alleged links to increased suicidal behaviour in young people

A much more interesting case reported in December 2020 related to the issue of 'antidepressant utilisation and risk of suicide in young people'. This followed national media coverage of an article disputing the efficacy of antidepressant medications and arguing that they cause harm to young people. The article claimed, 'There is clear evidence that more young Australians are taking antidepressants, and more young Australians are killing themselves and self-harming', implying that the two phenomena were causally linked.

My own assessment was that the article was based on poor tatistical, epidemiological and analytic methods. It included no proof of a causal link. For those interested in comparisons, I would highlight a similar type of analysis that we conducted in the 2000s, which was published in the prestigious *British Medical Journal*. It led to the opposite conclusion – that the wider prescribing of new antidepressants for adults was actually a proxy marker for greater medical and psychological treatments of depression, and that this may have been one factor contributing to falling suicide rates at the time.

An extensive review of this issue was conducted by the TGA. It consulted widely and highlighted the major methodological limitations of the research study. That is, the serious regulator did its job.

It concluded: 'The investigation found that while the increasing use of antidepressants in young people was a concern, the strength of the current evidence available was insufficient to conclude that a causal relationship existed between prescribing of antidepressants and rates of youth suicide.'

Needless to say, the TGA's final conclusion was not widely reported in our national media. Nor was the important additional advice: 'The ACM (Advisory Committee on Medicines) advised that there is a valid and important role for SSRIs and SNRIs in current clinical practice in treating moderate-to-severe depression in children and adolescents, supported by professional guidelines.'

NEIL COLE'S STORY

Depression is something that has plagued me all my life. I live, having done so for the last 20 years, free of it due to the medication that I am on. The contrast between being on effective medication and not is palpable. Unmedicated, I dip into a state of melancholy and despair. With it comes suicidal ideation, hopelessness and obsession with the terrible state I'm in.

I believe in the need to be on antidepressants to arrest any chance of the depression coming back. Even if I feel good, I know that if I go off the medication there will likely be a severe relapse.

While medication is the key to my wellness, I find exercise – in my case, running – to be beneficial. Watching the food I eat is also important; not having sugar is the hardest one for me to give up because it delivers highs and lows. Not having more than one cup of coffee a day.

Sleep is vital for me. Too much could mean I'm depressed. Not enough can lead to anxiety. I'm on mood stabilisers, which aid my sleep.

I believe in the biological nature of depression, and it is hereditary. My two late brothers suffered badly with depression, and it was only when they were on antidepressants that it abated.

The introduction of the SSRIs for me was a complete game-changer, as it was for many hundreds of people I know who are on one of them. Other medications hadn't worked for me.

I have been a public advocate for mental illness for 28 years, since as a member of parliament I went public about my mental illness. It is the medical treatment, with medication and counselling, that I have advocated for. People are best to be medicated, then we can work on other issues such as background that might be relevant to their low mood.

Experiences of those receiving antidepressants from their regular physicians

Second, we rely on post-registration (and post-marketing) reports of adverse events in a much broader group of those living with clinical depression (characterised by age, sex, alcohol or drug use and concurrent physical or other psychiatric illnesses) and who have been prescribed specific medicines or other physical treatments, like the new brain stimulation techniques.

Third, we rely on first-person and public reports from those who take the medicines. It's common in the traditional media, in personal blogs, on social media and in more extensive personal accounts, to find widespread but anecdotal reports of both benefits and side-effects being attributed to the various compounds. There are now organised movements to bring these first-person accounts together in more systematic ways. Given the very large number of people worldwide taking these compounds, this is potentially a very important data source (see AGDS below).

What do clinicians think about the relative value of different antidepressant medicines?

Fourth, we rely on clinicians reporting what people with clinical depression are saying back to those who prescribed the medicines. The doctors then share that information among their colleagues, their professional organisations and their particular sub-speciality groups (like child psychiatry or geriatric psychiatry). They can detect differences between the findings of the initial clinical trials and the broader 'real world' experiences.

The views of practitioners have important impacts on:

- which antidepressants become popular. For example, psychiatrists strongly support the use of the newer SNRIs like venlafaxine for more severe cases despite its more significant side-effect profile and later difficulties with withdrawal phenomena;
- which ones don't progress far. For example, psychiatrists were very sceptical about the efficacy of new noradrenaline reuptake inhibitors (NRIs), like reboxetine, and are sceptical about the efficacy of new melatoninergic agents like agomelatine. This is despite the fact that both of these compounds may have far fewer side-effects or other potential benefits like motor activation or alertness (for reboxetine) or enhanced sleep and circadian rhythms (for agomelatine); and,
- which ones get used in different settings. For example, mirtazapine is very popular in family practice, presumably due to

its sedative effects. By contrast, it is unpopular among psychiatrists due to the perception of lower efficacy and its association with more pronounced weight gain.

Direct surveys of clinicians' impressions are extended by the formal development of consensus practice guidelines. In Australia, these have been recently updated to present the best available evidence from formal trials and clinical experience.

These are interesting as they try really hard to escape the turf wars of self-care versus psychological care versus medical care. They recommend the appropriate use of all strategies for the more severe or recurrent forms of clinical depression. Further, they attempt to provide much greater differentiation between different classes of antidepressants – the world of medicines is no longer dominated simply by SSRIs, and their big brother SNRIs. They try to make the case as to why, when you consider both efficacy *and* side-effect profile together, you may well chose different classes of compounds for different clinical scenarios.

Fifth, we see very high-profile enquiries into specific cases – typically by forensic services, namely the Coroners Courts in Australia – following a suicide, homicide or other major incident. In these cases, it is often alleged that either ingestion of the medicine or, conversely, withdrawal from the medicine, has played a causative role in these tragic incidents.

The Australian Genetics of Depression Study: what do 20,000 Australians *really* experience?

So, given our desire to better collate the experiences of those with clinical depression who take antidepressant medicines, we have capitalised on Australians' willingness to volunteer for genetic studies (see Chapter 10) and asked them to provide us with a 'warts-and-all' summary of the positive and negative aspects of these experiences.

In this study led by Professor Nick Martin and his team at the Queensland Institute of Medical Research, 20,689 Australians were recruited (75 per cent female, average age of 43 years). They completed online surveys about their depressive symptoms and their experiences with treatments. Those who consented were then sent a saliva kit in the mail so that they could contribute their DNA to this national program. Of those who enrolled, 95 per cent were given a diagnosis of depression by a medical practitioner and 88 per cent met formal criteria for a lifetime depressive episode. As is common in real life settings, 68 per cent also met criteria for another psychiatric disorder (overwhelmingly general anxiety, panic, social anxiety or PTSD).

The peak ages for onset of depression in this group were 10–20 years, consistent with the international epidemiology that most people have their first episode much earlier than historic texts, and much media reporting, would predict. Depression is increasingly a young person's problem – even though the therapist couches and psychiatrists clinics are largely occupied by middle-aged and older people.

Depression was also a recurring problem. Four per cent of the participants had had only one depressive episode, with the median (middle) number of episodes being six, while the most commonly reported number was more than 13! The median duration of each episode was 12 weeks – much longer than the two weeks required by most classification systems to assign a formal diagnosis. More than 10 per cent reported that their worst episode had lasted more than a year. In other words, these volunteers were more likely to have severe or recurrent disorders, relatively early age of onset and then depression persisting into mid-life.

Given our interest in how depression may run in families (see Chapter 10), in this group 70 per cent reported that a first-degree relative (parent, sibling, child) also had a mental disorder – most commonly depression, but also anxiety or bipolar disorder.

But what about their experiences with antidepressant medicines? Not surprisingly, 95 per cent reported taking an antidepressant largely for depression but also for anxiety. The average number of antidepressants that they'd tried was 2.75 but the range was very wide (from one to 14). Only 33 per cent of the group had ever taken just one antidepressant, while 42 per cent reported that they had tried three or more compounds. This is consistent with the broader clinical trials research, where only about one-third of people do really well with their first antidepressant they take. By far, the most commonly prescribed antidepressants were SSRIs (notably sertraline, escitalopram, fluoxetine, citalopram and paroxetine) and SNRIs (venlafaxine and desvenlafaxine).

So, do antidepressants work for most people? Across the ten most commonly prescribed antidepressants, approximately two-thirds reported that the drugs worked either 'very well' (about 25 per cent) or 'moderately well' (35–40 per cent). These figures were generally better for the common SSRIs and SNRIs than for some of the older agents, like amitriptyline.

Importantly, approximately 75 per cent of respondents reported relief of particular symptoms, things like low mood, loss of pleasure, fatigue, poor sleep or suicidal thinking. That is, in these people with more severe, recurrent or persistent clinical depression – for the vast majority – the medicines did exactly what they are designed to do.

But the other side of the coin is the side-effect cost. Noting that the great majority of the sample had experiences with SSRIs or SNRIs, the most common side-effects that participants attributed to the medicines were reduced sex drive (35 per cent), weight gain (26 per cent), dry mouth (22 per cent), nausea (18 per cent), drowsiness (16 per cent), insomnia (16 per cent) and headache (14 per cent). While all of these are problematic, not all would be expected to be persistent or severe, though some (notably nausea and headache) may lead to early discontinuation of the medicine.

The more worrying adverse effects that participants attributed to the medicines were suicidal thoughts (12 per cent), agitation (11 per cent) and suicide attempt (four per cent). Approximately 40 per cent of the participants had to either cease medication or change medications due to intolerable side-effects.

Our interpretation of this very large dataset of Australians with clinical depression and who have considerable experience with the most common antidepressant agents is that while most derive very significant benefits, finding the best antidepressant usually takes several goes, and that most people continue to live with an ongoing side-effect burden – with particular emphasis on sexual dysfunction and weight gain.

TAKE-OUT TIPS

- Most people who take antidepressant medicines find one that works and experience much relief from their main symptoms.
- Most peole who choose to keep taking antidepressants experience some side-effects, most commonly sexual in nature or relating to weight gain.

23

Right Care, First Time

'How the hell do I get out of this hole, and how soon can I get back to work?'

Not uncommonly, I'm asked to meet urgently with a high-profile professional, politician, community or business leader. Recently, I was halfway through my usual explanation to a highly successful business leader – Bill – when he abruptly stopped me in my tracks: 'Ian, can we just cut to the chase – how the hell do I get out of this hole and how soon can I get back to work?'

At the end of the day, they are the essential questions.

While sitting with a very distressed mother (Helen) of a young woman (Anna) with a nasty teenage-onset psychotic depression, Helen cried out, 'The staff say she is getting better – what do they mean? I can't see any evidence. When you say we'll trial the next treatment, how will you know that she's better?'

As Anna had engaged in a chaotic suicidal act earlier that day, Helen felt that the priorities of the treating team and the parents were really not shared. Not surprisingly, her first priority was her daughter's safety.

But paradoxically, Helen was very reluctant to consider other treatments that may have long-term side-effects, like weight gain, sedation or short-term memory difficulties with physical treatments (like TMS or ECT) through to more significant issues like suppression of Anna's natural immunity from experimental immunotherapy.

Anna herself expressed reservations about various treatments, based on the experiences of other young people she knew. These included one other girl's report of persisting memory problems that she attributed to physical treatments, and two kilos of weight gain on medication.

It was never 'psychology versus medicine', and it certainly isn't now

Sitting with a senior advisor to government, I recently found myself in the usual defensive position of trying to justify our current treatments. His general view was that most of our treatments are ineffective, and that even for those that are more efficacious, the longer-term side-effects are intolerable. At one level, that makes him an influential supporter of further clinical research. There is no doubt that we need better options, but, in truth, that makes clinical psychiatry just like every other area of medicine.

Sadly, though, it also reflects the fact that even some of our most ardent supporters provide a rather unbalanced representation of where treatments are really at. The truth is that when we do provide the best medical and psychological care now available, we achieve much better outcomes than when we provide no treatment.

Overwhelmingly, the best treatment options emphasise link self-help, psychological and behavioural therapies, plus appropriate medical interventions, to achieve the best results. The more personalised the approach and the more intensive tracking of individuals, the better the results.

Garry McDonald: personalised, pragmatic and effective care

When I was CEO of Beyond Blue, I had the great pleasure of touring parts of regional Australia with the actor and comedian (and Beyond Blue board member) Garry McDonald – one of our living natural treasures who has his own lived experience of severe anxiety and episodic clinical depression. Garry's story was well known to many Australians in the early 2000s, having been one of our most successful comedic actors, creating the legendary Norman Gunston character and appearing with Ruth Cracknell in *Mother and Son.*

Sadly, just at the start of a new TV venture, he had a recurrence of his illness, and the show was pulled from national television – a professional and personal disaster. Following his recovery, it was great fun for me to appear as a 'warm-up' act at community meetings to raise awareness of depression. I was the dry clinician, the academic doctor. My role was to provide a brief summary of the symptoms of depression, its impact on families, and generally encourage people to seek treatment.

These country audiences were very polite, but they really warmed up when Garry took the stage. They had flocked in to see his 'show' and hear him speak. He gave a great personal outline of underlying and persisting anxiety being the big risk factor for depression in his life (classic anxious arousal leading to depression. So, between episodes of depression, he makes great use of high-quality cognitive behaviour therapy, yoga and meditation to control his anxiety and challenge his dysfunctional thoughts.

Often, this very telling explanation of his personal journey led to this question from the audience: 'So, you don't need to take medication?'

Garry's matter-of-fact reply: 'No, when I'm really depressed, I take the medication. It works.' It often left the audience silenced – perhaps not what some had expected to hear. He was equally straight, and funny, about cognitive therapy, noting that when you need to use it, use it. Sometimes you get the point after one session, sometimes after a whole lot more – but once you've got the point, just use it and get on with it.

Garry's whole tone was such a welcome relief from the usual nonsense: no great drama, employ the strategies that work for you, get on with your life.

Do we really listen to the positive outcome stories?

Not all such public outings go so well. I've been in others where members of the audience are keen to share their negative experiences, often with medications. The reality is that while individual experiences are variable, and negative experiences drive people to warn others, many very good experiences are not shared. Even worse, those who tell their good outcome stories are often actively devalued. Compared with other areas, like cancer or heart disease, we still have a very long way to go to bring these real and positive stories into the public domain.

When clinical psychiatrist and psychotherapist Peter Kramer published his international bestseller *Listening to Prozac* in 1993, there was an immediate backlash from the anti-medication community. While the book was easily attacked as a traitor to the true cause (namely unlocking the past psychological conflicts that cause depression), to me it was much more relevant that the author was open to hearing what was being experienced by those taking these medications.

These days, we have the potential to move well beyond deep personal narratives and present the collective picture from tens of thousands of Australians (see AGDS – Chapter 22). The bottom line: for those with clinical depression, particularly where it recurs or persists, the vast majority derive significant benefits, while living with (largely tolerable) side-effects.

Another major public figure, John Brogden, who is now chairman of Lifeline, Australia's long-standing, leading crisis support service, presents a riveting tale of his own mood disorder, and suicide attempt. More importantly, he details the challenges of living with the condition and the extent to which he needs to make use of all available strategies – medicines, lifestyle adjustments like diet and exercise, access to high-quality professional care, family and professional support – to be a productive member of a community. Sadly, that community still engages in active discrimination against those who have revealed their mental ill-health, even after they have recovered.

BELINDA'S STORY

Belinda was brought to my office by one of our very smart non-medical workers, who normally focuses on helping young people get back to school. But she was old enough and wise enough to know that Belinda's school attendance problems and declining performance were way off the normal range of anxiety and depression explanations.

Belinda was falling asleep during school lessons, having unusual out-of-body experiences and feeling increasingly desperate about her future. She had hoped to do well in her end-of-secondary-school exams and go on to university. As those hopes seemed dashed by her unexplained illness, she was increasingly depressed and having thoughts of self-harm. She had attended a children's hospital for medical investigations, as it had been suggested that she may have a form of epilepsy. The results of those tests were inconclusive, and she was sent back to her local doctor with the notation: 'No clear cause found.'

On meeting Belinda and her very attentive, engaged mother and older sister, it was clear we had only scratched the surface of Belinda's altered behaviour (a markedly disturbed sleep–wake cycle, extreme recent-onset compulsive behaviours, severe ruminations and visual hallucinations), and the depth of her depression and her suicide risk. She rapidly deteriorated, with the onset of more severe and impulsive attempts at self-harm, paranoid ideas about her own family members and prolonged periods of being largely unable to communicate at all.

We arranged her urgent hospitalisation through a specialist group (led by Liz Scott) that focuses on much more detailed medical examination of such cases. Relatively quickly, we were able to determine that Belinda had a rare form of autoimmune disease attacking her thyroid gland and brain. We recommended new forms of immunotherapy, as conventional antidepressant and antipsychotic treatment were only resulting in more side effects without delivering clear benefits.

Belinda's dad, who had been described to me previously as a 'very difficult father', came to see me urgently – he was concerned about exposing his daughter to new treatments (including the suppression of her immune system) that may have very serious long-term health impacts. He was intelligent, educated and challenging. He wasn't simply inclined to accept our best clinical advice. I think the 'difficult' label had been applied largely because our professionals had not sat down long enough to listen to his own ideas about what was causing his daughter's difficulties (social isolation and declining school performance) and contrast them with our conventional explanations (teenage-onset anxiety and depression). Throughout the complicated course of Belinda's subsequent hospitalisation and immunotherapy, he continued to insist on an active dialogue about the merits of pursuing this course versus other alternatives – a perfectly reasonable position to take.

Despite many desperate days, many close calls and residual cognitive difficulties, Belinda did respond to complex immunotherapy. She gradually returned to her original plan to complete school and go on to higher education. We have followed her closely for some years now, through various ups and downs, and recurrent periods of illness. But she has made a very remarkable recovery.

Some years ago, my partner Liz and I wandered into a major department store close to Christmas. To our great surprise, we ran into Belinda and her mother, who just happened to be passing through. Belinda was working as a temporary shop assistant – before her planned return to higher education in the New Year. I hadn't seen Belinda in some time, though Liz had continued to monitor her progress. For both of us, this was the best Christmas present of all – to see Belinda out in the world leading a thoroughly 'normal' life. She was headed towards the next phase – now with the real prospect of reaching her full potential.

In a side conversation with Belinda's mum, who was shedding tears of joy and relief, we all reflected that without access to high-quality, prolonged, multidisciplinary care – medical, psychiatric, psychological, nursing and educational support – Belinda would not still be with us, let alone moving on to new things in her life.

What you need to ask when you go to get help

So, at any time a person presents for care, what do you really need to know? What are the things that you (or hopefully the person accompanying you to care) need to ask? Getting the right answers upfront is essential. It's best if someone you care about goes with you. They can really help you to get answers to these ten questions.

1. What model(s) of illness, and of care, do you work with?
2. What are you best at doing, and what types of things might you ask other professionals to do?
3. Do you work closely, as a team, with other practitioners or organisations? How do you share my information with them?
4. Can you get more information about me from laboratory, psychology or brain tests?
5. What's your best understanding of the things that we need to focus on to:
   - get me out of this hole in the short-term?
   - keep me well in the longer-term?
6. Are there other treatment options available, different from the ones that you normally recommend?
7. Do you have ways to track how things are going for me, and can I access them? And which things do they track – my symptoms or my daily functioning?
8. Can we agree about those things that matter most to me, so that we are both really clear about my goals?
9. What ways do I have of contacting you if things suddenly get worse? Will I be able to text you, or is there another way?
10. How can other people who care about me (partner, family, carers) best provide relevant information to you? What will you share with them in return?

Hopefully, you've entered a care system that does actively track your progress, in person or with more modern tracking tools and personalised IT. Just remember, this is a personal journey. It's highly likely that we don't yet have all the information, and things will emerge along the way that will influence our decisions.

As this is a very individual n=1 experiment (meaning it is uniquely about you and not the 'average' person), if your situation is already complicated, I would also push towards going to a clinical research centre or centre of excellence. No matter what treatment they provide, they get better outcomes. They are the people who concede that they don't have all the answers (hence the need for more research) and they are also the ones most prepared to step outside simplistic guidelines or the standard 'cookbook' approaches to care.

You will need agreement with the treating team – always look for a team and not one stand-alone clinician – about what is the model of your illness that they are working with and how does it relate to your specific circumstances? I'm always staggered by the blank faces that confront me when I ask this question of people who have been to many other professionals. We all need to be on the same page. We need to be well-informed about the assumptions that are in operation. We need genuine agreement about where we are headed.

Once we've got the model of care straight, we need to be in agreement about the desired short-term (getting out of the hole) and longer-term goals (or 'clinical outcomes' in our business-speak). That may seem obvious, but treatment can often be very short-term (and aim for some reduction in depressive symptoms) and may not involve planning the best sequence of treatment options over the longer journey.

Illness type, stage and trajectory: not simply a diagnosis

In our model, we focus on five key domains (see Figure 6 overleaf) for both assessment and ongoing tracking of the things that matter. The question 'What's the diagnosis?' dominates specialist psychiatry.

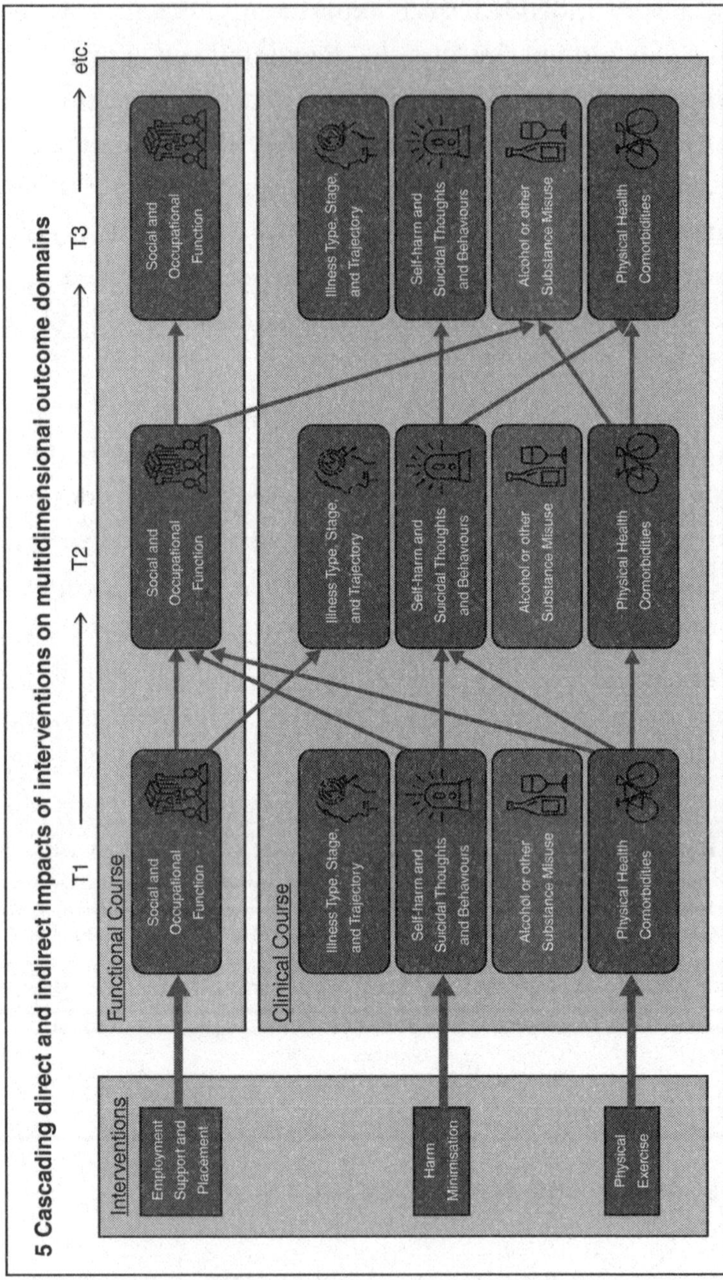

Icons from www.flaticon.com: alarm bell, bicycle and magnifying glass/brain made by Freepik; wine bottle/glass made by srip; team education made by Eucalyp. Interventions which target individual multidimensional outcome domains are likely to have specific and direct impacts, as well as indirect impacts which cascade over time (indicated by time points [T] 1 to 3). Here, we demonstrate three hypothetical paths stemming from three distinct targeted interventions. Path 1 (green) demonstrates that employment support and placement can have a direct effect on social and occupational function that is sustained over multiple time points and has flow-on effects on the future illness type, stage and trajectory, and alcohol or other substance misuse. Path 2 (blue) shows that harm reduction can have a direct and enduring effect on self-harm, suicidal thoughts and behaviours, and also has downstream impacts on social and occupational function and physical health. Path 3 (grey) demonstrates that an exercise intervention can directly improve physical health with future positive effects on social and occupational function, self-harm, suicidal thoughts and behaviours, and alcohol or other substance misuse. ◆

Figure 6

Source: *Medical Journal of Australia*, Rohleder, C. et al, 'Personalising Care Options in Youth Mental Health', vol 211(9), S35.

For us, the diagnosis is just one part of our model – we call it 'Illness type, stage and trajectory' (see also Figure 3 back on page 233).

Within this domain, particularly for young people, we put much greater emphasis on clinical stage (see Figure 3), and the personal or lifelong trajectory (see Figure 4 on page 234). For those in early stages, we focus largely on psychological and behavioural interventions, embedded within appropriate family, social, educational or employment support. The interventions required are low risk but also provide the opportunity to prevent progression to later stages (see Figure 5 on page 298). In our longitudinal studies of those who are already receiving care, while some progression is still common, progression to a much worse outcome is uncommon.

For those who already have a formal diagnosis of clinical depression, we ramp up the psychological–behavioural interventions and consider which medicines may be relevant. These include SSRIs for those with the most common anxiety depression types and non-SSRI agents for those with more circadian or neurodevelopmental trajectories.

Here, the holes are often already deep and the prospects of progression or recurrence much increased. Given the substantial risk of progression at this stage, it is really important to emphasise that there are two key tasks. First, find the quickest way out of the hole – the ladder – but second, ensure that the best possible protective strategies are in place, to reduce the chance of illness persistence, or further progression.

Once individuals have crossed over to the arena of recurrent, persistent or progressive illness we make the assumption that no care, very brief episodes of care or inadequate or poor quality care cannot deliver full recovery.

So clinical staging has two main objectives. The first is to promote early intervention, relieve the current situation and prevent recurrence or progression. The second is to ensure that those who have already progressed to major, persistent or recurrent syndromes receive the most appropriate and intensive interventions to achieve full recovery. Sadly, on most occasions – within our current health care systems – we often fail on both counts.

Illness type

The illness 'type' question is also critical – although, like diagnosis itself, this is very much a work in progress. Again, this is strongly influenced by our work with young people where they are much closer in time to the illness onset, and their lives and their biology have not yet been fundamentally altered by the illness itself. We focus on three fairly general categories – anxious depression, circadian–bipolar, neurodevelopmental–psychotic – that may well influence the type and sequence of treatment (medical and psychological) selection (see Table opposite).

Our working assumption is that these broad types have closer relationships to the underlying brain and body mechanisms that drive the onset and progression of illness. If we've got this right, then providing more specific treatments targeted at these mechanisms should deliver faster recovery and reduce recurrence.

So, for anxious depression, medical or psychological interventions (like SSRIs, mindfulness, meditation, progressive muscle relaxation and/or cognitive therapy) that reduce central nervous system arousal and linked HPA activation may be most relevant. For those with more circadian features, the targets are those SCN-pineal gland and other brain-driven regulators of our sleep–wake cycle – so exposure to morning sunlight, daytime physical activity or the prescription of the natural sleep hormone melatonin may be best. For the neurodevelopmental–psychotic path, those processes linked to social cognition and misperceptions in the

	Self-care strategies	Psychological, behavioural and social		Pharmacological	
		First Choice	**Second Choice**	**First Choice**	**Second Choice**
Anxious-Arousal	• Digital interventions • Mindfulness • Meditation • Physical Activity • Sleep–wake cycle monitoring • Reduction in alcohol, sedatives and other substance use.	• Brief CBT-based therapies • Guided digital interventions for anxiety or depression • Education and employment engagement.	• More specific, skilled or prolonged psychological therapies • Specific exposure and response prevention therapies • Rumination-focused therapies • Individual placement and support in education or employment.	• Selective Serotonin Reuptake Inhibitors (SSRIs) – like fluoxetine, sertraline, escitalopram.	• Selective Serotonin and Norepinephrine Reuptake Inhibitors (SNRIs) – like venlafaxine and desvenlafaxine, duloxetine.
Circadian-Bipolar	• Digital interventions for sleep, fatigue and activity • Physical activity (morning-focus) • 24-hour sleep-wake cycle interventions • Morning light exposure.	• Brief CBT-based therapies for insomnia, sleep-wake cycle • Guided digital interventions for sleep–wake cycle and physical activity • Behavioural activation • Regular, daily education and employment engagement.	• Specific chronobiological therapies – sleep restriction, light therapies, 24-hour behavioural therapies • Social rhythm therapies • Rumination-focused therapies • Individual placement and support in education or employment.	• Melatonin (immediate or slow release) • Melatonin analogues – like agomelatine	• Lithium • Mood-stabilisers – like lamotrigine • Wakefulness medications – like modafinil • Atypical antipsychotic agents – like quetiapine.
Neuro-developmental-Psychosis	• Digital interventions for socialisation and connection.	• Social skills training • Regular, daily education and employment engagement.	• Individual placement and support in education or employment.	• Selective Serotonin Reuptake Inhibitors (SSRIs) – like fluoxetine, sertraline, escitalopram.	• Atypical antipsychotic agents - like quetiapine • Mood-stabilisers – like lamotrigine.

Table: Recommendations for choices of treatments for different types of clinical depression.

Source: *Medical Journal of Australia*, Rohleder, C. et al, 'Personalising Care Options in Youth Mental Health', vol 211(9), S35.

environment – like social skills training or supported education or employment – may be more helpful.

By contrast, most formal diagnoses, including those for clinical depression, rest on the concept of thresholds. Once you have a certain number of symptoms or clinical signs of a certain type you become a 'case' and that is often the starting point for a 'cookbook approach' to treatment selection. Often you can pass the threshold for multiple diagnoses (now termed comorbidity), notably for co-occurring anxiety disorders, personality dysfunction or substance misuse.

The 'threshold' approach doesn't recognise earlier forms of the same type (i.e. sub-threshold cases) and, hence, delays treatment selection until that threshold is reached. The evidence for any very specific relationship between each formal diagnosis and any specific underlying cause is weak. Hence our preference for much broader, more inclusive and more dimensional illness 'types'.

The five domains of real interest – the path to personalised care

The domain of 'illness type, trajectory and stage' sits beside the other four: social and occupational function; self-harm, suicidal thoughts and behaviours; alcohol and other substance misuse; and physical health. As outlined in Figure 6 back on page 362, these domains have important interactions with each other over time, and it's unlikely that you can be really well (or 'recovered', to answer Helen's pointed question) if we are not making substantive progress on all five.

To understand where all of these dimensions are at when you enter care, someone has to be really interested. Often clinicians or their organisations say things like, 'I don't do treatments for alcohol or drug problems, or I'm not interested (or qualified) to comment on your physical health.' I recently had a trainee in psychiatry inform me, 'I'm not comfortable performing physical examinations', even when this was a necessary part of the clinical assessment. Often there are critical physical signs of major neurological disorders, or indications of major side effects of medications, that need to be assessed by the clinical psychiatrist (we are medical doctors after all).

At times, we've had mental health campaigns propagate the myth that suicidality and clinical depression are not tightly linked. We've had mental health services say that suicide prevention (notably the concept of promoting 'zero suicide in care') is not their responsibility. A whole range of clinicians have informed me that their job is to treat the 'illness' and not sort out whether the person with depression gets back to work or school.

Jay's story: 'I just want to get back to uni.'

Jay is a 22-year-old man, who due to the severity of his mental health problems as a teenager and the surrounding social chaos (separated parents, living with grandparent) dropped out of high school at age 16. He had been attending our various youth services for most of the previous three years. During that time, he engaged with various forms of cognitive-behavioural therapy and more intensive and psychoanalytically orientated psychotherapy. Given his chaotic early life, his mother's frequent hospital admissions and the consequences of his father's alcohol abuse, it was not surprising that he was still greatly distressed by these childhood experiences. He had lots to talk about!

But, as is fairly typical at the start of my own interactions with young people, I asked him, 'So, Jay, what do you really want to do?'

His reply was quick and direct: 'I just want to get back to uni.' (Given Jay's academic capacity and despite his early departure from school, this pathway was an entirely reasonable goal.)

My reply: 'Has our service helped you with that?'

Jay's response: 'The people in the service have been really nice, but no-one has ever really asked . . .'

I don't make the assumption that all the information about the five domains outlined above can come solely from the person with the illness – and particularly not when they are at their lowest point. On most occasions, others such as partners ('We haven't had sex in months', 'She doesn't call her friends anymore', 'She won't go out with our friends', 'He's talking about death all the time'); family ('She's in major financial trouble and borrowing from us', 'He's stopped visiting his mother', 'He's screaming at the kids every night') or other carers ('He's drinking heavily now – that's a real change'), can provide critical information.

Partners, parents or families are often excluded from providing this crucial information. The main reasons are largely false assumptions about privacy and confidentiality. I do make it clear to the person I am treating, and all available family members, that I welcome their input at any time. I do make it clear that I may not be able to share information I have access to from the person themselves – that is still their choice. But there is so much information that only partners, close friends and family have access to, and it is vital to making the best treatment choices.

Clinically, there are other factors, including: family history of depression, bipolar disorder, psychosis, addiction or suicide, along with preferential responses to specific treatments, past history of sexual or physical violence or abuse, and previous history of non-response to specific medical or psychological treatments, that need to be known. Most importantly, it is important to explore the personal or family preferences for treatments – and the reasoning that may sit behind those preferences.

Clinical assessment often needs to be augmented by laboratory tests, brain imaging, neuropsychological tests or objective sleep–wake cycle measures. Sadly, clinical psychiatry and psychology are notorious for their under-utilisation of these techniques. Perhaps it is the ongoing legacy of Cartesian dualism ('it's really all in the mind') or just a failure of clinicians to engage with the insights that can be delivered by better understanding of the biological changes – in brain and body – that accompany clinical depression.

Some years ago, particularly when I spent more time with older people, I used to provide those with clinical depression with their own coloured pictures of the brain scans we produced. These often showed reduced blood flow in parts of the frontal or temporal cortex, or structural changes in key brain regions or interruptions to the white matter cables between cortical areas (see Figure 1 on page 217). My instruction: 'Go home and stick these on the fridge, so next time someone says, "Just what is really wrong with you?", you can just point to the picture! By the way, you can also remind yourself, it's not your fault. You're not lazy, and with the right treatment, you will probably get a lot better.'

For many young people who have participated in our clinical research studies of their disturbed circadian system, we provide printouts of their activity patterns, or their underlying sleep hormone profile, which shows melatonin release under controlled light conditions. Next time, someone calls you lazy, or says you just need to get out of bed earlier and get active, you can point to these very significant disruptions of this most basic regulatory system (see Figure 2 on page 220).

In general medicine, highly personalised care is the new benchmark for a quality service. It's about what is best for you, not just the average treatment for the diagnostic category in which we have placed you. For effective management of your clinical depression, we need information about each of those five domains, from you or others that care about you. When we combine that with other key clinical and laboratory information, we are in the best place to start the journey to recovery.

Measurement-based care

My favourite line when making the argument for innovations in clinical care is, 'I know it sounds odd, but I don't care that much about those people who got better. What I really want to know is, who is *not* getting better and, most importantly, who is getting worse!' Just doing the same things when someone's illness is headed in the wrong direction is not okay. As quickly as possible, I want to know what illness course you are on. For young people, we have been developing maps of different trajectories, to aid our decision-making – when to persist with current efforts or quickly change course.

Prioritising the clinical care of those who do not improve or get worse assumes that the clinician actually knows you are headed the wrong way. In clinical medicine, we often assume that those with ongoing difficulties will just keep coming back, irrespective of prior experiences, cost, logistics or their own assumptions about their prospects for recovery.

I was reminded of this when revisiting my own orthopaedic surgeon who had been kind enough to repair my knee injury. He had very successfully done the same thing for the other knee a decade previously. On this occasion, though, the outcome was not nearly so good, and I was busy and didn't rush back. I just assumed the whole thing was not so successful – after all, I was a decade older, heavier and less physically fit.

But, some months later when I was about to embark on a more demanding trip, I decided to consult him again. Immediately, he provided an explanation for why things had not gone so well, provided additional and very effective short-term treatment and proceeded to arrange and deliver a much better longer-term solution.

There's nothing like personal experiences to cause you to stop and think – so, why wasn't measuring the outcome of the first procedure built in? Simple text messages or automated self-report systems would have done the trick. It would have saved me some months of unnecessary pain and impaired function. Orthopaedics, and other surgical or traditional medical procedures, may seem a whole lot simpler than mental health. But they aren't, really – we can ask just as readily, 'What is happening to you, how symptomatic are you and are you back at school or work?'

The reality in the 21st century is that the active tracking of these five domains through modern apps, online tools, activity trackers and other devices is entirely feasible – but more importantly, really useful! It is so much more real-time and appropriate compared with coming back in-person to a clinic at some much later date. It's also so much more informative than the type of very broad questions that get asked, such as, 'Well, how have things been since last time I saw you?'

I really want to know, as quickly as possible, if things go wrong. I encourage the use of these tracking systems, which can be linked to alerts or text messages, so that much harm is avoided. With real-time information from you, we can quickly get you back on the right track (or at least a different track) quickly. If I prescribe a new medication, I want to know what happens over the next 72 hours – if you become very agitated, I need to know and you and your family need to know what to do next (stop it, change it, be reviewed urgently by me, go to hospital or manage in other ways). If you develop other immediate side-effects – nausea, stomach upset, headache, worsening sleep – we need agreed-upon strategies to respond.

If I recommend a certain behavioural strategy that is very common around sleep–wake cycles and physical activity schedules,

I'm keen to know whether you can implement the plan, and whether it has led to benefits such as better mood, more energy or deeper sleep, or unexpected side-effects, such as increased fatigue or more musculoskeletal pain. If our plan is also linked with other things like increased exposure to morning light, change in regular bedtime, maintenance over the whole week and weekend, I'm keen to see the objective evidence of what you have been able to achieve. It's all part of our shared journey to determine what really works for you in this phase of your life.

This whole dynamic approach, which means adapting in real time to changing circumstances, is best described as 'measurement-based' care. When it is combined with the earlier concept of more personalised care, then you have the basis for a real journey to better outcomes! (See Figure 5 on page 298.)

Optimising non-specific care options

Many of the things I've just described (getting the best information about you, tracking the impacts of care, agreeing a specific treatment plan, focusing on your goals) are what we term the 'non-specific' treatments that accompany the best clinical care. They are labelled 'non-specific' as we do not expect them to have any direct effects on underlying disease mechanisms. We often don't really know how they lead to real benefits. But these non-specific options often deliver more benefits than the specific treatments – particular psychological therapies or individual medicines – that we spend so much time discussing.

Another great reason to attend a clinical research centre is that they are expert at maximising these non-specific – but real – effects. The evidence is clear: people who attend these centres live longer and better than those who receive standard care. It's the business-class section of the health industry! Those involved go to a whole lot more trouble to meet your specific needs – and often put you on the first, not last, seat available to your intended destination. They are not necessarily more expensive, as many are in public hospitals or larger private clinics. They may have limited availability or longer waiting lists, but often the wait is worth the effort. Of course, in an emergency or when you are actively suicidal, you need to connect with the care available.

Non-specific care includes many aspects which are trivialised or dismissed as placebo effects – but these things have all been shown to have real therapeutic benefits and include.

The benefits of really good non-specific care (which is typically maximised in clinical research centres) include: the expectation of a positive benefit from treatment; highly standardised and skilled assessment; independent review by more than one practitioner; time for detailed dialogue and questions with the clinical investigators; independent laboratory investigations; neuropsychological testing; active tracking of clinical outcomes; engagement of skilled clinicians; provision of detailed information about the illness and the merits of currently available treatments; information about novel or experimental treatments; formalisation of the process of informed consent to care; the passage of time as some conditions will improve spontaneously; active engagement of family members or carers; and engagement with other social organisations that focus on support from other community members who have made the same journey.

I am reminded of that last factor on many mornings when I'm walking through a harbourside park just as a group of Alcoholics Anonymous participants gather for their daily 'dose' of peer support. Long before the development of any specific (medical or psychological) treatments for alcohol or other drug dependence, many people found a road to recovery through these social organisations. To this day, despite the development of more specific treatments, the ongoing role of such organisations in the lives of those most affected is significant.

In the realm of mental illness, we have seen the development of various social groups, organised by people with lived experiences. Often, these focus on those with persistent psychotic disorders like schizophrenia, or groups who have other shared characteristics, like war veterans with post-traumatic stress disorder, rather than people with more episodic disorders, like bipolar disorder or clinical depression. But for those with major mood disorders, these groups are just as useful. Join one if you can.

In my early days as the CEO of Beyond Blue, one of my more socially orientated colleagues suggested that I focus our efforts on the development of such community-based and peer-informed support services. In fact, he went as far to say that we would be judged a failure if we did not give birth to a new social (non-professional, non-health-service based) movement.

Interestingly, our efforts to get such things off the ground ran into active pushback from health professionals and health services. While those groups were content with seeking information and feedback from those with lived experiences, there was real resistance to investing in their separate development. Fortunately, the early days of Beyond Blue did give birth to Blue Voices as a start to this movement.

Unfortunately, two decades later, we still don't really have such an active, on-the-ground social movement as one commonly sees around alcohol and drug addiction. This is despite the fact that the sharing of lived experiences, and the active support from those who have travelled similar journeys, have major benefits. So we do strongly encourage those with clinical depression and their families and carers to join those peer groups that are available.

In my view, the goal is to lift 'standard' care (which is typically budget-airline style – bring your own food and carry your own luggage) to 'business class' level, so that as many people as possible can derive the full therapeutic benefits.

Deliberate misuse of placebo data

For most people, a placebo is reduced to a very simple idea – the sugar pill in medication trials; the normal saline injection or the sham procedure in surgical or physical treatment trials. In theory, as it should have no effect on the underlying disease process, it should produce no benefit. But in clinical trials the placebo effect is real and significant! It happens because of the therapeutic benefits from all those non-specific elements of care described above. (These benefits are also maximised in clinical research centres that conduct clinical trials of new treatments.)

One of the most damaging aspects of the distorted public debate about the efficacy of antidepressant medicines is the active misrepresentation of the 'no difference from placebo' data or the slightly more tricky 'no clinically meaningful difference from placebo'. The casual reader might assume that people didn't get better. Actually, many people did, and in both arms of those clinical trials – that is, both those who received the active medicine and those who didn't.

The casual reader may also assume that the 'debate' is most relevant to all types of people with depression and that there is evidence across all these groups (i.e., children, youth, depression with active suicidal behaviour, psychotic depression, bipolar depression, post-natal depression, late-life depression, depression following stroke, cerebrovascular disease or in association with other medical conditions) demonstrating the ineffectiveness of antidepressant medications.

In clinical trials, the non-specific treatment effects are large, and they benefit those receiving the new active treatment *and* those receiving the placebo. Exactly the same thing is observed in other medical conditions such as chronic pain, back injuries, gut disturbances, insomnia, nausea and migraine headache. Very few people in these settings then turn around and say treatments are useless; or worse, the conditions don't really exist – or worst of all, the people with these conditions do not really require clinical care.

The most preposterous extension of this argument has been that we should abandon the specific treatments and instead just prescribe placebos. Fortunately, the ethical implications (including the active deception of the person with depression), the false assumption that this has no potential ill-effects (see the 'nocebo' response below), the withholding of active treatments that are clearly effective, and the significant differences between different medicines (with quite different risk–benefit combinations) means that this has remained largely a rhetorical device rather than a real option.

In my own research career, one of the most fascinating examples of the placebo effect has been our studies of treatment of children with autism with the 'love hormone' oxytocin (administered intranasally). It turns out that this 'positive response' factor is as important in these trials as the other conditions we study, such as anxiety or depression. Similar effects have been observed in early dementia treatment trials – where again the expectation was of negligible placebo treatment effects.

It is a well-established principle in medicine that we do not require placebo-controlled trials in those areas where the differentiation between a positive effect and a disastrous outcome is clear (e.g. the prescription of antibiotics for bacterial meningitis, the surgical treatment of acute appendicitis, the prescription of chemotherapy for blood cancers). Placebo-controlled trials of new treatments are required ethically and scientifically when there is no proven effective treatment for a condition, when withholding treatment will not be associated with significant risks or when there are compelling methodological reasons – such as an anticipated high placebo response rate or a very uncertain natural course of the illness.

The latter situation, which is commonly the case in many clinical trials in psychiatry, also assumes that the person is not at risk of significant harm as a consequence of withholding existing treatments. Interestingly, in some areas such as schizophrenia (where existing antipsychotics are beneficial) or bipolar disorder (where lithium carbonate is effective) the assumption that we need more placebo-controlled trials of new agents is increasingly contested. The movement to comparative trials (comparing new agents with existing treatments), and add-on trials where new agents or placebo are added to existing therapies are often utilised.

For those experiencing severe clinical depression, depression associated with active suicidal behaviour or psychotic depression, enrolment into a standard placebo-controlled trial may be unethical. As a result, these people have typically been excluded from many registration trials for new antidepressant compounds. Older medicines (like the tricyclic antidepressants) or physical treatments (like ECT) are often used for these patients, as postponing effective treatment is associated with unacceptable risk. But an unfortunate outcome of this situation is that many with these more severe disorders believe wrongly that antidepressants or physical treatments have been shown to be ineffective in people with their problem.

There are other areas where there is only a very small number of relevant trials, most notably for children and young people. But the most significant large trial of fluoxetine (an SSRI) in young people, the Treatment for Adolescents with Depression Study (TADS), did clearly demonstrate the short and long-term benefits of both the medicine and professionally delivered cognitive behaviour therapy. Other small trials of another SSRI (sertraline) have demonstrated its safety and efficacy for anxiety disorders (which typically precede depression) in children and young people.

Independent reviews have noted that we actually have the least evidence of the benefits of specific treatments for older teenagers and young adults (18–25 years). Rather than howling against the provision of potentially effective treatments, it would be really useful if the efforts of many child and youth psychiatrists were directed at conducting real trials and growing the evidence base to guide future practice.

'Nocebo' effects

Another fascinating aspect of the scientific investigation of placebo effects is characterisation of its opposite or 'nocebo' effects, where a person's expectation of negative effects from an inactive treatment results in negative outcomes. So, in drug trials, such as those associated with antidepressant compounds, people receiving the sugar pill are more likely to report side-effects normally associated with the active compounds (things like nausea, headache, gut disturbance, insomnia and fatigue). Interestingly, these nocebo effects are subject to far less adverse commentary by critics of antidepressant therapies than those associated with placebo effects.

Such nocebo effects are also relevant in the debate about the accuracy of messages around the possible adverse effects of medical treatments for clinical depression. Practitioners obviously have a clear ethical requirement to provide the most accurate information available about the prevalence, severity and time-course of any significant adverse events associated with specific treatments.

Critics of these therapies do not operate within the same constraints. Very frequently, the rates and severity of common side-effects – weight gain, nausea, insomnia, sexual dysfunction – or rare side-effects – agitation, suicidal ideas – are exaggerated, not compared with the rates of the same problems in those who received placebo interventions, or linked back to the extent to which people with clinical depression had these problems *before* they were exposed to any specific treatment.

Once a person has received treatment, it is also highly likely that these problems will then be attributed to the intervention and not the ongoing illness of clinical depression. So, there is a real need to differentiate those problems that emerge, or are greatly increased, *after* exposure to specific treatments and to report accurately the different possible reasons as to why these may have occurred, how long they may persist and how they may be best managed.

Sadly, there is now a real danger that very deliberate misinformation increases the chance that people will experience and report adverse effects after commencing treatment. That is, the nocebo effect becomes operative in real clinical practice. In my own practice, I try to make use of several strategies to respond to this challenge.

These include:

- Providing accurate information about the true rate of side-effects, and their time course. Data from placebo-controlled trials give an indication of the true rates of each side-effect, and the size of the difference between the active treatment and placebo group;
- Accurately documenting the most important features (cognitive function, suicidal ideation, agitation, physical symptoms, emotional blunting, sexual function) before commencing each treatment. Some of my most important early research involved documenting the extent and severity of cognitive dysfunction prior to ECT, which typically went down – that is, cognitive functioning improved – following the administration of the treatment;
- Providing data from very large surveys (notably the AGDS study – see Chapter 22) on both the overall benefits and difficulties that people using these treatments experience;

- Enquiring actively as to which particular side-effects are of greatest relevance to you – and to incorporate these very personal preferences into treatment selection (see Julie's experiences below);
- Making clear which types of side-effects are dose-related, time-limited or able to be moderated by using other strategies. For some other adverse effects, such as sexual dysfunction when on SSRIs, there is no easy way out;
- Encouraging direct dialogue with others who have undergone the same therapies so that more real-life perspectives can be shared before using that treatment; and,
- Advising accurate recording, through diaries, apps, or systematic rating scales, of the type, severity and time course of any side-effects that emerge following exposure to different treatments.

Julie, aged 22 years, was a young nurse with a very severe clinical depression. Her illness had already resulted in disruptions to her education and was putting real pressure on her relationship with her male partner. Her withdrawal from social interactions with their friends was resulting in a greater reliance on positive feedback from her partner. A key aspect of that intimate relationship was the very positive nature of their sexual activity, despite the adverse impact of clinical depression on Julie's libido. As a health professional, Julie was very aware that SSRIs may well result in not being able to reach orgasm.

She stated quite politely but very firmly, 'If you prescribe me something that stops me orgasming, that's it! It's the only pleasurable thing I've got left. I'm out of here!'

Needless to say, the common clinical guidelines that recommend starting treatments with SSRIs (particularly in young people) were not a viable option in Julie's case.

Specific care options

So, you've probably just arrived at what you were hoping to read in the first place: which treatment options really work short- and long-term, for which people, in what sequence and over what time periods? Add to that the other important questions, such as what's the downside of each treatment option and what's the best specific treatment combinations. And then, what's new, what's still experimental, what's on the drawing board but moving into clinical trials?

Just in case you have been put off by the negative publicity, or you don't know many people who have got really well on treatment and returned to their productive lives (see the responses from our 20,000 plus people in the AGDS survey and the many personal accounts collected here), you're afraid about potential side-effects or you're really worried that you will be discriminated against if you use any specific treatment (by an employer, insurance company, religious or political group or some other social organisation), then, before we go any further, I'm very keen to say:

> You're about to make the best decision for a better life that you'll ever make! Having called for help (which itself was a great decision) – we're here to assist and stay the journey. It's not one easily taken alone. Living with severe depression is hell. Untreated clinical depression kills and disables. Treated depression empowers you to make the decisions you need to make, and live the life you choose to live – but, it may take a while.

As we race through all the questions and all the options, I have one other major piece of advice. The more types of treatment – self-care, behavioural, psychological, interpersonal, medicinal, physical – that are relevant to your situation and that you can effectively engage, the better the outcome (see Table on page 365).

As my kids often remark, 'Dad, don't be so binary!' This is not a case of choosing between medical versus behavioural versus psychological versus social options, but rather optimising your best treatment combinations. If we scored each treatment as a '2' and each type is relevant for you, the overall effect may be 2 × 2 × 2 × 2, with a net result of +16! That's a whole lot better than just getting a net +2 by choosing just one option.

The most effective cancer therapies often involve self-care (such as a strong emphasis on diet and exercise), personal and family support, skilled surgery, focused radiotherapy, targeted chemotherapy *and* novel and highly personalised immunotherapies. For clinical depression, the best combinations often involve a selection of exercise, sleep–wake cycle management, light exposure, social engagement, peer support, antidepressants or mood stabilisers, psychological and interpersonal therapies, episodic TMS (or ECT) or adjunctive oestrogen. There are also many treatments that are novel (ketamine, brexanolone), experimental (immunotherapy, Transcranial Direct Current Stimulation (tDCS), orexin antagonists, psilocybin and other hallucinogens) or alternative (stimulants and vigilance enhancing agents) out there or on the way!

Effective self-care strategies

A whole range of self-care strategies are available. Which strategies are most suitable for any individual will vary. The timing for when people choose to take them up often depends on personal circumstances. Some are much more relevant to different illness stages (i.e. acutely or after recovery) or types (anxious or circadian depression). For the anxiety-arousal group, those things that focus on modulating the arousal response – like meditation, mindfulness, yoga (the relaxation-focused kind) on-line CBT, on-line insomnia management, group participation, moderating alcohol and other sedative use – are all attractive.

For those with the more circadian types, daily physical activity, yoga (the more physical kind), morning light exposure, regular sleep cycles, are particularly effective.

For those with neurodevelopmental difficulties, participation in education, employment and social group-based activities are significant.

For all groups, very active personal monitoring of mood, anxiety, sleep and physical activity patterns are really useful. What I really encourage is the 'n=1 personal experiment'. That is, choose the ones you like and then find out whether they really work for you!

Effective medicines

As a clinical psychiatrist with a very specific interest in treating in clinical depression in youth (12–25 years), middle aged or older people (over 70 years), I'm often asked two things:

First, 'Do the drugs really work?' Short answer: 'Yes, but with some side-effects.'

Second, 'If you were me, which one would you take first?' Now that is a much more difficult question!

The real question is, which one do I think is best suited to your situation? For me that's a complex algorithm of age, sex, illness type, comorbidity, physical health status, clinical stage, prior experiences, family history of response to treatments and personal preferences – particularly with regard to desired benefits (alertness, energy, better sleep, reduced anxiety) and tolerance of side-effects (like weight gain, sexual dysfunction, drowsiness-sedation or daytime fatigue).

Fortunately, we now have five things going in our favour:

- Almost 30 years of clinical experience with the least toxic, least sedating and most easily administered 'new agents' that target the monoamine systems, namely the SSRIs and SNRIs;

- A whole range of new classes of antidepressant, mood stabiliser, stimulant and antipsychotic compounds developed over the last decade;
- Much older compounds that are now almost 60 years old that still have important roles to play in very specific situations (the tricyclic agents, monoamine oxidase inhibitors and lithium carbonate);
- A wide choice of 'add-on' agents (including lithium, estrogen, thyroid hormone, newer antipsychotics) that may augment the effects of the major antidepressant agents; and,
- New experimental approaches that operate outside the traditional biochemical models of what may be effective (see below). These include a range of immunological, anti-inflammatory, anti-infective agents as well as other new neurobiological targets – such as those promoting the generation of new nerve cell connections.

In the most extensive review of 21 antidepressants used in the acute treatment of major depression (by Andrea Cipriani and colleagues in the *Lancet* journal in 2018), the authors examined the results from 522 trials, which had included 116,477 participants.

I'd suggest that it provides a comprehensive summary of:

- The overall effectiveness of antidepressant medicines – *yes, they do work*!
- Rankings of the relative efficacy of different drugs
- Rankings of the relative acceptability (meaning less likely to drop out of treatment).

The bottom line was that we have a wide range of medicines that work, with varying degrees of efficacy and acceptability. So, any good doctor in this area can outline why a particular medicine is the best place to start for your problems or where to go next if things are not working.

The recently published (2020) RANZCP clinical practice guidelines also provide an accessible overview of the major choices available, attempting to link desired benefits more directly with the choice of compound. For example, escitalopram (an SSRI) for anxiety, vortioxetine (SSRI and serotonin receptor modulator) for cognitive difficulties, agomelatine (melatonin agonist) for sleep disturbance, amitriptyline (tricyclic) for pain and venlafaxine (an SNRI) for melancholia (or very severe depression).

It then also tries to emphasise the choices if you are trying to minimise specific types of side-effects. For example: for less sedation use SSRIs or melatoninergic agents; for less weight gain use SSRIs, SNRIs or melatoninergic agents; for less sexual dysfunction use non-SSRI or SNRI agents; and, for less cardiac (heart) side-effects use SSRIs and melatoninergic agents.

The bottom line is that those drugs that seem to be more powerful or efficacious – the SNRIs and tricyclics – often have the most toxic side-effects. By contrast, those with lower side-effect burden – the SSRIs and melatoninergic agents – are often considered to be less effective in severe depression.

So, for our three illness types-trajectories – which medicines are best?

Since we don't treat clinical depression as one single entity, the larger comparative studies only provide limited insights into these questions. We do have a preferred approach to matching probably illness-type with first-up, second and later novel or experimental approaches to medication selection (see table).

Basically, for the anxious depressions, where moderation of the anxious-stress response is critical, SSRIs (first with lower side-effects) and SNRIs (for more severe forms) are the usual choices.

For the circadian-type depressions (and with strong overlap

with bipolar depression), the SSRI and SNRI approaches are often problematic. They are far less effective and can lead to more disturbed sleep, increased anxiety or agitation and more unstable 24-hour sleep–wake cycles. Consequently, we have been enthusiasts for melatoninergic agents such as agomelatine. But, in these cases, the big issue is whether to prescribe a traditional antidepressant at all, an alternative mood stabiliser (like lamotrigine, pregabalin, or lithium) or a combination of a mood stabiliser and an antidepressant agent.

For the neurodevelopmental–psychotic spectrum, various types of antidepressants may be relevant depending on the symptom profile, but the big issue becomes whether there is any place for an antipsychotic agent alone or in combination with an antidepressant.

The special case of children

There is more public debate about the use of antidepressants in children and young people than in any other aspect of this work. First, it's important to understand that when antidepressants are prescribed in young children – meaning under the age of five years – that's not for the treatment of depression. Rather, it is usually related to neurodevelopmental (like autism) or physical disability problems.

Second, when prescribing does commence for those in the pre-pubertal 5–12 year group, general anxiety rather than depression is usually the target. At times, it may also be childhood onset obsessive-compulsive disorder, a most disabling condition. Here the SSRI agents are most effective.

Third, for the ages that really matter, meaning over the age of 12 years, the international clinical trial data are limited. However, the most recent very large review (2020 *Lancet*, by Xinyu Zhou, et al.) looked at the data from 71 trials and 9510 participants, noting that in most studies the depressive disorders were moderate to severe.

This was a really interesting review, as it focused on comparing drug, non-drug and combination treatments. Its conclusion: an SSRI medicine (fluoxetine) alone or in combination with CBT was the best option.

The big side-effect issues

In many of my clinical discussions, the big issue is not really whether the medicines may have benefits but rather how to avoid the big side-effect issues, namely: sexual dysfunction; weight gain; agitation or suicidal ideation; and emotional blunting (or 'personality' changes). So, here's my clinical guides:

- Sexual dysfunction: This is a major problem on SSRIs and SNRIs and there is no easy way out. People do try and vary doses and do try to add other agents to assist. Mostly, if it's a major ongoing issue (severe loss of libido; significantly delayed ejaculation in men; unable to orgasm in women) I'm likely to recommend changing medicines to a non-SSRI type;
- Weight gain: For most antidepressants (except mirtazapine), when not prescribed alongside other agents like antipsychotics (quetiapine, olanzapine) or some mood stabilisers (pregabalin), the weight gain is slow. So, great attention to diet and exercise and close monitoring of weight and metabolic status are critical;
- Agitation or suicidal ideation: When this is severe, develops as a new phenomenon or as an exacerbation of phenomena that were already present, it can be a medical emergency. So, the first thing is to be ready to respond – which may include immediately stopping the antidepressant, adding an anxiety or agitation-reducing agent or arranging emergency (possibly hospital-based care). While this can occur in those with anxious depression, it is our experience that it is more common and more severe in those with the circadian–bipolar illness type.

- Emotional blunting (see also Chapter 21 on myths). The real issue here is what exactly this means in practice and the extent to which the problem may be due to ongoing depression and not a loss of emotional depth that emerged after starting the drug. If it really is new, and is perceived by the person with depression to be a major ongoing problem, then it will most likely result in discontinuation of the offending (usually SSRI or SNRI) agent.

Effective physical therapies

The first really effective treatments we had for clinical depression were physical treatments – most notably convulsive therapy. The decision to induce convulsions was based on an earlier clinical observation – namely that people with epilepsy often experienced a significant improvement in their mood after having a spontaneous seizure.

The first attempts to turn this into a therapy involved chemicals, not electricity. As this was very dangerous, it rapidly gave way to the development of electroconvulsive therapy in Europe in the 1930s – long before the modern pharmacology revolution of the 1960s.

Despite its long track record of being a life-saving treatment for those with the most severe forms of clinical depression, the public perception is still strongly linked with notions of torture, deliberate harm, punishment and cruelty. The original administration of the treatment, prior to the development of modern anaesthetics, and importantly, specific muscle relaxation agents contributed to these widely held beliefs.

There is a great deal of research around the short- and longer-term benefits of ECT, as well as the issues related to side-effects. I've conducted some of this work, seeking to identify who might be most likely to respond well (those with motor changes or psychotic phenomena) and, conversely, who may not respond well (those with pre-existing brain changes due to underlying damage of their subcortical pathways).

The most commonly presented myth is that ECT results frequently in long-term memory problems (in people who had no prior cognitive or memory difficulties), followed closely by the assertion that it causes structural brain damage. These are not assertions supported by the available scientific literature.

Repetitive Transcranial Magnetic Stimulation (rTMS)

Another major development in physical therapies over the last two decades has been rTMS. Unlike ECT, rTMS is administered via a magnet on the side of the head while you are awake, sitting upright in what often looks like a dentist's chair. It delivers pulses of energy to the surface of the brain (the cortex) and is usually applied over areas of the frontal lobes. It is thought that these energy bursts stimulate nerve cells within those frontal and subcortical circuits (see Chapter 14) that moderate our mood. Treatments are often delivered daily for a period of 4–6 of weeks. Traditionally each treatment took about 30 minutes, but more intensive and shorter periods of treatment are now being offered. Side-effects are often mild (headache, sore scalp, light-headedness) but there is a very low risk (less than 1 per cent) of having a seizure. It is not a replacement for ECT, and in our experience, often younger people with more atypical types of depression respond best. We don't see a rapid response (quite unlike ECT or ketamine) but rather a slow cumulative response with good impacts on cognitive function (attention and memory), and return to other normal functions, like education and employment. The positive effects often last several months without needing to take many additional medicines.

Psilocybin, ayahuasca, LSD and other (new and old) hallucinogens

One of my great regrets in clinical psychiatry is that I came into the field one generation too late! For those leaders in the field who were active throughout the 1960s, the therapeutic possibilities of hallucinogenic compounds (LSD being the most popular) was well recognised. As was common at the time (and is now largely prohibited by modern ethics committees), the first place to try new substances was with yourself and your colleagues!

This emulated the original decision of Albert Hofmann, the Swiss chemist who intentionally ingested 250 micrograms of LSD in his laboratory in 1943. He then documented the physical and psychological effects of this first medically induced acid trip (which were profound, frightening and 'life-enhancing'). Hofmann was wise enough to ensure he was accompanied by an assistant, to call his own doctor when things got scary, and then seek to document accurately the effects of his own n=1 experiment.

This kind of firsthand experience with other more common (but not toxic) medical drugs was also encouraged when I was in medical school. If you were ever going to prescribe these things for other people, then you should have some real-world experiences. The reality at that time was of very mixed experiences – not only among my older colleagues, but also among those with existing illnesses (particularly psychotic disorders).

As the intention of ingesting such compounds is to induce a profoundly altered state of consciousness (disorientation, confusion, and altered mood), that is typically associated with visual and auditory hallucinations, it's not surprising that the experience may not be pleasant, but often very frightening – the 'bad trip'.

Of additional concern has always been the idea that these experiences may then recur at some later period, so-called 'flashbacks'. In those with a history of existing psychotic illnesses (or with other known risk factors to psychosis such as a strong family history, or the presence of another major psychiatric disorder like a severe mood disorder), there has always been the concern that exposure to these hallucinogens may precipitate a psychotic illness, exacerbate its severity or prolong its course.

Other social forces put an end to this line of psychopharmacology with the adoption in the US of the Controlled Substances Act in 1970. Internationally, these legal and regulatory processes resulted in serious disruption to systematic research for most of the next three decades. Right now, with interest being driven by those most affected by severe anxiety (like chronic PTSD) and depressive disorders, some serious psychopharmacologists and high-profile clinical research centres, the field is back in the news. Here in Australia, we have moved suddenly (and rather unexpectedly) to licence psilocybin for treatment-resistant depression. What happens next (the good, the bad and the ugly) will be of great public and international interest.

24

Conversations

I've been very privileged in my public roles with Beyond Blue, the national depression initiative, the National Mental Health Commission (2012–18) and other advisory and media roles to have had the opportunity for informative conversations with major public figures. We have been very fortunate that many of these people have also been willing to share their personal stories of clinical depression with the wider public. They are part of a much wider group who have come from all walks of life and have included well-recognised people in politics, business, sports, the creative arts and community leadership.

There have been many other public figures, or their family members, who I have encountered, advised or consulted with over the years. They are not included here as they have not chosen to tell their stories publicly. There are obvious reasons why people choose to protect their privacy on many health issues, including clinical depression. A more pernicious reason, which is shared with other mental disorders, is that stigma and potential discrimination persists.

My goal here is not to repeat the details of those personal accounts. Instead, I'm keen to highlight how they align with important points I've tried to make throughout the book. Together, they may provide insights that can be shared with others who find themselves in similar predicaments. I have also learnt a great deal from these conversations and, so, I'm keen to share my own perspectives as well.

What these people have in common has been their willingness to engage, not only in the process of contemplating one's own intrinsic vulnerabilities, but also to take the tougher journey toward a more stable and fulfilling future. These are very positive stories. They are genuine examples of working hard to leave personal devils behind.

When I started my own more public journey, talking about the clinical aspects of depression and its public health and health services policy implications, the main goal was to normalise discussions about common mental health problems. That is, to make a public discussion about clinical depression as normal as a health-based dialogue about breast cancer or heart disease. In Australia, we have made great progress with that objective, though for every individual (and their family) affected, the decisions to seek mental health care and then to talk openly about those experiences are an ongoing challenge.

Malcolm Turnbull: 29th Prime Minister of Australia

Malcolm has elegantly outlined his encounter with clinical depression, and its association with persistent suicidal ideas, in his 2020 autobiography, *A Bigger Picture.* The depression had its onset following the loss of his leadership of the Liberal Party in 2009. That loss turned his personal world upside down, thwarting his long-held ambition to be prime minister of Australia. Although he announced he would leave parliament, he had a sudden change of heart and stayed. On the election of the Abbott government in 2013, he became a senior minister, and then in September 2015 he successfully challenged for leadership of the Liberal Party. As a direct consequence, he became the 29th Prime Minister.

Although he was re-elected in July 2016, he was again overthrown by more conservative forces in 2018. The drama of all this, one chapter in the turbulent period of Australian politics over the last 15 years, has been well documented. What is less considered is the personal impact and how different people are affected, what they learn and what they do subsequently to thrive.

Although Malcolm chose not to reveal the impact of the first loss of leadership on his mental health at the time, or subsequently when he was prime minister, he has been kind enough to share not only what the experiences were like (see Chapter 2), just how alienating, persistent and unfamiliar it was and how hard it was to get out of that hole – 'I felt like I was clawing my way out of a pit with my fingernails; it was very hard' – but also his approach to dealing with its consequences and the steps he took to get professional assistance and then to reduce his own longer-term vulnerability.

As he outlined during a podcast with James O'Loghlin and me (*Minding Your Mind*, 9 October 2021 – and you may wish to listen to our later episode on vulnerability, 22 November 2022):

> Looking back – I obviously had been glum or mildly depressed in the past, but I had never experienced anything like the 'Slough of Despond' into which I sank in the first part of 2010.
>
> And I got really ill. I learnt a lot from it, and it was a pretty painful way to learn. But I think the most important thing I learnt was that you've got to be aware of your mental health.

Younger people today are probably more aware of it because we talk about it, but I had not grown up really thinking about it at all, in the sense of it being something that could happen to me. I was obviously aware of mental health as an issue, and I wasn't pretending that it didn't exist, but I hadn't personalised it. And I think the reality of what I learnt is that you have to be as aware of your mental health as you are of your physical health.

With mental health, I think, too often we just shrug things off and the big lesson was, one, you've got to be very aware of it and very aware of your vulnerabilities – which in my case is a vulnerability to depression – and so when you start feeling yourself getting depressed, or feel the early signs of it, you deploy some strategies to combat it.

If Malcolm hadn't taken such steps, one might have predicted that the impact of his loss of his role as Prime Minister might have been even more devastating than that resulting from the first loss. So, what were those critical steps? First was the active recognition of his personal vulnerability. In my career, I've met many men like Malcolm – high-flying, accustomed to success and public approval. Just like the rest of us, at some times in their lives, and often not for very obvious reasons, they crash. But many still believe that they are invincible, and as soon as they can, they resume their former life in a state of active denial. It helps if you can simply blame one unfortunate life event, those close to you or some other unexpected stress. 'It only happened because of the action of my company (my employer, my partner, my kids)'. This is usually followed by, 'I'll be fine now that I've left that company (my partner has left, the kids have moved out).'

Malcolm makes it clear that he accepted that mental ill-health, and particularly clinical depression, could happen to him – and that, yes, lightning can strike twice! So, when continuing in politics, and then deliberately while prime minister, he focused on daily strategies that would reduce that risk. Most prominently, these tactics included trying to live a normal daily routine, with family and a social life. He retained his main residence in Eastern Sydney close to family, friends, children and grandchildren, and worked on a daily schedule of morning light exposure and physical activity, like kayaking on Sydney Harbour, to maintain a regular sleep–wake cycle. Although this drew political criticism from his political foes ('Mr Harborside Mansion'), it did make good sense from a mental health and wellbeing perspective.

He articulated several key points for James and me in the *Minding Your Mind* podcast episode:

1. 'Don't make dramatic decisions when you're in a bad way – so getting out of parliament was the wrong thing to do [in 2009]. I would have been better off just sticking with it . . . When you know you're not thinking straight, when you are depressed, don't make momentous decisions. Try to just focus on getting yourself well again.'
2. 'I think exercise is terribly important – sunshine, getting into the outdoors. I walk a lot with Lucy, paddle a kayak . . . Sleeping is also very important.'
3. 'A lot of men identify themselves solely with their job.' Malcolm noted the line spoken by Robert Duvall in the film *Network* – 'I am a man without a corporation!' His takeaway was the importance of maintaining intimate relationships and family connections outside of work: 'I'm so lucky to be married to Lucy. It trumps everything else.'
4. 'You've got to have a strategy for being happy.' The emphasis here is not just on preventing the relapse of depression but focusing specifically on enjoying life every day through many small things – not just the big events.

When lightning did strike again in 2018, Malcolm quickly announced that he would leave parliament and soon after decided to leave the country during that turbulent period. Again, while this led to some criticism from opponents, it was clearly a decision to not stay in an environment loaded with risk. Instead, he had the clear intention of moving away from regret, and then potentially on to more productive pursuits. Despite the nature of the personal loss, these particular strategies appear, from a mental health perspective, to have served him well.

Geoff Gallop: 27th Premier of Western Australia

I have been fortunate to come to know Geoff Gallop since he moved to Sydney, following his departure from the top political job in Western Australia. Unlike Turnbull's story, Geoff's very public episode of depression didn't follow a major life event. At the time, he was at the top of his game in public life, having led the Labor Party to electoral victories in 2001 and 2005. In early 2006, he announced he was stepping down from his leadership role, and leaving parliament, to aid his recovery from depression.

There is an issue here that I have discussed not only with Geoff but with other major political figures, and some others in very high-profile and major decision-making roles. Is leaving the job necessary, or is stepping aside or taking leave while unwell (as you may do for other major medical problems) a real alternative? Opinions vary, though I suspect that we may be moving toward a time when total withdrawal is not so necessary.

Geoff has fascinating insights into his own journey with mental ill-health. Like Malcolm, he is very open about coming to terms with his own vulnerability. In Geoff's case, he focuses (like Garry McDonald – see Chapter 23) much more on his own underlying anxiety – or anxious temperament. That's been a lifelong issue – and something that's not likely to change much at this stage of life. While I tend to describe an anxious temperament as a vulnerability (in terms of increasing the risk of depression), it's important to say that real sensitivity, and a genuine awareness of and empathy for the impacts of social adversity on others, is also a virtue. Geoff is a living example of that virtue.

Geoff makes it clear that he actively engages with cognitive and behavioural strategies to manage his own anxiety, while also being really engaged with his own very active professional and personal world. He has made maximum use of professional help from skilled practitioners. For many people, anxiety leads to avoidance rather than engagement. I've had the pleasure of seeing Geoff in action at meetings of the Organisation for Economic Co-operation and Development (OECD) in Paris and witnessing him asking hard questions of major political, social and economic leaders. In his situation, anxiety is best dealt with by continuous engagement with a productive life.

Geoff is also very thoughtful about the challenges of dismantling the stigma and discrimination that surrounds mental ill-health. In a piece he prepared in May 2023, he noted: 'We need not just to convince our fellow citizens that prejudices are not only contrary to our views of right and wrong but also misguided in their estimation of what we can achieve through the power of enlightened endeavour. Compassion plus science is a powerful brew; let us be more serious about making it a day-to-day habit rather than an optional extra.'

Recommended Reading

If you want more detailed information about clinical depression, there are many reputable government-sponsored and academic websites, both in Australia and internationally. Locally, those operated by Beyond Blue; Orygen Youth Health; headspace National Youth Mental Health Foundation; the Black Dog Institute and our own Brain and Mind Centre are notable.

Preferred websites

- Brain and Mind Centre, University of Sydney: sydney.edu.au/brain-mind
- National Institute for Health and Care Excellence (NICE) in the UK: nice.org.uk/guidance/conditions-and-diseases/mental-health-and-behavioural-conditions
- National Institute of Mental Health (US): nimh.nih.gov/health/publications
- Beyond Blue, the national depression initiative: beyondblue.org.au
- Orygen Youth Health: oyh.org.au
- headspace, National Youth Mental Health Foundation: headspace.org.au

- Black Dog Institute: blackdoginstitute.org.au
- THIS WAY UP: thiswayup.org.au
- MindSpot: mindspot.org.au
- For further help in accessing care and information about mental health services in Australia, go to headtohealth.gov.au
- For an interesting historical perspective on the long and rich history of depression, a recent exhibition from the Royal Society of Medicine, 'The Golden Age of Melancholy' is most informative: rsm.ac.uk/media-releases/2023/the-golden-age-of-melancholy-royal-society-of-medicine-library

Books and journal articles

Hopefully this book has conveyed the centrality of personal and individual experiences of depression, and emphasised the value of listening to individuals who have benefited from available medical or psychological treatments and their personal journeys to recovery. I encourage those with depression to read the personal accounts of those who have travelled similar paths. Among them, I recommend: those written by my friend and colleague, Neil Cole, and notably *Colonel Surry's Insanity* and *Stability in Mind*, as well as his play *Alive at Williamstown Pier*; and the series by Alastair Campbell, the UK political advisor who worked closely with Tony Blair, particularly his short volume *The Happy Depressive*, as well as the novel *All in the Mind*. Graeme Cowan's book *Back from the Brink* is a very useful compilation of personal accounts.

A great deal of emphasis in this book is not simply on the brain as a 'neurological' machine (controlling movement, speech, sight, hearing, etc.) but rather on the development of the 'emotional and social brain' and our resultant emotional and cognitive processes. It's more about how the emotional brain grows (under genetic and environmental influences) and how it operates.

The neuroscience of our area continues to evolve rapidly, and we see new scientific insights published every month. These are well covered by leading science journals like *Science* and *Nature*. Their implications for humans, and particularly clinical psychiatry, are well covered by the

New England Journal of Medicine, *JAMA Psychiatry*, *Lancet Psychiatry* and *World Psychiatry*.

Really interesting reads on the social and emotional brain include works by Larry Young, an eminent scientist in the field, who is particularly well known for his work on the influence of oxytocin ('the love chemical') on animal and human behaviour. Another important writer in this explanation of brain functions and linked emotions is Joseph LeDoux.

Dan Blazer is one of the most thoughtful psychiatrists I have ever worked with. Much of his work has been devoted to how we understand the impact of social circumstances on depression, how we reconcile the social risk factors that are at work more broadly and the need to provide more effective psychological and medical treatments to those individuals affected. His book *The Age of Melancholy* is highly recommended.

Much of this book is devoted to the relevance of circadian rhythms (body clocks) to the onset and course of depressive disorders. For one of the most accessible books on the topic, try the very engaging and leading European researcher in the field, Till Roenneberg. For another, go to the Oxford neuroscientist Russell Foster. And if you are keen to hear things directly from a world leader in the field, go to this TED talk by legendary US biologist Joe Takahashi: youtube.com/watch?v=ocqn3wYTCRM.

Also discussed in detail in this book are the physiological (body) and neurological (brain) changes, not just psychological features that characterise common anxiety and depressive disorders. Much of my own research career has been tied up with these issues, and for those who may wish to look in more detail at these approaches, I'd suggest various works from Gordon Parker and colleagues, who established specialist services now overseen by the Black Dog Institute in Australia.

One of the most impactful books in the public discourse about depression in recent decades was Peter Kramer's *Listening to Prozac*. Written with the deep insights gained from time spent in long-term psychotherapeutic settings treating clients with chronic depression, it challenged many psychologically orientated thinkers to reconsider their own negative perceptions of the role of antidepressant medicines. *Ordinarily Well* is a must-read for those who are serious about the roles of medicines in treating depressive disorders. *Against Depression* is another notable book from this key author.

I've also emphasised the importance of early intervention for common anxiety and depressive disorders in this book. It rests on the key observation that most adult-type disorders commence during the teenage years – the period of life where we should focus much of our therapeutic effort. Our previous Australian of the Year, Professor Pat McGorry, and his Melbourne team have led the world in these efforts, and it has been a great pleasure to co-edit a book with Pat on 'clinical staging' – a tool we use to emphasise intervening before any disorder becomes overwhelming.

Our perspective, from the Brain and Mind Centre's Youth Mental Health and Technology team, on how to best manage the common mental disorders that arise in adolescence and early adult years is best summarised in our 2019 supplement to the *Medical Journal of Australia.*

- Bennett, Maxwell R. & Hacker, Peter M. S., *Philosophical Foundations of Neuroscience,* John Wiley & Sons Ltd, 2022.
- Blazer, Dan G., *The Age of Melancholy: 'Major depression' and its social origins,* London Routledge, 2014.
- Carpenter, Joanne S.; Crouse, Jacob J.; Scott, Elizabeth M.; Naismith, Sharon L.; Wilson, Chloe; Scott, Jan; Merikangas, Kathleen R.; Hickie, Ian B., 'Circadian depression: A mood disorder phenotype', *Neuroscience & Biobehavioral Reviews,* vol. 126, 2021, 79–101.
- Cole, Neil, *Colonel Surry's Insanity,* Beagles'DEN, 2010.
- Cole, Neil, *Stability in Mind: A memoir of politics and plays in the shadow of bipolar disorder,* New Holland Publishers, 2012.
- Cole, Neil, *Alive at Williamstown Pier,* Esson Press, 1999.
- Cowan, Graeme, *Back from the Brink: Australians tell their stories of overcoming depression,* Bird in Hand Media, Australia, 2007.
- Crouse, Jacob J.; Carpenter, Joanne S.; Song, Yun Ju C.; Hockey, Samuel J; Naismith, Sharon L.; Grunstein, Ronald R.; Scott, Elizabeth M.; Merikangas, Kathleen R.; Scott, Jan; Hickie, Ian B., 'Circadian rhythm sleep–wake disturbances and depression in young people: Implications for prevention and early intervention', *The Lancet Psychiatry,* vol. 8(9), pp. 813–823, 2021.

- Foster, Russell, *Life Time: The new science of the body clock, and how it can revolutionize your sleep and health*, Penguin Books, 2023.
- Hickie, Ian B.; Scott, Elizabeth M.; Cross, Shane P.; Iorfino, Frank; Davenport, Tracey A.; Guastella, Adam J.; Naismith, Sharon L.; Carpenter, Joanne S.; Rohleder, Cathrin; Crouse, Jacob J.; Hermens, Daniel F.; Koethe, D.; Markus, Leweke F.; Tickell, A.M.; Sawrikar, Vilas; Scott, Jan, 'Right care, first time: a highly personalised and measurement-based care model to manage youth mental health', *Medical Journal of Australia*, vol. 211(9): S3-S46, 2019.
- Insel, Thomas, *Healing: Our path from mental illness to mental health*, Penguin Books, 2022.
- Kramer, Peter D., *Listening to Prozac: A psychiatrist explores antidepressant drugs and the remaking of the self*, rev ed, Penguin Books, 1997.
- Kramer, Peter D., *Ordinarily Well: The case for antidepressants*, Farrar, Straus and Giroux, 2017.
- Kramer, Peter D., *Against Depression*, Penguin Books, 2006.
- LeDoux, Joseph E., *Anxious: Using the brain to understand and treat fear and anxiety*, Penguin Books, 2016.
- LeDoux, Joseph E., *The Emotional Brain: The mysterious underpinnings of emotional life*, Simon & Schuster, 1998.
- Parker, Gordon, and Hadzi-Pavlovic, Dusan, *Melancholia: A Disorder of Movement and Mood*, Cambridge University Press, 2021.
- McGorry, Patrick, and Hickie, Ian, *Clinical Staging in Psychiatry: Making diagnosis work for research and treatment*, Cambridge University Press, 2019.
- Morton, Rick, *One Hundred Years of Dirt*, Melbourne University Press, 2023.
- Morton, Rick, *My Year of Living Vulnerably*, HarperCollins Publishers, 2021.
- Rapee, Ron, *Helping Your Anxious Child: A step-by-step guide for parents*, New Harbinger Publications, 2022.
- Roenneberg, Till, *Internal Time: Chronotypes, social Jet Lag and why you're so tired*, Harvard University Press, 2017.
- Shorter, Edward, *A History of Psychiatry: From the era of the asylum to the age of prozac*, John Wiley & Sons, 1997.

- Shorter, Edward, *Before Prozac: The troubled history of mood disorders in psychiatry*, Oxford University Press, 2009.
- Uhlhaas, Peter J., and Wood, Stephen J., *Youth Mental Health: A paradigm for prevention and early intervention*, MIT Press Academic, 2020.
- Van der Kolk, Bessel, *The Body Keeps the Score*, Penguin Books, 2020.
- Wigney, Tess; Parker, Gordon; Eyers, Kerrie, *Journeys with the Black Dog: Inspirational stories of bringing depression to heel*, Allen & Unwin, 2017.
- Young, Larry, *The Chemistry Between Us: Love, sex and the science of attraction*, Penguin Books, 2014.

Acknowledgements

Many people have made this book possible. It's been a team effort.

My life partner, Dr Liz Scott, has traversed much of this personal and professional journey with me. As noted frequently here, it's the quality of your travelling companion that really matters when you face real adversity. I have indeed been very fortunate that Liz has been willing to stick with me. She has demonstrated great patience, intelligence, wisdom and warmth as we have ventured over many challenging terrains.

Liz leads our clinical team and reminds me daily that the goal is to provide the best possible care to the many young people who seek our help. Based on her acute clinical observations, and neuroscience and immunology background, she has often inspired some of our best research ideas.

As I've grown older I've come to understand that you learn much more from your children than you ever teach them. My kids are talented and diverse, and they love to challenge most of my views. The ongoing discourse and active debate with them keeps me young.

I am very fortunate to have had two extraordinary parents. My father, Johnno, was a Professor of Cardiology, devoted to rational enquiry, empiricism and pragmatism. He loved being a practising doctor and a teacher of clinical medicine, while also contributing to serious research and professional practice. He believed that those who benefit from easy access to education and resources have a personal obligation to be engaged in improving our society. Johnno definitely favoured fewer words and more effective actions. From his personal library, he passed on to me a copy of Robert Burton's 17th-century classic, *The Anatomy of Melancholia.*

My mother, Noelene, was the centre of warmth and care within our large family unit. Her kindness was central to our lives. Having been a nurse, she was also very familiar with the impacts of illness, demonstrating not just sympathy or sentimentality – she expressed *empathy.* She was ferocious in her personal response to social and health inequities and, like Johnno, favoured less complaining and more effective actions.

Many people who have lived with the experience of clinical depression have provided the real heart at the centre of this book. With their permission, and often in their own words, I've included their diverse journeys. It is still a poor substitute for the real-life journeys I have shared with them. It also struggles to capture what I have personally learnt – not simply about mental ill-health, but about myself and the wider world in which we all reside. I am greatly indebted to those individuals, and their families, for the privilege of having shared this part of their life with me.

While I have specifically named some because of their public contributions – thanks to Neil Cole, Jackie Crowe, Sam Hockey, Alexis Hutcheon, Jess Cottle, Rachel Laidler – many others will recognise their own stories here. Many families have directly supported our work publicly and financially. Their generosity is greatly appreciated.

We are fortunate in Australia to have had many high-profile figures share their personal experiences. I'm particularly grateful to Geoff Gallop (former Premier of Western Australia) and Malcolm Turnbull (former Prime Minister) for the time they have taken to share their very specific perspectives with me.

My professional life has rested heavily on the inspiration of many great psychiatrists. As a student at the University of NSW, the wide world and very human perspectives of key figures (Neil McConaghy, Gavin Andrews and Henry Brodaty), along with their commitment to research and empiricism, drew me in. As a training psychiatrist, I was very fortunate to join the start of the Mood Disorders Unit at Prince Henry Hospital (later to become the Black Dog Institute) in Sydney. That specialist group, and unique clinical research enterprise, was established by Gordon Parker and, along with Philip Mitchell, Philip Boyce, Kay Wilhelm, Dusan Hadzi-Pavlovic, Kerrie Evans and Catherine Hickie, it provided me with invaluable personal, academic and professional support.

I was very fortunate then to spend critical periods with key figures at Duke University in North Carolina (led by Dan Blazer and K. Ranga Krishnan) and, after returning to Australia, with Margaret Tobin at St George Hospital. Margaret's devotion to delivering better mental health care was an inspiration. Her early and tragic death was a great loss. Two of my longstanding and most talented research colleagues, Tracey Davenport and Professor Sharon Naismith, started that journey with Liz and me at St George Hospital. Their patience, good humour and wise counsel have been greatly appreciated.

Throughout these years, I was most fortunate to do ground-breaking clinical research with two inspiring physicians: Professors Andrew Lloyd (infectious diseases) and Denis Wakefield (immunology). Consequently, I've spent much of my career in the basic medical aspects of clinical depression and its physical-health ramifications. Hopefully, the centrality of that holistic way of thinking about mental and physical health is evident on every page of this book.

My jump from academia in 2000 to being the inaugural CEO of Beyond Blue, Australia's national depression initiative, provided me with the opportunity to engage seriously with the public discourse and health system challenges related to clinical depression. I am very grateful to the key political figures responsible, notably Jeff Kennett and Michael Woolridge, and the board and staff of that organisation for their support. Major changes have also resulted, most notably in our campaign to bring psychological care under our national health insurance scheme (Medicare) in 2001–02.

From that time onward, I've been very engaged continuously in public advocacy, underpinned by health systems research, for better and more equitable mental health care. It's a hard road, and the companionship on that journey of Grace Groom, John Mendoza, Sebastian Rosenberg, Pat McGorry and John Moran have been essential.

I was very fortunate to be recruited by Professor Max Bennett (a neuroscientist) in 2002-3 to establish with him and Professor John Pollard (Professor of Neurology) the Brain and Mind Research Institute at the University of Sydney. For over twenty years now it is has provided me with the substantive base from which my own academic, professional, and public roles have been able to flourish. Without that sustained institutional support the breadth of experiences and knowledge (in clinical medicine, brain imaging, genetics, immune activation, public policy, health systems research and digital technologies) reflected in this book would not have been possible.

My clinical and research focus is increasingly on the needs of children and young people. This was inspired by the internationally renowned work of my close friend and colleague, Professor Pat

McGorry, and his Melbourne team. Together with Pat, our groups have taken on major political and professional challenges but the results (including the establishment of headspace National Youth Mental Health Foundation and its network of over 150 clinical centres) have been well worth the effort. The emphasis in this book on the value of early intervention, and attending to the needs of children and young people, derive from this collaboration.

Internationally, two key people have inspired, challenged and supported much of my professional work, while also making major contributions to my personal and family life. Professors Kathleen Merikangas and Jan Scott are not to be messed with. They both pursue the facts, argue the case and then get on and do the empirical work needed to take things forward. Many of the real insights into mood disorders in this book are derived from their work. Over almost the same period, I've worked collaboratively with Professor Nick Martin and his genetic research colleagues in Queensland. Nick's generosity and his willingness (along with Professor Naomi Wray) to educate me is clearly reflected in the long sections here on genetic and environmental causes of mental ill-health.

My research and development team at the Brain and Mind Centre, and their intimate links with young people and families affected, are an inspiration. They make it a thrill to go to work each day. The organisational skills of Christine Song and Jacqui Hutcheon mean that I have time for things like books, podcasts and public advocacy to complement research, teaching and clinical practice. The contributions of each of our team leaders Frank Iorfino, Jacob Crouse, Joanne Occhipinti, Adam Skinner, Emily Selmon and Sarah McKenna are essential.

My co-presenter of the podcast 'Minding Your Mind' and co-author of the subsequent book *Minding Your Mind*, also published by Penguin Random House Australia is James O'Loghlin. James has spent much time and effort educating me on how to make these topics, and the underlying science, much more accessible to a wider audience.

My publisher/editor at Penguin Random House Australia, Brandon VanOver, inspired this exercise in the first place. He has toiled hard to keep me focused on the essential task – namely, sharing expert knowledge in readily accessible forms with those who might benefit most. Academic arguments are best conducted elsewhere. What the wider world really needs is clear communication about what we can all do now to change our worlds, thereby leaving our own devils far behind.